DATE DUE

Feminist subjects, multi-media

This stimulating collection is the first of its kind. It is a unique blend of theoretical writing with techniques of fiction, autobiography, poetry and artwork. Encompassing high and popular culture, it addresses the question: how are women represented, and how do we represent ourselves?

The authors look at a range of media from paintings and family photography, through opera, film and TV to novels and poetry. The traditional boundaries between the 'creative' and the 'critical' are challenged through a new combination of artistic, poetic and critical voices.

The first section deals with 'The politics of spectatorship' with essays on Frida Kahlo, the Impressionists, Surrealism and family snapshots. The second section, 'The politics of production/performance', looks at the popular film *Thelma and Louise*, natural history programmes and opera. The last section argues for feminist interventions at all levels of cultural production.

Feminist subjects, multi-media
Cultural methodologies

edited by
PENNY FLORENCE and DEE REYNOLDS

MANCHESTER UNIVERSITY PRESS
Manchester and New York

Distributed exclusively in USA and Canada by St. Martin's Press

Published by Manchester University Press
Oxford Road, Manchester M13 9PL, UK
and Room 400, 175 Fifth Avenue,
New York, NY 10010, USA

Distributed exclusively in the USA and Canada
by St. Martin's Press, Inc.,
175 Fifth Avenue, New York, NY 10010, USA

British Library Cataloguing-in-Publication Data
A catalogue record for this book is available
from the British Library

Library of Congress Cataloguing-in-Publication Data
Feminist subjects, multi-media : cultural methodologies /
    edited by Penny Florence and Dee Reynolds.
        p.   cm.
      ISBN 0-7190-4179-1 (hardback). — ISBN 0-7190-4180-5 (paperback)
      1. Feminism and the arts.   2. Feminist criticism.   I. Florence,
    Penny.   II. Reynolds, Dee.   III. Title: Feminist subjects,
    multimedia.
    NX180.F4F46   1995
    700'.1'03—dc20   93–50585

ISBN 0 7190 4179 1 *hardback*
ISBN 0 7190 4180 5 *paperback*

Typeset in Monotype Bell
by Servis Filmsetting Ltd, Manchester
Printed in Great Britain by
Bell & Bain Ltd, Glasgow

Contents

Repositioning feminist subjects

We would like to thank most warmly Malcolm Bowie, founding director of the Institute of Romance Studies, London University, for providing the kind of 'space-off' out of which this collection could grow.

Notes on contributors

Jean Andrews teaches Spanish Language, Literature and Culture at Goldsmith's College, University of London. Her research interests lie in comparative literature and literary themes in the performing and cinematic arts.

Jane Arthurs completed an MA in Film and Television Studies in 1984 at the Institute of Education, London. She then taught Video Production and Media Studies in Warrington and London before moving to the University of the West of England, Bristol as a lecturer in Cultural Studies. Her previous publications have been on gender, technology and women in the television industry.

Anthea Callen (University of Warwick) trained as a painter and printmaker before moving into research in art history; her PhD for the Courtauld Institute, on artists' materials and techniques in nineteenth-century France, is currently being revised for Phaidon Press. Other publications include *Angel in the Studio: Women in the Arts and Crafts Movement 1870–1914* (Astragal 1979), *Techniques of the Impressionists* (Orbis 1982) and, forthcoming, *The Spectacular Body: Science and Technique in the Work of Degas* (Yale, 1994). She is currently editing a series for Routledge on 'Visual Cultures', writing monographs on the female spectator, on perspective and pictorial space, and on art and anatomy; and still painting. . .

Kate Chedgzoy is a Lecturer in English at the University of Warwick. She has recently completed a doctoral thesis on cultural authority and the uses of Shakespeare, and is currently working on constructions of sexuality in early modern writing.

Barbara Crowther teaches Literature, Media and Cultural Studies in the Women's Studies division at the University of Wolverhampton. Her essay is part of a larger project on gender and representation in popular science. She is also working on the characteristics of girls' diary-writing.

Penny Florence is an independent scholar and filmmaker. She describes her film career as 'chequered', and she is now working mainly on her own in Hi 8 video. She is author of *Mallarmé, Manet and Redon. Visual and Aural Signs and the Generation of Meaning* (Cambridge University Press 1986), and various articles on painting, women's film, photography and writing. She has just taken up a position as Reader in Cultural Studies and Feminism at Falmouth College of Arts (formerly Falmouth School of Art and Design).

Jean Grant is a professional artist working in Liverpool. She has lectured at Goldsmith's College of Art, Croydon College of Art and Birmingham College of Art. Her current exhibitions include *Room to Manoeuvre* at The Grant Hall, Albert Dock, Liverpool (an audio-visual exhibition of work relating to *I am a Child of War*) and *Put Your Hand In and Feel the Darkness* (photographic installation) at the Open Eye Gallery, Liverpool.

Elizabeth Grosz is Director of the Institute of Critical and Cultural Studies, Monash University, Australia. She is the author of *Sexual subversions: Three French Feminists* (Allen and Unwin 1989); *Jacques Lacan: A Feminist Introduction* (Routledge 1990); and *Volatile Bodies: Toward a Corporeal Feminism* (Indiana University Press 1994).

Annette Kuhn is currently working on a book on memory work and productions of the self, *The Daughter's Lament*. For some years a freelance writer, lecturer and critic, she is now Reader in Film and Television Studies in the University of Glasgow.

Lynne Pearce teaches English and Women's Studies at Lancaster University. She is co-author of *Feminist Readings/Feminists Reading* (Harvester Wheatsheaf 1989) and author of *Woman/Image/Text* (Harvester Wheatsheaf 1991) and *Reading Dialogics* (Edward Arnold 1994). Her next project, *Feminism and the Politics of Reading*, will combine a selection of her published essays on 'reader positioning' with some new ones focusing, in particular, on the 'emotional politics' of the reading process.

Griselda Pollock, is Professor of the Social and Critical Histories of Art and Director of the Centre for Cultural Studies at the University of Leeds. She has written extensively on feminist issues in the histories of art and cultural representations, including *Old Mistresses, Women, Art and Ideology* (co-authored with Roszika Parker Pandora 1981) and *Vision and Difference* (Routledge 1988). Current projects involve 'differencing the canon' a feminist analysis of both women artists and 'modern masters' (forthcoming from Routledge).

Frances Presley is an experimental, feminist poet, whose work often explores the convergence of sex, poetry and painting. She has published two collections of poetry, *The Sex of Art* (North and South 1988), and *Hula Hoop* (The Other Press 1993). She lives in north London, where she is employed on a health and race project.

Susannah Radstone teaches in the department of Cultural Studies at the University of East London. Her essay in this collection will form part of the book she is currently writing, entitled *Ariadne's Thread: From Confession To Remembrance*, to be published by Routledge.

Dee Reynolds lectures in French at the University of Bristol. She specializes in comparative aesthetics and feminist approaches to aesthetics. She is the author of *Symbolist Aesthetics and Early Abstract Art: Sites of Imaginary Space* (Cambridge University Press, forthcoming) and is currently working on figures of dance in Symbolism and Expressionism.

Introduction

> Taking a small trowel out from my sack I began to dig in the roadside for the word that would open the secret of the Egg . . . I then understood that the word to address such a primitive and embryonic body would have to come from a language buried at the back of time. Leonora Carrington, *The Stone Door*[1]

Our aim in editing this collection is not to proclaim a new school of criticism, nor a new form of 'collected essay-art', or any such. It is to foreground consideration of how innovation by women in critical theory and methodology and in creativity participates in the dynamic of cultural change. In so doing, it should be no surprise that its own form is unconventional.

A primitive and embryonic body? Art at the back of time

Addressing the embryonic is doubtless a sophisticated business. Let it be clear that my choice of epigraph from Leonora Carrington does not imply that a woman active in culture is somehow like 'a bulky egg on legs', to borrow Christine Battersby's astounding quotation.[2] Nor do I subscribe to the idea that women (or notions of 'the female') are in some privileged relationship with the pre-verbal. Women are the inheritors of masculine culture, whether we will or no, as surely as we are of imperialism, and the way forward is inflected by the pasts of world culture. To be working at the same time to make visible what has been hidden and to make it possible to articulate the new is in itself a highly developed position with a complex history. The distinctiveness of women's culture includes its challenging relationship with a masculine inheritance. What the epigraph does imply is a recognition of the animating agency of the potential and of the unknown whenever a subject intervenes in meanings; this is the case whether I/you find ourselves in the role of writer/producer or reader/audience of any given text. Moreover, these are positions which shift and interact, and there is no clear separation between them. They are an example of the complexity and instability of intermeshing functions within which any subject currently operates in western culture. But the issues raised are particularly relevant within feminism, since they touch closely the problematic ways in which female subjects are positioned in different media, and position themselves. This collection is organised around such questions.

Carrington's 'primitive and embryonic body' also serves as a reminder of the paradoxical nature of possibly any cultural development, but certainly that of women's recorded culture. In addition to the vast differences between women's lived experience and how they make sense of it in the present, women's contribution to past culture, and the extent to which it is traceable either directly or indirectly, varies according to class and country. But common to us all is the need for self-representation within a world culture built on our denial and distortion, part of which is the tendency to homogenise, reducing differences between women to a chameleon femininity whose colours, while supposedly 'eternal', are responsive to the mutable needs of masculinity. Wherever we try to make our meanings we find to some extent that we have to get behind the way things are to reach the way things might become. It is in this sense as well as in the more abstract notion of an ever-present future at the back of time, that this collection participates in a process like that of Carrington's word to address the Egg, reaching backwards and forwards at the same time, from dis-placements both inside and outside at the same time. What I like about this way of describing women's positions in culture is that it puts us into language and signification in motion. Rather than emphasising blockage, it seeks to understand and make use of our experiences of what may be described as inhabiting differential space-times: where we situate ourselves, and where we are situated, do not necessarily coincide, either internally or in relation to others. There are many ways of forging the new from within a culture that finds increasingly subtle ways to deny the source of much of its most innovative creative energies, and of changing what meanings attach not only to 'being a woman', but to being active as a woman. Prominent among the issues raised is that of the self, the gendered self, and how it can be understood without perpetuating the dualistic ways of thinking that produce women as secondary, singular and fixed. Questioning the self invokes the social, especially in feminist approaches that try to discover a beyond to individualism. The contributions to this book approach questions of the self in politicised contexts, implicating definitions of the social in their mobilisation of a plurality of issues around spectatorship, performance and subjectivities.

One gritty consideration in feminist understandings of women's cultural interventions is widely implicit but less often pursued in writings or other commentaries of any kind about culture. It is that of whether and how new subject positions impact on form. This is a difficult question to approach without getting into technicalities, but it is raised in and by this collection. Several of the contributions are experimental, as is the collection itself. A proposition this book as a whole reflects upon is that a cultural movement dedicated to change will produce transitional forms, which would clearly demonstrate that control and hierarchisation of forms inhibit change. It is my belief that there is a connection between the reinvention of subjectivities and the erosion of the division between verbal and visual form. The same applies to a focus on the body, both in the sense of defining connections between the self and the gendered (female) body, and of testing the contours of the emergent transitional form against the cultural corpus in tension with its representations of the body. This is a theme which this collection both presents and represents.

The separated enclaves of cultural theory might well benefit from greater communication, as the essays collected here show. The book is not aimed exclusively at students of any one discipline, and one of our aims in bringing together a diversity of pieces is to draw innovative work to the attention of a wider audience than it might reach in a specialised collection. But moving between the various areas within which feminists are actively working to change and refine representation, it is striking how little permeates in the main from one to the other, even though the work has many common reference points. Pluralisation is not a virtue in and of itself; the formation of disciplines is part of a process of the institutionalisation of certain ways of thinking, and it has to be engaged with and developed to render it more relevant to women. This concerns not only women's studies, but also the growth of areas such as word-image studies, or the tension between the old idea of literature and its more recent role as one of 'the media'. This collection has come from artists, writers and critics from several academic disciplines, and from those with no current institutional affiliation. Even if we work independently, educational and cultural institutions necessarily affect how we can work if we wish to engage with the issues they have appropriated. My own experience of the relation between 'creative' and critical work has brought home to me that it remains insufficiently thought-out as a politicised issue for feminism in terms of the conditions that produce it. Specific conditions produce specific forms; that is a challenge taken up by women in cultural production wherever they situate themselves. We have to resist and engage at once, to speak into the future in a 'language buried at the back of time', but the precise ways of doing so vary according to the arena we work in, whether by choice or necessity.

'As sure as eggs is eggs'

There is no single cultural form that is *necessarily* more progressive than any other. The critical essay that sets out simply and clearly to transmit

cultural meanings where they may be inaccessible or obscure has its contribution to make as surely as the most innovatory. The same is true of,
say, the lyrical in art, or the straightforward narrative. 'Theory' used to be
thought of as masculine, and one of the important interventions feminists
have made has been to demonstrate how this hegemony was brought
about and maintained. How theory relates to what is called 'art', both in
itself and in its production is implicit in the form of this book and of several
of the contributions. Feminist artwork dealing explicitly with ideas has
been a prime target for the anti-feminist; put-downs include 'feminist
tract', 'preaching', 'tedious'. But literature or theatre of ideas has a long
and excellent tradition. A 'message' is not inevitably doomed to tumble
inspiration like Humpty-Dumpty. We would argue that within the development of a culture as a whole, the need for certain ideas-based forms is
historically produced. What is new about the current situation is not the
emergence of any single form, but rather it is the plurality of feminist
expressivity and commentary, and their common engagement with 'the
public'. By this I mean the awareness of material, institutional and semiotic factors which condition whether and how any given text can be
understood *by women*, and of how female audiences and readers participate
in the production of meaning. What is being said with this book is far more
about de-hierarchisation than it is about defining a new avant-garde. Some
of the contributions may *de facto* participate in a process of this kind, but
then I would argue that what is interesting and important here is the question why a given historical moment produces specific forms and shifts in
the constant realigning of cultural forms, why there should be an avant-
garde at all, rather than seeking to define and then freeze the definition.

The critic and the egg

Women have always had a voice and a culture, but it has been recondite.
Much of the feminist culture of the past twenty years has sought at the
same time to redefine what that voice might be as well as the subjectivity
with which it is in symbiotic formation; that is to say feminism has both
formed and been formed by women's changing senses of self and self-
representation, and it is impossible to say which, like the chicken and the
egg, came first. Indeed, part of what feminism is doing is to reframe such
questions to show that what matters and carries meaning is how the
answer is formulated. What is special about the present moment is that
women are reorienting this work to relocate it in relation to the public
sphere, aiming at the same time to transform that sphere and its meanings. While there are clearly senses in which this alterative approach to

patriarchal society's idea of itself has been present from the beginning of modern feminism, I would argue that there has been a significant development towards engagement with 'macro' social and power structures.

It is a moment which produces the role of the critic as various and innovatory, her function and methods sometimes as less clearly differentiated from those of the artists and writers alongside whom she struggles than has previously been the case, certainly since the last century. Such a *rapprochement* is paradoxical at a time when 'theory' has been in the ascendant in cultural studies within higher education, involving the kinds of specialised vocabulary and argumentation accessible only to those with particular academic training. This narrowing down has led many to be rightly critical of overly specialised and abstract ways of formulating the issues for women. But the work to be done requires multiple, coordinated strategies, and it is a mistake to reject all forms of difficult writing as elitist. The task, it seems to me, is rather to make the kinds of connection that allow the greatest possible access without oversimplification. There is a kind of levelling that constitutes distortion, which ultimately adds the insult of being patronising to the injury of obscuring real complexity. There is also an argument to be made for feminist interventions at all points and in all languages (or forms of discourse) now current. That includes the specialised, the academic and the theoretical. Our aim in collecting these chapters into a book is to combine thematic continuity with a stimulating and enjoyable variety of media and form so that the issues are to some extent enacted in the nature of the collection itself. By putting subjectivity into play in this way across a range of modes from the abstract to the autobiographical we hope to contribute to a productive dialogue between the various feminist articulations of how the forces at play in contemporary culture, and the values it manifests, are being both mobilised and changed by feminism.

Penny Florence

The collection

The authors in the first section, 'The politics of spectatorship', explore ways in which female spectators are positioned, both by the visual arts and other media, and by prevailing critical discourses. They propose possibilities for feminist interventions, which are frequently grounded in politicised readings of representations of the female body, perceived as a site of class, racial and historical discourses. This theme of the body will again be taken up by Elizabeth Grosz in the closing essay, in which her interrogation of psychoanalytic theory shows how a rewriting of the female body is crucial to feminist reshaping of patriarchal culture.

Griselda Pollock's piece takes the form of a series of letters to a 'Famous Professor' (Pollock is the addressor, not the addressee!), to a feminist scholar-friend, and to the nineteenth-century painter, Mary Cassatt. The distorted construction of artistic modernity as a male space is critiqued, partly as a product of paintings whose images of women and of social spaces cater to male desires, but also as a more recent product of the art historical discourses where such images are transposed into a male script. Pollock's epistolary drama unfolds in two parallel 'plots'. The production of space for a feminist subject of art history (one level) involves the uncovering of repressed meanings within representations of female subjects and of emerging nineteenth-century feminism (the other level). Using as a rhetorical device Freud's concept of the 'talking cure', Pollock sets out to discover the silenced voices of gender, race and class, whose discourses expose the fetishism and commodification at work in the myth of Paris constructed by late nineteenth-century Impressionist painters. This enterprise could not be undertaken without a dialogue with female Impressionists and specifically the work of Mary Cassatt. Mary Cassatt's painting, 'Woman in Black', contains a striking image of a woman looking, her gaze directed towards the 'elsewhere', the 'space off' emblematic of the 'elsewhere' of the subject of feminism. In Manet's painting, 'Un bar aux Folies-Bergère', Pollock discovers an intertextual 'repetition' of this image, which prompts a number of questions and opens a dialogue between the 'Bar' and contemporary (nineteenth-century) feminist discourses. This search for an 'elsewhere' to the 'Bar' leads Pollock to her denouement in the ungloved, work-worn hands of the barmaid, which 'give the game away', undermining fetishism and giving the lie to the monolithic, mythical discourse of modernism constructed by (male) art historians.

Kate Chedgzoy's essay on Frida Kahlo discusses further problems of spectatorship in terms of post-colonial thinking. Chedgzoy sets out to account for the unique intensity of feminist critical responses to Kahlo's images, and to show that white western feminist accounts of Kahlo's work – like her own – need to give more weight to Kahlo's political location and agency as the subject of her artistic practice. She demonstrates that psychoanalytic theory can be useful in analysing the ways in which Kahlo's paintings position the viewer, but it must be politicised through the inscription of the social, particularly issues of gender and race. The relation between the picture and the spectator is discussed in terms of

Kristeva's theory of the 'abject', whose power lies in a combination of fear of and desire for dissolution of identity, epitomised in the relation of women to the body of the mother. However, the body is not a transcendent given, and the female body is abjected as the 'm/other' of patriarchal masculinity. Chedgzoy draws on the politicised (though, as she points out, gender-blind) Bakhtinian concept of carnival, embedded in the 'grotesque' body, to support her argument that Kahlo's paintings of birth, miscarriage, the 'grotesque' and suffering body represent the process by which the female body is socialised and rendered abject by the technological gaze of patriarchal culture. Kahlo, however, used this inscription of the grotesque to 'make a spectacle of herself' in ways which actually enhanced her control over her art and life. Her body was displayed as an art work in itself. Moreover, by choosing to identify herself with the Tehuantepec, an indigenous Mexican people and the most matriarchal of Mexican Indian cultures, whose costumes she wore, Kahlo challenged the Europeanising politics of the pre-revolutionary regime. For Chedgzoy, then, a feminist approach to Kahlo demands a critical awareness of the racial and cultural specificity of the context of production, a context from which gender politics cannot be separated.

Two of Frances Presley's poems, 'Leonora at the Serpentine' and 'Imago', are responses to painterly images: the work of two women Surrealist artists, Leonora Carrington and Meret Oppenheim. As in the previous essays, the visual images are explored in words, but the poetic form allows greater licence and more ambiguity, presenting the reader (as the paintings present the spectator) with suggestive images to unravel. It is significant that these women painters are Surrealists, since Surrealist art has long been considered a predominantly male domain. Despite the active presence of women, their role has only recently claimed more critical attention. The poem 'Leonora at the Serpentine' evokes memorable images of Carrington's remarkable, dreamlike paintings, while using these images to probe quizzically and ironically the gender issues which they raise and which continue to permeate 'the world of dreams': 'the patriarchs have stopped enumerating/or have they?/is the world of dreams nothing/but newer and busier patriarchs:/ digital sequence under our feet?' 'Imago', whose form is pictorially evocative, is written to be read in conjunction with Presley's own commentary, which in turn comprises a commentary by Oppenheim on the image in question. 'Free Union' is an ingenious play on André Breton's poem, 'L'union libre', described by Presley as 'a surrealist idea reversed'. Here, the Surrealist transformation of woman into a mythical, sensual and transcendental object is deftly and humourously parodied by being translated into a celebration of male anatomy, comprising the stereotypical features of poetic worship of the female body, hair and eyes, as well as more specifically male appendages, such as the 'beard of burnt paper/ever curling away from its own expansion'.

Annette Kuhn takes the theme of spectatorship further, exploring the spectator/subject relation through analysing family photographs of herself. She shows how these photographic images, centred on representations of the body and its adornment, can be read as sites of power struggles between mother and daughter. The mother uses her authority both to present the child to be photographed looking as she wants her to be seen, and also to shape (by trimming) and inscribe the pictures themselves. Kuhn's readings of the pictures indicate how the daughter's body functions as a screen for the mother's desires, and show how 'dressing up' is part of the *production* of female identity (which is then passed off as part of the 'naturalised order of gender difference'), rather than simply the adornment of the female child: 'the clothes make the woman'. The female child, however, can reject this process and become 'a disappointment to her mother'. Kuhn's narration of her experience of spectatorship itself re-enacts this gesture.

In the final piece of this section, Penny Florence takes up an actual historical incident between Berthe Morisot and Edouard Manet and uses fictional techniques to probe the kinds of meaning it invokes. Morisot had asked Manet for his advice about a painting, and he had astonished and distressed her by taking over and feverishly repainting the figure of her mother. The theme of matricide is central to this piece, both as bodily actuality and historical metaphor. Her contribution is in the form of a 'video-poem', a visual dramatisation of the incident through the eyes of a contemporary white videomaker and through images deriving from paintings by the two artists, or inspired by them. As such it is itself about spectatorship and visual meanings. The differing roles of black and white women as artist, model and 'muse' are brought into play through Morisot herself, who sat for Manet several times, and through two of his other models, Victorine Meurend and Jeanne Duval, who was the inspiration for a cycle of poems by her lover, Charles Baudelaire.

The following section, 'Politics of production/performance', extends the spectrum of media, encompassing both 'popular' and 'high' culture (film, TV and opera), and engages with the question of women's involvement and (lack of) power at the institutional levels which control production/performance. Moreover, Jane Arthur's piece addresses the issue of the relation within feminism itself of 'popular' and 'professional' strands, as it emerged in debates over the controversial film, *Thelma and Louise*. There was disagreement among reviewers as to whether this film provided an empowering model for female spectators (an opinion reinforced by the vociferous response of female audiences) or whether it reproduced patriarchal structures of meaning, where women's transgression is punished by death. Its popularity and its status as Hollywood entertainment were not in doubt, but reactions to this were different. For some, the entertainment value rendered the underlying 'women's rights issues' more persuasive or more palatable, in explicit contrast to what was represented as the dour, humourless face of academic feminism, while for other (feminist) reviewers, its very popularity cast doubts on its 'authenticity' as a feminist film. While recognising the film's ideological limitations and the dangers of depoliticisation which its Hollywood context entails, Arthurs argues persuasively that the historical changes whereby feminism has broadened to encompass a wider class spectrum and has become a more diffused current within society, 'necessitate a mode of address that connects with popular culture'. It is crucial for feminism to intervene at the centre as well as in the margins. Further controversy was generated by the fact that *Thelma and Louise*, although scripted by a woman, Kallie Khouri, was directed by a man, Ridley Scott. Arthurs points out that the complexity of film-making means that there is 'a multiplicity of "authors", all of whom will have some influence on the final text'. A film can have positive value for feminism without being exclusively female authored. However, because mainstream filmmakers enjoy better conditions and can exert far more influence than those working on the margins, long term radical effects will require the presence of greater numbers of women in areas of the industry that have sufficient finance to reach large sectors of the population.

Concerns of power and control over performance and the means of production resurface in Barbara Crowther's treatment of natural history programmes, which sets out to expose the gendered agenda of this highly popular and influential genre, as exemplified in David Attenborough's blockbuster, the Trials of Life. The gender bias here extends right from the 'hero' culture which dominates the programmes' production to the politics of the living room, where programme choice is often the prerogative of the 'biggest'. Natural history programmes are in fact more popular with male than with female viewers, a preference which comes to seem highly logical as Crowther charts the encoding of gender bias and misogyny through analyses of narrative format, language and rhetoric.

These strategies are also analysed in the contexts of the positioning of women within supposedly 'objective' scientific culture, and of the gender implications of the adoption of sociobiological models. Crowther puts forward constructive proposals for less exclusive approaches to the making and formats of natural history programmes, which could better serve women's interests, but emphasises that a prerequisite for change must be the involvement of more women in the production process.

Opera, generally considered a 'high' cultural form, has in recent years expanded further into 'popular' culture, especially through film versions. Opera is of special interest to feminists in that it has traditionally been a favourite of women, and also in that the great stars of opera – its 'primadonnas' – are female. Taking as her starting point the writings of Catherine Clément on opera, Jean Andrews explores the figure of Carmen (possibly the most popular opera heroine of all time) and traces her portrayal in the film versions by Francesco Rosi and by Antonio Gades and Carlos Saura, and in the stage version performed under the direction of Nuria Espert at Covent Garden. Clément sees 'hysteria' both as a positive characteristic of the 'feminine' and as central to opera, although she considers that great male figures like Don Giovanni and Orpheus are akin to female 'hysterics'. While in agreement with the spirit of Clément's approach, Andrews questions her insufficiently critical espousal of Romantic stereotypes of femininity. However, Clément's analysis of opera is also grounded on its misogynist plots, which, in her view, highlight the superiority of women. Opera heroines are victims and must die because they are a danger to men: 'their aspirations to independence are intolerable'. Carmen, whom Clément considers as the most feminist, the most independent-minded of opera's doomed heroines, is destined to die because she is a woman who refuses to conform. Andrews' readings of the three versions of the opera show how this defiance can also operate at the level of performance. In the film versions (particularly in the Rosi film), the female performers have to reproduce femininity as imagined by the male, and Carmen is 'on show' for the gaze of the male spectator. In the Nuria Espert production, on the other hand, Carmen's ambiguity is not that of the enigmatic *femme fatale*: on the contrary, she refuses to submit to the male gaze, and it is Don José, rather than Carmen (Maria Ewing) who is 'on show'. Here, the irrational power of the feminine is aligned with the power of the dangerous female, the outsider who threatens patriarchal power structures, thereby creating a powerful feminist production of Carmen. Andrews notes, however, that such performances are likely to remain the exception in the foreseeable future, since funding for opera is largely in the hands of traditionalists.

The essays in the final section, 'Repositioning feminist subjects', explore new possibilities for mobilising feminist subjectivity. All the pieces are 'subject-centred', through their presentation in the first person, their reflexive exploration of the critic-as-subject, or their reconceptualisation of subject formation itself. Memory and its significance for feminism is a recurrent theme. It is central to Jean Grant's art work, while Susannah Radstone's piece proposes a challenging new perspective on the role of 'remembrance' in the constitution of female subjectivity. Finally, Elizabeth Grosz's provocative essay argues powerfully for the possibility of intervening in the social construction of subjectivity through a 'rewriting' of the female body as positivity rather than as lack.

Lynne Pearce's 'I the reader: text, context and the balance of power' begins as a critique of the apparent freedom offered by the 'death of the author', conducted in the form of a humourously ironic backward look at her own history as reader and critic of both verbal and visual texts. Her espousal of the concept of the 'death of the author' and of (Bakhtinian) polyphony blinded her, as she later realised, to the power structures created by the setting up of dominant reading positions by the text itself. These positions, however misogynist (as exemplified in Pre-Raphaelite art and literature), could be 'deconstructed' by a variety of reading strategies which enabled the female reader to reappropriate the text – or could they? Reading texts against the grain of their historical production does not erase their inscription of a 'preferred reader'. Exploring this concept further through feminist writing leads to the discovery of a new dimension of 'polyphony', which is now recognised as being both plural and hierarchical, but also shifting: even within feminist writing, the implied 'preferred' reader is multiple: black, white, heterosexual, lesbian, middle class, working class, and so on. The feminist subject position, then, is not one but many, and the reader's freedom is an unstable negotiation between positions. It is the strategic understanding of this dynamic which constitutes the politics of reading.

Jean Grant's highly original art work brings together personal and national history. The continuing presence of her own past is explored as part of the history of a nation. The loss of her father, who died in World War II, was potentially redeemed by the legacy of peacetime structures such as that of the welfare state, but these structures are now themselves undergoing dismemberment. Grant also explores her conflicting position as an artist and a woman, isolated within art institutions and yielding for a time to pressures to devote herself to domestic responsibilities rather than to making art. But her making of art has continued, producing here images which are at once abstract and lyrical, and which intersect with the narrative to condemn the use of images to glorify war. It is perhaps not surprising that at exhibitions of work related to this piece, Grant is often approached by women with experience of war tragedies who report that for the first time they have encountered art work which addresses their experience at a deep level.

Susannah Radstone's essay explores the constitution of 'female selves' through feminist 'memory work' which is both remembering and antici-pating. Crucially, Radstone differentiates remembrance from nostalgia. She reads the story of Medea in order to uncover the hidden myths of psychoanalysis itself, where (as she shows through analysis of Jane Flax's and Valerie Walkerdine's treatment of remembrance), remembrance often conceals nostalgia for the figure of an archaic, powerful mother, remem-bered as both 'other' and 'self'. Similarly, Toni Morrison's *Beloved* can be read as a re-presentation of the mother figure as subject and object of nos-talgic desire. Radstone discusses the treatment of nostalgia in Mary Jacobus, for whom feminine desire as nostalgia is produced at a moment of *Nachträglichkeit*: a remembering of the pre-Oedipal from the side of the Oedipal. The object of desire emerges as the phallic mother, and female desire risks reinscribing the fiction of the uncastrated woman at the cost of denying sexual difference. The task of feminist remembrance, on the other hand, is to remember what nostalgia forgets: it is sustained by nos-talgia, but works through it to the 'beyond' of the 'other country' (Carol Ann Duffy, 'In Your Mind'). Radstone traces the workings of this process in two literary texts, Drusilla Modjeska's 'Poppy' and Eva Hoffmann's *Lost in Translation.*

Elizabeth Grosz begins by challenging and deconstructing the bound-aries between the psychical and the sociocultural constitution of subjects as masculine or feminine. Working through and beyond the existing con-fines of psychoanalysis, Grosz argues that the body itself is the ground for the *social* production of subjects, for constructing our sense of 'self'. For Freud, the ego is constituted by the subject's relation to his/her own body, which already internalises the relation to the 'm/other'. In this sense, the ego is 'the meeting point, the conjunction, between the body and the social'. Not only is the ego inseparable from the body, but the body is in itself 'meaningful', as a result of the libido or sexual energy the subject has invested in it. Moreover, the body of the other provides a model for the representation of one's own body. This representation is a function, not merely of sensation or perception, but also of fantasy and desire, which are themselves inseparable from the cultural contexts through which they are constituted. In fact, the biological body exists for the subject only through the mediation of sociocultural images. Each individual's self-conception is directly linked to the social meaning and value of the sexed body; indeed, gender cannot be separated from the sexed body. Significantly, although Freud offers a model of the relation between body and world for the male, there is no such representation for women. Lacan recognises the lack of a model of subjectivity specific to the female body, but he argues that this is an inevitable outcome of 'the dominance of the penis in the shaping of the body image'. Grosz counters, however, that the phallus cannot have the same meaning for the girl as for the boy, and that although psychoanalysis describes and explains the 'mutilated body image' which results from the construction of the female body as lack, it does not recognise that this construction is specific to patriarchal culture. The female body is *socially* constituted and 'written', and can therefore potentially be 'rewritten' as a positivity.

By challenging and intervening in representational systems across the media, feminists actively engage in a 'rewriting' of female subjects. Through its presentation of a cross-section of such activity, this collection aims to open up new perspectives in feminist cultural methodologies.

Dee Reynolds

Notes

1. Leonora Carrington, *The Seventh Horse and Other Tales*, London, Virago (1989) p. 86.
2. Christine Battersby, *Gender and Genius. Towards a Feminist Aesthetics*, London, The Women's Press (1989) p. 20. Battersby is critiquing the masculinist version of culture exemplified by Paul Abelman, according to which a woman cannot be culturally creative without going against female nature. Incredibly, he was writing in 1983.

The politics of spectatorship

Fig. 1.1 *A Bar at the Folies Bergère* Edouard Manet (1881–82)
Courtauld Institute Galleries, London

1 The 'View from Elsewhere': Extracts from a semi-public correspondence about the politics of feminist spectatorship

GRISELDA POLLOCK

I Letter to a famous professor, or, Through the looking glass
Dear Sir,
Well, here I am, at last, in front of one of the most valued and valuable paintings in the Courtauld Institute Galleries, London, The Bar at the Folies Bergère *by Edouard Manet (1881–2) (Fig. 1.1). It is obviously one of the canonical images for modernist art history, and the painting has acquired a symbolic function in the social history of art. But the way in which* The Bar *has been discussed exposes the limits within which all existing art histories operate in regard to questions of sexuality and representation, the interface of class and gender, the association between spectatorship and power.[1] Given all that has been said about this painting, all the significance it has acquired, what can I say about it? As I stand in front of* The Bar *and the discursive field to which it is central, where can I be? What I am asking about are the possibilities for a female spectator, and further, for a* **feminist** *relation to this work and to the art historical practices which have defined its significance in all the existing histories of modernism? I do not know if you read much feminist theory. Of course, I do, since it is there that a I find the critical reading and writing practices through which I forge a way to do something like art history, to intervene against it as much as into it. Let me quote you a passage I read recently which set me thinking.*

> The problem, which is a problem for all feminist scholars and teachers, is . . . that most of the available theories of reading, writing, sexuality, ideology, or any other cultural production are built on male narratives of gender, whether Oedipal or anti-oedipal, bound by the heterosexual contract; narratives which persistently reproduce themselves in feminist theories. They *tend to*, and will do so unless one constantly resists, suspicious of their drift. Which is why the critique of all discourses concerning gender, including those promoted as feminist, continues to be as vital a part of feminism as the ongoing effort to create new spaces of discourse, to rewrite cultural narratives, and to define the terms of another perspective – a view from 'elsewhere'. Teresa de Lauretis, *Technologies of Gender*[2]

I started writing about it and I shall quote what I have done so far:

For Teresa de Lauretis **gender** is a semiotic construction which takes place through the interlaced processes of representation and self-representation. Gender is produced in the constant play of material social practices, institutions, apparatuses, whose representations are absorbed subjectively by individuals as they are addressed by what she calls, borrowing and adapting from Foucault, the 'technologies of gender'. De Lauretis identifies the cinema as such an apparatus, for instance, and shows why the concept of spectatorship has become a vitally important area for feminist contestation of the gendering processes of cinema, as well as for a theorised analysis of the power of 'address' in film-making in general. 'All western Art and high culture is the "engraving" of the constructions of gender', she argues, while also asserting that the academy, intellectual and artistic practices and radical theories may equally be technologies producing gender. Such areas can also become a place for a radical deconstruction – once their function in the social process of gender formation is recognised and the implications for all practising within their ambits is acknowledged.

Here is where I would identify my current concerns – the effects on me, as a woman, of studying art history, entering the narratives and practices of the discipline as well as those of the artistic practices art history attempts to study. The apparatuses of art and the academy address me as a potential participant in terms which are the product of current gender constructions. Just as the cinema positions its anticipated spectators, so too the narratives of art history propose modes of viewing and study, showing me how to look at paintings, how to see their meanings, how to be placed in front of art works. They define a position for knowing which is fundamentally a highly specific and selective form of gaze.

Feminism has provided an 'elsewhere'. Over the last twenty years, feminist art history has slowly and often painfully found ways to resist the relation to the image which is proposed in dominant forms of art history. Feminist art histories, now plural and engaged in serious theoretical and political debate, have identified other narratives to study and found new spaces to research. We look at the omitted and neglected work of artists who were women while we also redefine the work of canonical artists who were men. We name the ways in which gender is enacted in both the practices of art-making and its reception. Feminism has been the politically motivated production of critical representations of gender. These have in turn changed the very producers of such critical representations as the new discourses we were inventing collectively as a movement and as a community within and outside the academy acted back upon us,

addressing us not as art historians who are women, but as political subjects, as feminists.

But as De Lauretis suggests, there is no place 'outside' the institution
which can guarantee the value of the discourses feminists produce.
Feminist analysis must be its own perpetual provocation and auto-criti-
cism. Feminism is itself a construction of gender, vulnerable to the institutional spaces and ideological materials with which it works. I am forced
to ask myself, can I be a feminist and an art historian – or have they
become mutually contradictory categories?

De Lauretis provides a provisional answer which allows my re-engage-
ment with the high ground of art history:

> For that 'elsewhere' is not some distant mythic past or some utopian future
> history; it is the elsewhere of discourse here and now, the blind spots, or the
> space-off, of its representations. I think of it as the margins of hegemonic dis-
> courses, social spaces carved in the interstices of institutions and in the chinks
> and cracks of the power-knowledge apparati.[3]

This space-off is not outside of discourse, or beyond ideology, a reality
external to it. 'What I mean instead,' she writes, 'is movement from the
space represented by/in a representation, by/in a discourse, by/in a
sex/gender system, to the space not represented yet implied (unseen) in
them.'[4]

What is it that we are looking for in this elsewhere? It is surely not
some real notion of woman repressed in a dominant white patriarchal
culture, and not merely the concrete realities of women in their cultural
diversities to set against the monolithic and imperialising abstraction
Woman. No more is it a purely speculative femininity at present only
imagined in feminist theory and literature. De Lauretis has in mind a
subject produced by feminism:

> By the phrase 'the subject of feminism' I mean a conception or an under-
> standing of the (female) subject as not only distinct from Woman with the
> capital letter, the *representation* of an essence inherent in all women (which
> has been seen as Nature, Mother, Mystery, Evil Incarnate, Object of
> [Masculine] Desire and Knowledge, Proper Womanhood, Femininity *et
> cetera*), but also distinct from women, the real historical beings and social sub-
> jects who are defined by the technology of gender and actually engendered
> social relations. The subject of feminism I have in mind is one *not* so defined,
> one whose definition or conception in is progress, in this and other feminist
> critical texts.[5]

The subject of feminism is a theoretical construct – a product of what
we are thinking and writing in the political configurations of the present.

Those of us living under the sign Woman, and identifying as women through representation and self-representation in contemporary culture, are engaged in a process of producing this subject of feminism, through the discursive positions we create, through the forms of address feminist writing can signify, through the look we cast over the spaces of representation, at them as much as away from them.

What I want to write about The Bar *is, therefore, not a piece of feminist art history, a demonstration of a feminist methodology and not an example of an orthodoxy. It will be a practice of reading and writing which will contribute to the production of a feminist subject – a position for viewing and seeing the painting in question and its cultural conditions of existence which will stretch the contradictions inherent in the technology of gender serviced by both modernist painting and modernist art history. In finding an elsewhere in the painting and an elsewhere in nineteenth-century feminist discourse from which to re-view the painting at work, I hope to contribute to demythologising the history of the nineteenth century. The point is not that gender is any more fundamental than the social relations of class, race, or sexuality. What I want to emphasise is, however, that it is* **as** *fundamental, as determining, and I contend that feminism, now undergoing its own process of radical self-criticism around issues of class, race and sexuality, is the political and discursive space where the fabric of textured inequalities and exploitations are being addressed.*

Let me try an opening out on you:

The narratives of class and gender within which The *Bar at the Folies Bergère* (Fig. 1.1) was produced in France in 1881, and those operative in present day art histories, coincide on the body of the barmaid, the monumental figurative centre of the painting. She provides the invitation to the presumed or, what should be called, the preferred spectator. A narrative reading of the painting defines her as a barmaid attending to a customer. 'What do you want?', she asks, which, read metaphorically, clearly means 'What do you desire?' (Fig. 1.2). Yet this impassive, still figure balks any confident knowledge. She remains an enigma that only further incites repeated art historical attention to the play of mirrors and reflections to generate the possibility that **she** is what the viewer desires. T. J. Clark's compelling reading of the historical specificity of this social space of the café-concert as paradigmatic of the *populaire* as the bourgeoisie consumed it, and the petite bourgeosie performed it, defines the painting as a tissue of uncertainties which never merely become a matter of pure ambiguity. The barmaid is calcu-

Fig. 1.2 Detail from *A Bar at the Folies Bergère*
Edouard Manet
Courtauld Institute Galleries, London

lated to function as 'detached', in a way which allows the customer to think she is one more such object which money can buy, and in a sense it is part of her duties to maintain that illusion.[6] In his study *Impressionism*, Robert Herbert reads the impossible reflection as an explicit sexual fantasy. The reflected barmaid's more responsive pose signifies the potential acquiescence envisioned by the desiring man: 'In the mirror, her more yielding nature is revealed, detached as it were from her body by the man's power of wish-fulfillment . . . We can't really be that man, yet because we are in the position he would occupy in front of the bar, he becomes our second self' (Fig. 1.2). At the point at which the regimes of representation of the commodity and masculine desire historically interpenetrate, these interpretations work within a gender ideology. The 'we' of the texts is the collectivity of men who can in fantasy and scholarship identify with the *Homme du Monde*, man of the world, *flâneur* and dandy who painted it and whose surrogate stands

ominously in the extreme right-hand side of the painting, offering his
implied place for the viewer to occupy.

I cannot be where he is, or might be. I can belong only to the 'you' and
the 'her', like the audience for Freud's undelivered lecture on 'Femininity'
of 1933:

> Throughout history people have knocked their head against the riddle of the
> nature of femininity –
> 'Heads in hieroglyphic bonnets,
> Heads in turbans and black birettas,
> Heads in wigs and a thousand others
> Wretched, sweating heads of humans . . .'
> Nor will *you* have escaped worrying over this problem – those of you who
> are men; to those of you who are women this will not apply – you are
> yourselves the problem.[7]

The painting is apparently a full sign, promising meaning – about Manet's
art, about avant-garde painting, and above all about Paris. It offers an
image of a social space catering to masculine desire. It is also, however, an
ambiguous sign, defaulting on its semiotic promise. Only through the
complex of significations projected onto and by this historically and
socially constituted female body can its discomforting dissonances be
contained. A painting which writers confidently proclaim offers the
essence of Paris does so precisely because of an ideological elision between
the city, Paris and a female image, *La Parisienne.* She is an embodiment of
bourgeois men's fantasies about female availability in which woman is like
a blank page upon which is inscribed a masculine script through the social
hieroglyphics of fashion. As a historical articulation of the accelerating
temporality characteristic of modernity, fashion then, as now, contains
within it notions of both commodity and masquerade – indeed it is a
precise formulation of the one as the other, and vice versa.

Furthermore, City and Woman are conflated through the signifying
relations of sex and money for which the body of *La Parisienne* was both
sign and conduit. These relations constitute the semiotic, and hence political, mastery of the masculine bourgeois subject – fictionalised as Man and
given a specifically modern garb as the man of the world. The myth of
Paris was produced by men such as Baudelaire, Zola, Dumas, the
Goncourts, Houssaye, Proust, Degas, Grevin, Huysmans, Mallarmé and
Manet. It has been adopted as the myth of modernist and social art
history. Doing the latter provides vicarious access to the former – a myth
of access to a world through vicarious consumption of its principle image
and fantasy – the available and desirable modern woman. Clark was right,

and more precise than Herbert: that sexual fantasy is riven with the matter of class.

I have never written much on Manet before. He belongs to them, the art histor-ians, the big others. These are men, for the most part, who seem to feel at home in the world of late-nineteenth-century French culture. They make it their own pro-fessional territory. It feeds and satisfies their fantasies of a society of men of the world, dandies, and of women of the half-world, the demi-mondaines. *Doing something on Manet, a colleague commented to me, when I first mentioned I was going to write about* The Bar at the Folies Bergère *is like a trip to a brothel; it is a rite of passage. This has become even more insistent and problematic in the aftermath of writers on Manet and modernity like Clark (coming to us via Knopff and Thames and Hudson) and Herbert (courtesy of Yale University Press). I have dared to talk about Manet a little in lectures and seminars. In the more informal spaces of the classroom, I can build up the confidence to advance a few ideas of my own about these critical and peculiar works and their historical moment. But I have literally never dared to conceive of writing – going public – with one of 'their' prize and paradigmatic names, who belongs in those grand schemes that run from Manet to [another] Pollock.*

Such a confession is no mere feint or device. The apprehension is real. My anxiety at dealing with this artist and this painting is genuine, because it is ulti-mately political. It is important not to underestimate the level at which I per-sonally experience the conflicts between feminism and art history. I have introjected a lack which stems from initially misunderstanding why I did not 'naturally' understand the goings on and fantasies of early modernist Paris and its paintings. What could I identify with when that culture made women its badge, not the agents of its meaning, but the cipher for those produced by the men of the world?

Despite my professional training which placed Manet so centrally on the agenda of the period in which I chose to specialise as a postgraduate student, there is a powerful censorship at work, something akin to Virginia Woolf's 'Angel in the House'. This was the voice of cultural conscience, of conventional femi-ninity, which shadowed her initial attempts at writing, encouraging her to conform to the admiring and supportive role prescribed for women. 'Be sympa-thetic; be tender; flatter; deceive; use all the arts and wiles of your sex. Never let anyone guess you have a mind of your own. Above all, be pure.' Virginia Woolf says she had to murder this phantom, else it would have taken the heart out of her writing.[8]

Women art historians have of course written about Manet.[9] *But in borrowed clothes, we have masqueraded as men, and lent our considerable scholarship to the perpetuation of the mythologies of modernism. We are well schooled in the professional transvestitism which the discipline requires of us — so that we either adopt the positions of viewing offered by the works of art and assumed in art history, or we masochistically accept our objectification by identifying with the image. Through this may come the pleasure of formal appreciation of the painting's masterful performance as a piece of painting. Seduced by the beauty of art, we accede to an image of femininity or femininity as an image. Or else we can divest ourselves of that femininity and internalise the viewpoint of the father. Feminism interrupts this spectatorship by providing a language in which to critique the image and to insist upon the sexual differentiation of spectatorship.*[10]

*Censored by the hegemony of modernist art histories, I have found an indirect way to have some access to nineteenth-century French culture by looking to (what seemed like) its margins. There, overlooked by the men whose scholarship has defined the field, were women modernists, notably Mary Cassatt and Berthe Morisot. They made me bold. To begin to understand their practice, I had to come to terms with what the big others had made their own, modernism. Once I looked at modernism from the vantage point of women modernists, of women **and** modernity, modernism looked very different. It was not nearly so monolithic and alien. It could contain elements of my own imaginary, my own experiences of urban life, with its prohibited spaces, its dread of that ubiquitous, proprietorial and offensive male gaze, but also its specific pleasures of female sociability, fashion, public entertainment, travel, science, education and so forth.*

Such a re-vision of modernism and modernity was made possible by the revitalisation of feminism rooted in that nineteenth-century moment of modernity. The emergent bourgeoisie produced a particularly vicious and confining concept of femininity, but its triumph incited the challenge to it in the form of women's social movements and the intellectual and artistic developments collectively known as feminism. Never merely a struggle about the voting rights of women, feminism in its largest intellectual sense is a struggle around enunciations of femininity, in fact, a critique of representation and sexual difference. Instead of battling with the bourgeois problematic of 'What is woman?', feminism utilised the modern preoccupation with change to explore what women could be or become. Excavating historical variation in the past and cultural diversity in their own presents, using current evolutionary theory to their purpose, feminists resisted the fixity of ideological notions of women's eternal nature by arguing that as woman is a social and historical category, what she is could be changed.[11]

Ignored or overlooked by the keenest scholars of modernity, we are obliged to recognise belatedly that feminism was one of the major symptoms of modernity, deeply rooted in the discourses and politics of which modernism as cultural form was the product.

In several earlier texts, I have focused on the formations of femininity within modern bourgeois culture, exploring its resources for women producers of that class to enunciate the specificity of their social and psychic positioning within a critical engagement with the consciousness and social practices of bourgeois modernity.[12] In this essay, I want to confront art history's submission to a mythic – a classed and gendered – version of modernity by shadowing The Bar at the Folies Bergère, *Manet and art history with the discourses of historical feminism which all three repressed.*

I'm off to the British Library to do some more reading.

Yours sincerely . . . .

II Letter to a feminist scholar, or, What do women want?

Dear Friend,

I was at the British Library the other day doing some research for an essay I have agreed to write about Manet's The Bar at the Folies Bergère. *Yes, I can well imagine, you are shocked. I never thought I would come to this, doing 'real art history' again after so long in the polemics and pleasures of feminist theory, writing always about art history, not talking about the pictures like you're sup- posed to. I feel the Courtauld and all its disciplines are far enough behind me now to dare do it. Besides, I always felt bad that I did not do any real research, you know, like you do at the Bibliothèque Nationale and so forth. So here, I am, in the British Library Reading room, sitting at the computer, doing a search for books about women and especially feminism in France in the nineteenth century. I'm getting very frustrated. None of the key words I try bring up any titles. Do they have no books on women and feminism? I recall Virginia Woolf being acid about just how many books are written about women. Eventually I get angry and in a fit of clearly Freudian rage I stamp out on the keys:* **What do Women Want?** *To my complete amazement, up comes one item, a book with exactly that title.*

On the 10 April 1869, a liberal bourgeois feminist, Maria Desraimes, pub- lished a lecture which was significantly titled 'Qu'est-ce que veulent les femmes?' Desraimes was born in 1828, four years before Manet. She was the daughter of republican, anti-clerical parents who were keen followers of Voltaire's rationalism. From them, she received a 'modern' education. In this formation she typifies the forces which made possible the altered relation between the terms 'women' and 'modernity'. Desraimes' question predates Freud's famous formulation of his own perplexity about 'what a woman wants' by more than half a century and shows that his blindness to women's desire was partly self-inflicted. By the 1930s there was plenty of evidence from the women's movement of what women desired.[13] It is a coincidence of considerable significance that Berthe Pappenheim, the real name of the patient 'Anna O', helped by Freud's colleague, Josef Breuer, underwent the first successful analysis in 1880–81, the very year in which Manet was painting *The Bar*. It was she who formulated the therapeutic process of, and name for, the 'talking cure', what became psychoanalysis itself. Through being listened to, Berthe Pappenheim overcame her socially induced, psychically experienced and physically manifested ill-nesses, by being able to articulate that she wanted to do something with her education. Indeed her case poses the important question: is feminism itself the 'talking cure' for women, the means to give voice to what the culture represses, leaving us bodies in trouble with patriarchal language, with its complex social ramifications embedded within its symbolic system? Berthe Pappenheim spoke four languages and Breuer commented on her being 'markedly intelligent with an astonishingly quick grasp of things and a penetrating intuiton' as well having 'great poetic and imag-inative gifts',[14] all of which were repressed by the closed horizons offered to the middle-class woman of a wealthy Orthodox Jewish family. The crisis of her illness manifested itself in an inability to speak at all. After her 'self'-treatment, she became a feminist activist, founder of the German League of Jewish Women, and translator of Mary Wollstonecraft's *Vindication of the Rights of Women* (1792).[15]

Maria Desraimes's answer to her own question derived from that same lineage, the feminist appropriation of the Enlightenment discourse of natural rights: women want '*le droit et la liberté*' ('rights and freedom'). Significantly, her concept of liberty included freedom from the linguistic dominance of men, from the fate of being represented. Women desire to represent themselves.[16]

> *Ce que les femmes veulent, c'est que les hommes cessent de baser leur grandeur sur l'amoindrissement systématique des femmes ... c'est de ne point être elevées, enseignées, façonnées suivant un type de convention, type conçu dans la cervelle des poètes, des romanciers, des artistes, et par conséquent dépourvu de réalité.*[17]
> [What women want is that men stop building their own elevated status on the systematic debasement of women; what women want is not to be brought up, instructed, and fashioned according to a convention, a type conceived in the brains of poets, novelists, artists, and as a result, entirely unrelated to reality.]

Maria Desraimes had participated in the foundation in 1866 of the first feminist organisation in France, La Société pour la Revendication des

Droits de la Femme (Society for the Promotion of the Rights of Women), whose chief purpose was to foster women's education. In 1870 she cofounded the Association pour le Droit des Femmes and was part of the Congrès Français International du Droit des Femmes which coincided with the International Exhibition held in Paris in 1878. It was over the question of the vote that this congress was split and Hubertine Auclert withdrew to found her own magazine and promote the political rights of women. During the elections of 1881, while *The Bar* was being painted and exhibited, French women campaigned for the vote. In 1884 three women were actually elected, but the election was later deemed unconstitutional. The debate in France over women's voting rights was complicated by continual anxieties about the security of the republican cause, and thus opposition to female suffrage was often posed in the name of a defence of the republic against **unenlightened** women who were under the sway of the priests.[18] These were women not yet reformed by modernity, who would sustain an antithetical, that is fixed and Catholic concept of femininity. For the modernist feminists of this liberal bourgeois constituency, education and thus rationality and modernity, were the necessary prerequisites for women's rights and their 'intellectual' liberty. Socialist feminists like Hubertine Auclert had a greater commitment to enfranchisement as the means to legislative changes to alter women's lack of economic freedom. Working women were in need less of cultural liberation than of the means to secure concrete necessities in relation to wages, work conditions and legal rights. Yet the radical communards and socialists, like Paule Minck, resisted suffrage and encouraged women to work within revolutionary groups to challenge domestic slavery and the authority of men at home as much as at work. The critical point, however, is that women were in need of a change in their status *vis-à-vis* representation, whether we use the term politically or discursively. Some wanted to represent themselves through the vote and political activity; others through the word and the image. The condition for both was the product of the conjunction of women's interests and the possibilities offered by modernity. Orators and writers like Hubertine Auclert, Paule Minck, Louise Michel, and Maria Desraimes took an active part in both class and gender struggle on the battlefield of representation.

The feminist movement, its debates, publications and conferences constitute, therefore, an erasure in the typical histories of modernity. Yet feminism is very much a presence in the history of Mary Cassatt. It informed her politically self-conscious programme of work and exhibition policies.

It directed actions in the support of independence in art and women's suffrage in politics. Feminism is part of her mural *Modern Woman* for the Women's Pavilion of the Columbian World Fair in Chicago in 1893 (significantly now lost but showing as its central subject 'Women Plucking the Fruits of Knowledge and Science'). Feminism is also a presence in the women intellectuals whose names we encounter only as models for painters such as Renoir, *Séverine*, for instance. Feminism is boldly voiced in the uncensored entries in the diaries of Marie Bashkirtseff about her meetings with Hubertine Auclert and her art reviews for Auclert's feminist journal *La Citoyenne*.[19] The other Parisiennes were these women intellectuals and artists who campaigned against the economic, political, professional and educational limitations that rendered women vulnerable to sexual exploitation, which modernist culture mythologised in its endless parade of grisettes, lorettes, cocottes, its partial version of *La Parisienne*

In sisterhood . . .

III Letter to a famous professor, or, Looking away
Dear Sir,

Against the mythic image of Paris and Parisiennes, circulated by all the masculinist art histories, I have found that I can interpose the feminist movement which equally forms part of the historical possibilities of modernist culture. Feminism constitutes the content of a 'space off', placed beyond the frame of these modernist discourses, yet none the less implied by it. The challenge to the class and gender power of bourgeois men posed by feminism in the nineteenth century is the phantom that shadows the works and images of the 'men of the world'. Feminism is the structuring absence. To be ignorant of this is to consume uncritically the mythology they produced in that intense period of gender struggle when women mounted a sustained attack on male bourgeois society.

Viewed from the elsewhere of feminism, La Parisienne *is, therefore, only a fragment of the history of women in the nineteenth century. The women who played this role were culled from those precarious professions available to pretty working-class women where they sold not their labour power but their appearance and their bodies – as prostitutes as well as performers, as mannequins and walking advertisements for couturiers and the fashions of the* grands magasins, *sometimes overdressed, at others naked as the Venus which made the fame of Zola's eponymous novel* Nana.[20]

Novelene Ross's study of *The Bar at the Folies Bergère* concludes with 'the most significant dimension of the painting – the provocative mystique of the barmaid'.[21] I cannot contest the fact that the monumental figure in the foreground is an arresting figure. Her position and purpose must be central to any understanding of the painting's project and effect. That she is a female figure, coded as a barmaid in that environment of potential as well as actual sexual commerce, provides the grounds for reading the painting's complex representation of the spaces of modernity which can be defined as those socially ambivalent and interstitial places of cross-class sexual exchange and their related fantasies.[22] In her chapter on the painting itself, significantly titled, 'The Woman at the Counter', Ross says everything very clearly:

> In the last major painting of his career, Manet paid eloquent tribute to *La Parisienne*, who was the chief deity of that world. *Un Bar aux Folies Bergère* could not have been more modern, for it distilled that element of the myth which sustained the clichés of popular art, motivated the naturalism of the avant-garde, and confirmed Manet's personal delight at being a man of his own time. The girl at the bar is a descendent of Monier's grisette, and the kingdom over which she presides bears a name that still evokes the promise of that delicious wickedness which is the secret charm of every great city, but most especially of Paris. When Manet decided to paint the subject of the Folies Bergère, it had already become synonymous with the seductions of *La Parisienne* and the boulevards.[23]

Paris is *La Parisienne*. To the *hommes du monde* like Charles Baudelaire, Paris was a City of Women. But the inversion is also appropriate: Woman was like the city, a sexual geography, with each part of the body, from face to pudenda, having an equivalent social location – from the Bois de Boulogne and the loges at the Opera via the *coulisses* and the *café-concert* to the brothels and stews.[24] This kind of conflation was current in the discourse and fantasies of the masculine literati. Archival work in popular journalism of the time finds appropriate evidence. In *La Vie Moderne* (24 August 1874) a reporter writes on the Folies Bergère asserting that the place is the 'microcosm of Paris', 'where sophisticated men of all cultures felt at home': 'Everyone understands the universal language spoken at the Folies Bergère, because it is the language of pleasure'.[25] Whether actual or fantastic, this pleasure was erotic (for heterosexual men). It was projected onto the architecture of display and consumption which was not only the pathway for the circulation of commodities and the site where capital accumulated into spectacle. These were precisely the spaces for a complex economy of subjectivities and sexualities for which the body of Woman was the key currency.[26]

Enough of me for now.

Yours etc . . .

IV Letter to a feminist scholar friend, or, Men never make passes at girls who use glasses . . .

Dear Friend,
I have made quite a breakthrough in my work on women and modernity.

Woman was the major sign of the masculine bourgeois's relation to urbanity and pleasure. Woman was the object of male exchanges taking place in the spaces of entertainment and recreation. Bourgeois women were, however, themselves consumers and participants. In a previous essay on women and modernity I posed the question: could a bourgeois woman paint *The Bar*, or conceive of it as a representation of her relation to modernity?[27] The answer must be negative. But when I stand in front of *The Bar*, I am drawn into that modernist play of peripheral reflections and find my look attracted to the margins and background of this canonical image. And there, we can find many fashionably dressed women in this crowd, summarily sketched, glimpsed only through the looking glass, made secondary to the barmaid who fills both the foreground of the painting and imaginations of scholars to the exclusion of all else. Like the Afro-Caribbean maidservant (modelled by a woman we know as Laure) in *Olympia* of 1863, the fact that there are several signifying female figures in the painting seems invisible to many commentators.[28]

There in the background are some clues, if not direct citations about how a nineteenth-century bourgeois woman might represent the elements of this space with which she could identify, on the edges of the permitted spaces of femininity. Over the shoulder of the barmaid, beyond her in the reflected space of the audience, set amidst the glitter of chandeliers and glowing gas-lit globes, are at least three women (Fig. 1.3). One is painted in striking whites, her pale face and blond hair set off with a rakishly-angled black hat. Leaning on the balustrade, her arms are encased in elegant lemon-coloured gloves. She has been identified by Tabarant as Méry Laurent, now more fully dressed than at her debut. Adolphe Tabarant, the Manet archivist, who identified so completely with his subject and used Manet's history as a vicarious recovery of his own, writes:

> Méry Laurent. She was one of the most captivating young beauties of the end of the Empire. Born in Nancy in 1851, her doorway to the world of galanterie was through the stage. In 1867, as the Universal Exposition made Paris one vast brothel, she appeared at the Varieties in the very scantily-clad role of Venus in the play *Le Belle Hélène.* She was just seventeen. How gorgeously seductive she was! The famous American dentist Thomas Evans made her his mistress and their arrangement lasted quite a while.[29]

Fig. 1.3 Detail from *A Bar at the Folies Bergère* Edouard Manet
Courtauld Institute Galleries, London

Just behind her, even more sketchily annotated is the head and shoulders of a woman in a tawny jacket and black hat. This figure Tabarant names as Jeanne de Marsy. And then there is a third woman, dressed in black, with muted grey gloves. She is looking through a lorgnette while she gazes towards the stage. It has taken me some time to find this figure, and to name her the metaphorical female spectator with which I – a feminist in the present – can identify in this representation of modernity. I think she is a quotation from, or an overt reference to an image by Mary Cassatt. What can this mean, to have found this reference, here of all paintings?
More later,
In sisterhood . . .

V Letter to a historical person, or, Now, but also then . . .
Dear Miss Cassatt,
I do hope you don't mind my presumption in writing to you after all these years. I have had many imaginary conversations with you. I find myself coming back over and over again to one of your paintings, Woman in Black at the Opera *(Fig. 1.4). Nowadays we date it to about 1880. I have found it again, displaced, in a most surprising place and I want to run a few*

Fig. 1.4 *Woman in Black at the Opera*
Mary Cassatt (1880)
Museum of Fine Arts, Boston

*thoughts by you to see if what I am finding in your painting, as a feminist in
my reading present, means anything to you as an artist in the moment of its
production.*

*Just to the left of the barmaid's left shoulder, in Edouard's [Manet] The Bar
at the Folies Bergère is a fragment of a woman, looking through her lorgnette
at the stage. Her presence is both subtle yet clearly stated. She seems to signify a
dialogic moment, a game played in your artistic community between two men,
MM. Manet and Degas, competing for the definitive realisation of a painting of
modern life. You will remember that in the mid-1860s Edgar [Degas] sketched
a scene at the racecourse, showing Manet – easily recognisable – standing beside
a woman holding a lorgnette (1867, British Museum, London). His female com-
panion is but a vague outline. Nonetheless, it was she and not Manet who became
an obsessive object for Degas who began the composition At The Races (1868,
Weill Bros Inc. Montgomery Alabama) in the later 1860s and left it much
repainted and badly conserved in his studio where it was found at his death in
1917. To me it reveals an attempt to make a big modern subject picture out of the*

little sketch. But it seems that compositionally and psychologically, Degas could not sustain the sexual rivalry (what we now would call an Oedipal triangulation – forgive this rather twentieth-century jargon; I wonder, did you ever read any Freud?) which this composition created between Manet, the woman, and himself as the spectator of their pairing, who was discovered peering at them when the woman's lorgnette captured him in her view. He is the voyeur discovered. He painted out the woman with lorgnette, before finally abandoning a canvas which, when cleaned, revealed sixteen layers of paint, eloquent testimony to both the obsession and the difficulty of resolving a painting of modern life in which a woman looks directly at the spectator. There are, however, several other canvases in which Degas's attraction to the figure of the woman with lorgnette was repeatedly enacted. In these she was isolated and obsessively refashioned so that her gaze was reserved for, tamed to be forever focused on, the artist himself. By this device, **she** *is now captured and fixed by the viewer's look. The viewer discovers* **her** *looking. This reverses the threat inherent in the multi-figure composition, where an Oedipal coupling excludes the observer of the primal scene. Psychically freighted as this single female has become, it could never lead to a solution to the big painting; it remained a powerful fragment.*[30]

I am wondering if Manet's Bar at the Folies Bergère *was his answer to Degas's abortive exploration of a way to locate the trope of a woman's gaze within the ambit of an utterly modern scenario. Once* The Bar *had been painted, it seemed to provide a definitive solution to the problem of making a painting about a woman looking. No wonder Degas abandoned the project and turned his still-wet canvas to the wall.*

But there was another artist who was party to this fascination and competition in the 1870s and 1880s. You, Mary Cassatt. You used the theatre as a setting for this woman looking, the theatre being an available public space for a woman of your class. You, however, inflected the question of woman and spectatorship within the spaces of modernity quite differently.[31] *In 1879 you began to paint* Woman in Black at the Opera. *A modern art historian, Novelene Ross, writes, 'Manet apparently appreciated Mary Cassatt's theatre imagery to such an extent that he represented the principal figure of A* Woman in Black at the Opera *among the spectators in the background scene of* The Bar.[32]

In a paper I have just published on your painting I argue that your painting is a woman's or a feminine viewpoint within the spaces and frames of what Baudelaire called 'modernité'.[33] *Like Degas's images, your work also articulates the dialectics of desire around both an active scopophilia (looking for the object of desire) and a passive exhibitionism (finding security and identity within the embrace of the (m)other's gaze). I apologise, I am again lapsing into late-twentieth-century feminist theory. I conclude that the difference between*

Degas's (and also Renoir's versions of this theme, as in La Loge *(1874, Courtauld Institute Galleries, London) and yours, Miss Cassatt, must be read in terms of the* **specificity** *of a femininity shaped by both social and psychic forces typical of late-nineteenth-century America and Europe. The woman in black looks across the compressed foreground space of the canvas and thus out of the picture. She might be looking at the stage. But the actual composition makes that act of looking assertive and thus it seems to imply much more than mere attention to the stage. The direction of her gaze implies a space not seen by the viewer, not fully included in the painting, yet signified by that intense attention which turns so decisively away from the spectator's look. Her pose bars entry to the picture and distracts the viewer. It denies the anticipated ease of looking pos-sessively at a painting – and a woman – and disrupts the expected relation to the woman's desired complicity with our looking at her. This composition can be read as an allegory of women's desire which exceeds the frame or field of vision offered to women within a patriarchal culture. Your modern woman as specta-tor looks across the space of the image to something beyond its frame which we the viewers cannot see. The painting gives us an image of 'What women want'. Whatever it is can only be implied – and recognised by those with eyes to follow that glance 'elsewhere'. Of necessity, what women want falls outside the repre-sentational schemes, those conventions against which Maria Desraimes was inveighing when she wrote that women want to be free of definition by men. Women desire more than the existing social and semiotic frames permit to those they position in or under the rule of bourgeois femininity. This 'beyond' or excess can be read as expressing both the social demands around which the many women's movements in the nineteenth century were organised, and the psychic desires articulated creatively by artists, poets, novelists for the means to overcome the limits set upon feminine sexualities and their access to power and collective self-determination.*

Was Edouard, as it now seems, already there before us in grasping the possi-bilities of your Woman in Black*? Inscribing into the background of his paint-ing, not the eager male peering annoyingly at the woman in black in your parodic scene, Miss Cassatt, but a female viewer, who is not interested in the transaction between dandy and* serveuse *in the foreground. This figure installs in the paint-ing a woman looking, who is distanced and diminished by the compositional devices Manet has chosen. She is there, nonetheless, to be retrieved by those who desire to find the other Parisiennes and she is looking at and for something beyond the presumed/assumed masculine viewer's frame of vision . . . imagination . . . desire? She looks at that 'elsewhere' which undermines the 'natural' centrality of the interchange which fills the inverted foreground.*

*   **Yours with great respect,***

VI Letter to a feminist scholar and friend, or, Women's pleasure and the pleasures of women

Dear Friend,

I've hit a problem. Tracing the genealogy and its difference from Mary Cassatt's Woman in Black *to the background spectator in Manet's* The Bar, *I find myself asking if I am right to read her as an active, feminist presence in the heartlands of modernism. This woman looking can be read in two quite different ways. On the one hand, looking to the space off signifies the inscription of female desire for the* **more** *for which feminism stands; on the other, she is 'just looking', part of the society of the spectacle.*[34]

Of course bourgeois women were participants in modernity's special forms of spectatorship and consumption. Rather than the brothel and the café, the street or the bar, however, shopping was the privileged site. I have just reread Zola's novel Au Bonheur des Dames *(echoes here of what women want desire?). This aptly named department store becomes a modern substitute for the Church, where the unenlightened, unmodern feminine woman might spend her time in appropriate disciplines and devotions. The department store was called a* cathédrale du commerce moderne, *a place where the new women could spend the entire day. This kind of 'modern' woman, the consumer, replaced her submission to priest and Church with her overstimulated desire for goods, for clothes, for the dispensing of money, or just the pleasures of looking.*

Do you know Rachel Bowlby's study of several late-nineteenth-century novels, Just Looking, *which focuses on the relations of women to consumption through the new retail industries of the* grands magasins?.[35] *Bowlby makes a historical link between shopping and cultural forms of spectatorship within the expansion of capital into areas of leisure. It is here that the distinctions which appeared so critical then and remain vivid now to male art historians evaporate. For men it was vital to be able to distinguish between a woman who sells herself as a sexual commodity and one who is not part of the flow of money and commodities. But through the processes of mass expansion of fashion and shopping, the division became faint indeed. Bowlby argues that 'women's contradictory and crucial part in "the oldest trade in the world" – at once commodity, worker and (sometimes) entrepreneur – can be taken as emblematic of their significance in the modern commercial revolution.'[36] As Walter Benjamin has argued, the prostitute contains the ambiguities of social relations and relations between people and goods characteristic of the age of capital; she is both saleswoman and wares in one.[37] The prostitute is the paradigm, however, of a condition to which all women were being subjected. In metropolitan capitalist economies was added the further dimension 'that it was above all to women that new commerce made its appeal'.[38] Bowlby concludes: 'They were to become in a sense like prostitutes in their active, commodified self-display; and also to take on the one role almost never theirs in actual prostitution: that of consumer.*[39]

Through shopping, women participated in the covetous and eroticised looking which we now define as paradigmatically the modern condition of the capital of the nineteenth century. They were also solicited by the spectacles in the café-concerts *and music halls. But through consumption, it is easy to erase the distinction between the subject and the object. Women shopped the better to make themselves perform their spectacular role in the modern city, some through marriage or courtesanship, displaying someone else's wealth appropriated from other women's labour, performing the rituals of fashion in which those relations of production were fetishised and celebrated. Women shopped in order to become the bearers of their culture's meanings. They modelled it; their bodies were literally remodelled through fashion and its undergarments to emit the required signs of artifice and the infinite unnaturalness and inventiveness of the commodity.*[40] *Yet the growth of shops and mass manufacture has also been identified with creating confusion in the city street. Fashion was no longer the badge of wealth – the sign of 'distinction'.*[41] *Clothes would disguise the social difference inscribed on the bodies of women of different classes at a moment when the sexual female body and the feminine body were categorically differentiated by the polarisation in bourgeois ideology between* la femme *(unspoiled goods, purchased and privately possessed) and* la fille *(desiring, errant, free to be exploited). These are the divided figures of femininity and sexuality. Under the sign Woman fell opposing modes which masked any real social differences between women, and signified instead their common if various subjection to the dominant class and gender's divisive control and use of women. Consumption and spectacle were part of an erosion of the ideological distinctions, with the result that all women appeared 'sexual', their desires incited through consumption. By the same token they were being eroticised through fashion and through their pleasure in participating in the play of leisure. Thus the categories mingled that should have been carefully kept apart. Women of the bourgeoisie slummed with their husbands in the* café-concerts *where other women's husbands kerb-crawled for sexual services amongst the range of working women who worked in the entertainment industry or used it as a means of earning an extra living by servicing the bourgeois sexual economy.*

I was surprised when I realised just how fascinated Manet and his circle were by fashion. They never treated fashion as mere feminine frivolity. I have come to formulate it thus: for men, fashion was the point at which modernity and its uses of femininity converged as spectacle for men while operating as masquerade for women. Baudelaire's Painter of Modern Life *(1863) stresses the central role of fashion in the very definition of the modern.*[42] *Mallarmé founded a fashion journal,* La Dernière Mode *in 1874, which lasted eight issues. He wrote fashion criticism under the pseudonym Miss Satin.*[43] *Antonin Proust's memoirs of his friend Manet, include some anecdotes which reveal his engagement with women's clothes as a part of his artistic imaginary. Indeed Proust records Manet's plan to paint a pendant to his portrait of Jeanne de Marsy, exhibited at the Salon in 1882 with* The Bar, *under the title* Spring. *Proust recalls Manet saying: 'I'm going to do* Autumn *using Méry Laurent. I went to talk to her about it yesterday. . . . She has had a pelisse made. What a garment, my friend, all tawny brown with a gold lining. I was stupefied.'*[44]

Jeanne de Marsy also appears in The Bar, *according to Novelene Ross.*[45] *Adolphe Tabarant also waxes lyrical about Jeanne de Marsy:*

> *But another feminine face was going to enchant the studio in the following weeks and it was the face of Jeanne de Marsy, exquisite model of the exquisite allegorical portrait,* Spring. *. . . really beautiful, dainty, smartly dressed, shameless and impudent, a butterfly of the boulevards . . . But what an outcome!* Spring: *Jeanne de Marsy, bust-length, in profile, her saucy face looking left, with its pert little nose. She wears a cream-coloured bonnet, bordered with frills and surmounted with daisies and roses all mingled in with black ribbons [and so forth with a detailed fashion analysis] . . . This painting is bewitching [literally, an enchantress – 'cette peinture enchanteresse').*[46]

Tabarant was not untypical, writing his history of Manet. He wrote from within a similar cultural and gender formation. Compare this review by Maurice Du Seigneur in L'Artiste *June 1 1882:*

> *Since we are speaking of living flowers, let me introduce you to* Jeanne *by Edouard Manet [this was the title in the Salon livret]. She is not a woman, she is a bouquet, truly a visual perfume. Manet's defenders are delirious, his detractors stupefied, and Mlle Jeanne strolls past them, proud and coquettish, in profile, her eyes alight, her nose turned up, her lips parted, with a winning air. A parasol, long suede gloves, not quite twenty years of age, and a full, fine figure. That describes her.*[47]

Here you will notice that common conflation of femininity and flowers, and all the other rhetorical devices by which 'Jeanne' does not signify a person, but an idea, a fantasy created as an effect of costume, of fashion.[48] *The grammar of the penultimate sentence is particularly striking. It lacks a verb, and metonymically collates a commodity, a fashion accessory, a sexually desirable body-shape and the signifiers of youth to define and consume a her – a modern package of desirability.*[49] *But it is crucial not to be taken in by the power of the fantasy. The painting is not the one evoked by such prose. In conversation about this painting, Laura Mulvey noticed that the set of the face refuses to collaborate with the image of* La Parisienne *which flowers and fashionable figure seem to promise.*[50]

Yours, in haste, as time is running out.

In sisterhood . . .

VII Letter to a historical person, or, Masquerade and fetishism

Dear Miss Cassatt, may I call you Mary?

Sorry to bother you again with all these questions, but having access to someone on the spot, as it were, is really so helpful. Today we can hardly read the codes of fashion and etiquette which so ruled your lives. We think the body is so stable, so fundamental that it can hardly change as much as it has – or at least the language of the body, gesture and dress have altered dramatically over the last one hundred and fifty years and with it the very meanings of femininity and masculinity as we live them through the body, or as it were embody the codes of our historical moment of sexual difference. Women now inhabit a quite different femininity. We have legs nowadays. We don't have to wear hats and hardly ever wear gloves, except when it's really cold.

I have been reading the reviews of Edouard's [Manet] Spring, that portrait of Jeanne de Marsy he showed with The Bar *at the Salon of 1882. One reviewer makes a note of her gloves. I feel that is significant. I am wondering if details of fashion functioned in painting of Manet's time to establish that nuance of class and identity – 'distinction'. They seem to create a distance which is at once a question of class in relation to the women in the painting, and an instatement of the male producer's class and gender interests. Fashionable dress seems to work both as a disguise for and a displacement of recognition of the status of the body who models it. Fashion clothed the working woman's sexualised body with the garments which were meant to function as a seamless unity with the feminine, the bourgeois body. Fashion thus worked as a kind of fetish for men. One of your younger contemporaries, Sigmund Freud – I mentioned him before – really developed this idea rather after your time so you will just have to take my word for it. Fetishism colonises the whole female body, refiguring it as total artifice, denying its nature, even while, as is the case with the painting titled* Spring, *the female body is made to signify the very idea of the natural.*[51]

Fetishism is now seen as one of the characteristic structures of nineteenth-century representation and it has been invoked by art historians in regard to Manet's painting.[52] *It is almost self-consciously evident in* The Bar *in the other woman present of whom I have not yet spoken. The trapeze artist, the actual performer who is truly marginalised, represented only by a fragment, her stunning lime green boots and carefully denaturalised legs, encased in the tights so beloved by Baudelaire. (Fig. 1.1) Fragmentary sketches from Manet's café-haunting days reveal a partiality for stockinged and booted female feet. A contemporary feminist art historian, Linda Nochlin, links the trapeze artist with Manet's preference for the use of synedoche – in which the part of the woman stands for the whole.*[53] *But for male viewers, I am assured this feature works metonymically, that is,*

Fig. 1.5 Detail from *A Bar at the Folies
Bergère* Edouard Manet
Courtauld Institute, London

*suggesting by means of continguity what lies elsewhere, beyond the frame, at the
top of her legs.*

*Other body parts, clothed and naked, are critical to the semiotics of The Bar.
In the painting, the fashionable woman in white with her rakishly set black hat
holds up her hands. They are gloved, as are those of the third spectator, the woman
with opera glasses, the citation not from his own work, but from yours, Mary.
Your bourgeois, or would-be bourgeois lady, also wears gloves.*

*Following this thematic, seeking to find an 'elsewhere' in the painting, I come
back to the centre and the foreground and admit to a perennial fascination with
the hands of the barmaid (Fig. 1.5). They are ungloved. They are hard pressed
against the counter on which she rests. This is no casual pose, but one full of significance within the overall composition itself, and in relation to the evidence of
other paintings which reveal Manet's longstanding obsession with hands.*[54]

Do let me know your views on these hands.

Yours in friendship . . .

VIII Letter to a famous professor, or, Handling the argument
Dear Sir,
*Just to report some further progress on the Bar essay. I have decided to focus on
the hands of the barmaid.*

My attention to hands – or their synedoche, as so little is in fact portrayed
of the hands – as a matter of semiotic interest in a construction of 'Manet',

must seem a little perverse, given that attention normally focuses on quite other components of the female body – the face and figure. In contemporary interpretation, much is made of the elegance of the barmaid's figure in her stylish, and 'of the moment' *Folies* uniform, which, as a current fashion, we also see modelled in Manet's *Portrait of Madame Michel Levy* (1882, National Gallery of Art, Washington DC).[55] Another art historian has argued that it is fashion and cosmetics which provide the disguise within which the barmaid's class eludes us and it is this which enables her to play the paradigmatic role in the 'game of classlessness' which was the appeal of the spaces of the popular. Perhaps I can quote the relevant passage:

> [I]t is the face of fashion, first of all, made up to agree with others quite like it ... Fashion is a good and necessary disguise: it is hard to be sure of anything else about the barmaid, in particular what class she might belong to ... The face that she wears is the face of the popular ... It is a face whose character derives from its not being bourgeois, and having that fact almost be hidden ... fashion and reserve would keep one's face from having any identity, from identity in general.[56]

I am not sure that I can agree here. I can concur that fashion was experienced in the nineteenth century as a kind of erosion of distinction between the bourgeoisie and those *nouvelles couches sociales* who could now afford the mass-produced replicas of the haute couture.[57] But men of Manet's class and social habits knew fashion as an aesthetisation of the commodity relations in which they actually or in fantasy engaged with *La Parisienne*. Take for example the forthright Ernest Chesneau writing in the *Annuaire Illustré des Beaux-Arts* who found no such ambiguity in the barmaid. She was quite simply '*vulgaire*'; that is, she did not perform the masquerade necessary to sustain the illusion of *La Parisienne*. 'It is not permitted to be more of a *fille* than the creature installed behind the marble counter of the bar laden with fruits and bottles. It is not in this that you will see the essential merit of the work'.[58]

Nothing could be more different from the gloved, bonnetted, made-up perfection of Jeanne alias Spring and her sisters in the audience, in the celebratory feminine side of *The Bar*'s background, than the stark nakedness of the barmaid's arms and hands plonked forcefully and gracelessly on the counter so that only the bulging mounds of Venus, as the fleshy parts below the thumb are named, ridge up against the counter's edge (Fig. 1.6). In the paradoxical conventions of bourgeois society, women could bare their chests and upper arms in ballgowns, but their lower arms and hands had to gloved, as a kind of compensation and permission

Fig. 1.6 Detail from *A Bar at the Folies Bergère* Edouard Manet
Courtauld Institute, London

for such display. Hands thus acquired a symbolic significance in the sexual geography of the female body totally unfamiliar to us today. To go about ungloved was akin to leaving your body naked. Such exposure was a classed sign which functioned metonymically for both nakedness and vulgarity, as Chesneau so roundly stated. We know from a wide range of literary and photographic evidence that for some bourgeois men at least this itself was an erotic sight.[59] But these naked hands would work to different effect in the context of a 'painting of modern life'. If he is right, the painting panders to the enigma of a femininity, which is both available, and yet is dressed in the mode of those fashionable women who are not simply for sale. The painting uses this tease as its central semiotic device. With respect, to concur with your reading would merely be to rehearse the fetishistic structure of feminine masquerade, which I have outlined above. The barmaid's hands – how they are painted as much as their position – disrupt that conflation and its negotiated pleasures and lead me to disagree finally with the reading cited above.

Fig. 1.7 Sketch for *A Bar at the Folies Bergère* Edouard Manet (1881)
Stedelijk Museum, Amsterdam

In her important work on Manet's working processes, Juliet Wilson
Bareau uses X-rays of the painting to show how late the decision was
taken about the final position of the barmaid's hands. The small sketch
of the composition (Fig. 1.7) shows what has been called a 'blowsy
madame' with her hands crossed in front of her waist.[60] Perhaps that was
an almost clichéd position for a salewomen or *dame de comptoir*, waiting
to attend to the request of the hatted gentleman at whom her gaze would
seem to be directed.[61] The reflection and the figure match well so that
the reflection provides a narrative explanation of her gaze off screen.
What is she looking at? She is looking at the customer who has just
approached. Her arms express that patient subservience as well as an
etiquette of neatness.

There can be no doubt that turning the barmaid's face to the front and
thus dislocating the narrative was a very clever move on Manet's part.
It is the gambit which lifted his final café painting from the anecdotal

banality of a Béraud to that canonical pedestal as 'modern', making it modern by turning it into spectacle. The 'space off' into which the woman absently gazes is still, however, projected by what is shown on canvas, in its fictive space. The painting cannily implies and implicates the social spectator in front of the canvas at the place of exhibition, i.e. at the Salon, making that viewer part of the fictive space of exchange in front of the counter at the Folies Bergère, rehearsing the similar device used before in *Olympia* (1863). At the same time, the expressionlessness of the woman disarms her looking (Fig. 1.3). She is not the gaze, and has not got a gaze, but rather embodies a 'look' in the fashion sense. She appears but does not see. The dropped eyelids prevent her from looking at us in a way which would be brazen, like the stare of Olympia.

This guarded non-look is Manet's resolution of what he has been trying to do with the café as a modern subject. It is his answer to Degas's racecourse settings, namely a modern woman looking – yet not agressively or menacingly – at the viewer. Manet's solution is much more subtle than Degas's device of obscuring the women's eyes with the monstrous extruberance of binoculars. But just over her shoulder, to the left, is a little reminder of that other woman, Mary Cassatt and her representation of a woman actively desiring to see.

When Manet reworked his sketch for *The Bar* and dislocated the barmaid from the reflection's banal explanation of her actions, he retained the crossed arms. From the X-ray, however, it seems that the clichéd pose of the sketch was already being worked on and the barmaid appears to be clasping her left hand with her right hand well above the wrist. The coding of this gesture within a semiotics of a contemporary sexual economy is suggested in a print by J. L. Forain, *Aux Folies-Bergère*, in which a top-hatted gent accosts a fashionably dressed woman, significantly seen in profile with her head set off by a big-brimmed black hat, whose right hand lightly flicks across her left arm. He asks 'What's your name, dearie.' and she replies, 'Zoe . . .'. Her hands, significantly, are encased in black gloves.[62] The final position of the hands of the barmaid pressing hard onto the edge of the counter so that the fleshy parts below the thumb are emphasised dramatically alters both the meaning of the barmaid and the signification of the composition as a whole.

In the sketch, there was originally no counter in front of the barmaid. Behind the barmaid was the only reflection of the gallery. In the final work, the barmaid's pose allows us to see through her arms to the reflected countertop and its contents, which appear suspended above the lower floor of the Folies. In the final painting, the barmaid is sandwiched between the scintillating glasses and bottles and their ghostly doubles. Were it not for the hands, that is. Multiplying the spatial oddities may have been served by changing the pose of the hands. But the figure itself becomes a lot less elegant, defiantly different from Jeanne's and Méry's poses here and near by, in the other Manet painting at the Salon. While breaking away from the established iconography of the *dame de comptoir*, this figure acquires the kind of frankness which occurs, as John Tagg has argued, in contemporary photography of non-bourgeois people. The frontal awkwardness signifies as a lack of that bodily poise which was the mark of class.[63]

The pose reads, therefore, within the semiotics both of gender and class, or rather precisely at the point of their historically overdetermined conjunction. The barmaid's hands are working hands. Tinged with colour, they are the counterpoint to the cosmetically induced pallor of her face and chest. And they give the game away. Masquerade as the imbrication of commodity and sexual fetishism is betrayed by these errant signs of the labouring class. Fetishism is disrupted by physical signs of manual labour. In Manet's *The Bar*, the positioning and detailing of the working-class hands arises out of an aesthetic of fidelity to the contradictions of the modern life which Manet lived, as a man of the world, but which, as an artist, he also scrutinised in order to devise for it some telling aesthetic form. This oddity at the centre of the painting attracts my gaze and unexpectedly allows me to reconnect with the feminist writers of the time. In their polemics, they emphasised the correlation between the economic exploitation of women in the labour process as unskilled, low-paid workers and their vulnerability to sexual exploitation through being forced to sell not just their undervalued labour on the market, but their bodies. Julie Daubie's crucial text *La Femme Pauvre aux Dix-Neuvième Siècle* was published in 1866 and went to a second edition in 1869–70. Writing in the 1860s, again concurrently with Manet's production, Daubie argued that poverty, and not feminine weakness for money, or love of finery, drove women into prostitution.[64]

And here is Paule Minck writing in 1869 one of her most famous essays, 'Les Mouches et les Araignées' [The Flies and the Spiders], in which she charts the relations of gender exploitation between bourgeoisie and workers across factory, home and café.

La mouche, c'est cette modeste fillette qui veut rester sage et vivre honnête en tra-vaillant, mais qui ne peut trouver l'ouvrage qu'en cédant aux honteux désirs du

contre-maître ou du patron qui l'occupe, et qui ensuite la jette loin de lui et l'aban-
donne – avec un enfant bien souvent – sitôt que la satiété ou la crainte du scandale
se fait sentir.

  L'araignée, c'est ce jeune dandy du boulevard, ce fils de famille impudent et cynique,
ce valétudinaire blasé, dépravé, qui plonge, en riant, une pure enfant dans la fange et
se fait un jeu, un honneur de débaucher les femmes honnêtes[65]

The fly is the modest young woman who wants to behave well and make an
honest living at work, but who cannot find work but in yielding to the shameful desires of the overseer or her boss, who ultimately casts her aside and
abandons her – often with a child – as soon as he has had his fill or becomes
afraid of scandal.

  The spider is the young dandy or *boulevardier*, the son of a cynical and impudent family, this blasé, depraved valetudinary, who mirthfully plunges a pure
child into the mire, and plays with her, making it a point of honour to debauch
honest women.

By these uncompromisingly proletarian hands, **work** is signified in
this space of **leisure**, **façade** and **social hieroglyphics**, at the *Bar aux
Folies Bergère*. Work is their very antithesis. It is what contradicts the
fantasy of an effortlessly produced and perfect image, the fetish which the
masquerade of femininity is meant to offer to men. Actresses like Méry
Laurent and Jeanne de Marsy were adored because they could perform
the myth of *La Parisienne* which Manet so obsessively rehearsed in his
paintings in his last years. As his sexually contracted illness took its toll,
he painted about twenty oils and pastels heads of women of the *demi-
monde*. Suzon, the model for the barmaid, was also subjected to this
regime of representation, appearing in her daytime clothes, in profile,
Suzon (1881, Musée des Beaux-Arts, Dijon). But she was also employed
to model in his last statement on modern life because she was an actual
barmaid. She came in the daytime to Manet's studio to model the pose in
which she worked at nightime. Huysmans' criticism of *The Bar* was aimed
precisely at the way that fact of its material production could not be
avoided. He complained about Manet's painting in no uncertain terms.
The *Folies* can only exist in the evening, he argued, a dreamworld made
fairy-tale with gas and electricity. Why, he fumes, must Manet ruin that
dream with a painting so obviously produced in **daylight** – a mock up, in
the studio, a fabrication of a place, which is however, too real, too prosaic,
too naked, too undressed so that the social relations which are the conditions of the erotic fantasy cannot be conjured away? He concludes:
'Treated in this unadulterated fashion it is absurd.'[66] Where there should
be fantasy, there is a distressing prosaic actuality. The hands are the place
where this negation occurs.

Art historians have not, however, noticed, it seems, the significant dis-juncture between the space represented – the Folies Bergère – and the space of representation which is the actual painting. The picture-as-text so pointedly provides an image and form for Parisian modernity, and yet it disjoins the social actuality and the fantasy through these aberrant details of the working-woman's hands revealed by the studio day-light-ing. Art historical versions/visions of this painting confirm and delight in the myth of Paris which this image reworks for us. They use it to get close to Manet and vicariously enter the world he enjoyed socially as a bourgeois man of his time. But the painting is itself a site of work, as T. J. Clark so usefully pointed out in his influential essay 'On the Social History of Art.'[67] Using heavily loaded ideological materials from *La Vie Moderne*, Manet's painting works those resources, allowing me, the woman specta-tor it does not directly address, to glimpse in its spaces off, and at its margins, another history, and to find another, even a *feminist*, identifica-tion within its frame.

I don't believe we can ascribe this foresight or intelligence simply to Manet. But it has to be grasped as part of 'Manet', the structure of meaning derived from a body of work by our critical and symptomatic reading of that oeuvre. Women spectators were historically part of the painting's possible audience at the Salon. And they were also part of its imagined public, foreshadowed by the women spectators in the painting itself. Manet knew Cassatt and women like her, campaigning for the vote and for independence in art. Just like Freud knew what women wanted but equally disavowed it, concluding his essay on 'Some Psychical Consequences of the Anatomical Distinction between the Sexes' (1925) with a firm negation of even bourgeois feminist demands: 'We must not allow ourselves to be deflected from such conclusions by the denials of the feminists, who are anxious to force us to regard the two sexes as com-pletely equal in position and worth.'[68]

Yours, in hope of some useful comments . . .

IX Letter to a feminist scholar, or, Answering the sphinx
Dear Friend,

I am really excited by what I have been doing. I have found a way to go back to the historical materials of the nineteenth century without being inhibited by the limitations of the masculinist versions of the social history of art which have, nonetheless, always provided me with the basic model for materialist historical analysis. I have looked away from their Manet and their visions of his paint-ing, following the gaze of the woman with the lorgnette to Mary Cassatt but also to Maria Desraimes, Louise Michel, Hubertine Auclert, Séverine, Paule Minck and to the women, like Suzon perhaps, with whom they campaigned to end the sexual exploitation of women by improving working-women's access to other means of subsistence – well-paid work. The nineteenth-century women's movement was much more focused on the issue of women's right to work than on the politics of the body, which characterises the theoretical originality of the contemporary discourses of feminism in the late-twentieth century. The right to work without sexual harrassment, the right to adequate means of self-support, were then, and still are now, the basic conditions for women's rights and liberty. That's what is outside the frame of modernist mythologies. But it is there in the painting of The Bar, *obliquely and indirectly signified by the devices which Manet had made his very signature as an artist – the fact that a painting is the product of his labour and the paid labour of Suzon in a concrete social space. The mock-up of the bar in his studio on the Rue St Petersbourg, is an artifice, which, by being laconically depicted in the painting as such, undoes the myth of modern Paris – a little – for those who do not eagerly take their place in the painting or the myth, but wonder if there was something else for the barmaid to look at and for. Instead of addressing her customer and asking what* **he** *wanted, maybe she dreamed of his asking what* **she** *needed, and what she as a working-class woman actually desired – what her fantasies of pleasure, ease and gratification might be.*[69] *If Suzon did not know, Maria Desraimes had published her suggestions in the year Suzon's current employer had exhibited at the Salon another working woman with her sleeves rolled up for work, in the background and shadows of a painting which celebrated his alter-ego, his son the dandy, looking off into the urban space in which he would feel so much 'at home', I am thinking of* Déjeuner dans l'Atelier *(1869 Neue Pinakotek, Munich).*

When I was preparing my essay on The Bar, *I kept going back to Teresa de Lauretis and her argument that feminist theory provides a 'view from elsewhere', which is neither mythic nor utopian. It is the elsewhere of discourse here and now, the blind spots, the almost invisible centre, like the barmaid's hands, or the space off yet always already inscribed within existing representations. I am struggling with the paradox, looking to solve the riddle for the sphinx. Within the feminist consciousness that emerged in the 1970s, we began asking questions about women's relation to patriarchal culture. In her brilliant film* Riddles of the Sphinx *(1976) Laura Mulvey positioned women as a voice off, like the sphinx outside the city gates, silenced and made monstrous at modernity's margins.*[70] *But we have since revised that powerful but ultimately negative image of our dilemma. We can now view dominant cultural discourses and practices, traditional and critical, from a politically and historically generated else-*

where, feminism, which is nonetheless right here. Neither centre nor periphery, women's histories have to be understood as complexly part of the fabric of historical discourses, institutions and practices. There are equally historical conditions which have determined whether that presence is visible or not, veiled or simply repressed by the hegemonic interests which dominate the apparatuses of power and knowledge. As part of the project of constructing the 'subject of feminism', I want, like Mary Cassatt in her painting, to write across the texts of history, the desire of women to be seen – in all the uncomfortable complexity of the pain and injuries of class, race, and gender – as subjects of history and subjects in history.
In sisterhood and hope . . .

Notes

1. Novelene Ross, *Manet's* Bar at the Folies-Bergère *and the Myths of Popular Illustration* Ann Arbor, Michigan UMI Research Press (1982) provides a review of the interpretations of this painting up to 1980. In addition it is worth noting several more readings of the painting. A. C. Hanson *Manet and the Modern Tradition* New Haven, Yale University Press (1977); T. J. Clark 'The Bar at the Folies Bergère' in J. Beauroy *et al* (eds), *The Wolf and the Lamb: Popular Culture in France from the Old Regime to the Twentieth Century* Anma Libri, Stanford French and Italian Studies 1976, Vol. III; T. J. Clark *The Painting of Modern Life: Paris in the Art of Manet and his Followers*, London, Thames and Hudson (1984); R. Herbert *Impressionism, Art, Leisure and Parisian Society* New Haven, Yale University Press, (1988); P. Florence, *Mallarmé, Manet and Redon: Visual and Aural Signs and the Generation of Meaning* Cambridge, Cambridge University Press (1986); Jeremy Gilbert-Rolfe 'Edouard Manet and the pleasure problematic' *Arts Magazine*, February 1988, vol. 62 no. 2, pp. 40–4; David Carrier 'Art History in the mirror stage: Interpreting *Un Bar aux Folies Bergère*, History and Theory, vol. XXIX, 1990 pp. 297–320.
2. T. de Lauretis, *Technologies of Gender* London, MacMillan (1987) p. 25.
3. Ibid p. 25.
4. Ibid p. 26.
5. Ibid pp. 9–10.
6. T. J. Clark, *The Painting of Modern Life: Paris in the Art of Manet and his Followers* London, Thames and Hudson (1984) pp. 254–5.
7. S. Freud, 'Femininity' in *New Introductory Lectures on Psychoanalysis* [1933] London, Pelican Freud Library, ed. J. Strachey, vol. 2 (1973) p. 146. The quotation is from H. Heine, *Nordsee.*
8. Virginia Woolf, 'Women and Fiction' [1929] in M. Barrett (ed.) *Virginia Woolf: Women and Writing* London, Women's Press (1979) pp. 59–60.
9. One of the major studies of Manet is Anne Coffin Hanson *Manet and the Modern Tradition* New Haven, Yale University Press (1977).
10. There are some exceptions which date from the inception of the women's movement. Eunice Lipton, for instance, provides a feminist reevaluation of Manet in her important article, 'Manet – a radicalised female imagery' *Art Forum* March 1975, vol. 13, pp. 48–53. She offered a reading, for women, of Manet's radical rupture with codes of representation, but one that still left the great artist central to the text of art history.

See also Linda Nochlin, 'A thoroughly modern masked ball' *Art in America* November 1983, vol. 71, pp. 188–201, for an important feminist reading of the relations between bourgeois men and working women in places of entertainment.

11. Lisa Tickner, *The Spectacle of Women: Imagery of the Suffrage Campaign 1907–1914* London, Chatto & Windus, (1987) provides a superb analysis of women suffragists' relation to these debates, especially in Ch. 4.

12. G. Pollock 'Modernity and the spaces of femininity' in *Vision and Difference: Feminism, Femininity and the Histories of Art* London, Routledge (1988) pp. 50–90.

13. Freud's question occurs in a letter to Marie Bonaparte: 'The great question that has not been answered, and which I have not yet been able to answer, despite my thirty years research into the feminine soul, is "What does a woman want?" [*Was will das Weib?*]', cited in Ernest Jones *The Life and Work of Sigmund Freud* [1953–7] London, Pelican Books (1964) p. 474. Lacan devoted a seminar to this question *Le séminaire Livre XX*, Paris, 1975; see also S. Heath 'Difference', *Screen* 1978, vol. 19 no. 3, pp. 51–112.

14. Cited in E. Showalter, *The Female Malady: Women, Madness and English Culture 1830–1980* London, Virago (1987), p. 155.

15. Dianne Hunter, 'Hysteria, psychoanalysis and feminism: The case of Anna O', *Feminist Studies* 1983 vol. 9, pp. 465–88.

16. This point is made with intended reference to K. Marx *The Eighteenth Brumaire of Louis Bonaparte* [1852] in *Marx and Engels Selected Works* London, Lawrence and Wishart (1968) p. 171, writing of the peasantry of France, who suffered a uniform life, culture and oppression, but did not constitute a class in themselves and therefore 'cannot represent themselves but they must be represented'.

17. Maria Desraimes, *Ce que veulent les femmes: Articles et Conférences de 1869–1894* ed. O. Krakavitch, Paris, Syros (1981) p. xx.

18. Paule Minck, another leading feminist orator and organiser, but of more revolutionary and anarchist tendency, equally opposed Auclert and the suffrage campaigners because women's vote would be 'le jeu du parti clerical' see *Paule Minck Communarde et Féministe 1839–1901* Alain Dalotel (ed.) Paris, Syros (1981). I am grateful to Adrian Rifkin for bringing this text to my attention.

19. Nancy Mowll Mathews, *Cassatt and Her Circle* New York, Abbeville Press (1984); *Séverine: Choix de Papiers* Evelyne Le Garrec (ed.), Paris, Editions Tierce (1982); Evelyne Le Garrec, *Séverine une Rebelle 1855–1929*, Paris, Editions du Scuil, 1982; Claire Goldberg Moses, *French Feminism in the Nineteenth Century*, New York, SUNY Press (1984); *The Diaries of Marie Bashkirtseff*, M. Blind (ed.) London, Virago, 1984.

20. In Emile Zola's novel *Nana*. Paris (1879) ch. 1.

21. Novelene Ross *Manet's* Bar at the Folies Bergère *and the Myths of Popular Illustration* Ann Arbor, Michigan, UMI Research Press (1982) p. 13.

22. For discussion of prostitution on site see P. Derval, *The Folies Bergère* trans. Lucienne Hill, London, Methuen (1955); see also F. Caradec and A. Weill, *Le Café-Concert*, Paris (1980).

23. Ibid p. 75.

24. See G. Pollock, 'Modernity and the spaces of femininity' op. cit. There is an important correspondence between what I am trying to construct here at the level of cultural myth and its puncturing and the work of feminist historians such as Christine Stansell, whose book on the history of working women in New York in the nineteenth century is titled *City of Women*, New York, Alfred H. Knopf (1986).

25. Ibid p. 75.

26. I am referring here both to T. J. Clark, op cit., and to the work of Marxist social geographer David Harvey, *Consciousness and the Urban Experience: Studies in the History and Theory of Capitalist Urbanisation*, Oxford, Basil Blackwell (1985).

27. G. Pollock, 'Modernity and the spaces of femininity' op. cit. pp. 54–5.
28. Heather Dawkins, *Sexuality, Degas and Women's History* University of Leeds PhD (1991). Ch. 3, offers an important revision to the historical meanings of two women in the painting, suggesting a perceived lesbian relationship and thus an exclusive, female sexuality signified by the painting.
29. Adolphe Tabarant *Manet et Ses Oeuvres* Paris, Gallimard (1947) pp. 426–7. I must acknowledge Adrian Rifkin's unpublished paper given at the Toulouse Lautrec Symposia at the Courtauld Institute London and University of Leeds, October and December 1991, in which he explained the way in which the early twentieth-century historians of the musical-hall culture of late-nineteenth and early-twentieth-century Paris used the texts they wrote both to reclaim and to distance themselves from their own beginnings. See his book *Street Noises* Manchester University Press (1992).
30. See my 'The gaze and a question of difference: Woman with lorgnette in the work of Degas and Cassatt' in R. Kendall and G. Pollock (eds), *Dealing with Degas: Representations of Women and the Politics of Vision* London, Pandora Press (1991).
31. Novelene Ross, *Manet's* Bar at the Folies Bergère *and the Myths of Popular Illustration* Ann Arbor, Michigan UMI Research Press (1982) pp. 6–7, suggests that Mary Cassatt's entry into the Impressionist circle through Degas in 1879 may have stimulated Manet's interest in theatre scenes and the use of mirrors. Cassatt exhibited *Lydia in a Loge Wearing a Pearl Necklace* at the fourth Impressionist exhibition. Ross cites Nils Ramstedt Jn, *Edouard Manet's* Bar at the Folies Bergère, University of California, Santa Barbara (1971) as the scholar who first advanced the idea of Cassatt's influence on Manet.
32. Ross op. cit. p. 7.
33. See note 31.
34. I am clearly indebted here to the work of T. J. Clark, *The Painting of Modern Life* op. cit.
35. Rachel Bowlby, *Just Looking* London, Methuen (1985) p. 6.
36. Ibid. p. 10.
37. Walter Benjamin, *Charles Baudelaire: Lyric Poet in the Era of High Capitalism* trans. Harry Zohn, London, New Left Books (1973).
38. Bowlby p. 11.
39. Ibid.
40. D. Kunzle *Fashion and Fetishism* New Jersey, Rowman (1981) provides important material for taking these observations much further. His work confirms the possibilities of serious and theoretically informed analysis of fashion in relation to a semiotics and politics of the body and social fabrications of both image and identity. These themes have been richly taken up in feminist writings on fashion, see, for example, E. Wilson, *Adorned in Dreams* London, Virago (1988).
41. In Baudelaire's erotic itinerary through the night spots of Paris, narrated in his *The Painter of Modern Life* [1863], he writes of the mistress of a spiv, who lacks nothing to become a grande dame, except that everything, which is 'distinction', 'that "practically nothing" being in fact "practically everything", for it is *distinction.*' This is clearly a matter of class and hence of gender, since class determined the forms of exploitation to which men would feel free to subject women. See edition edited by J. Mayne, Oxford, Phaidon Books (1962), p. 35.
42. His essay begins with a chapter entitled 'Beauty, fashion and happiness'.
43. *La Dernière Mode* is reprinted in facsimile, Paris, Editions Ramsay (1978).
44. Antonin Proust, *Edouard Manet: Souvenirs* [1913] cited in Thérèse Ann Gronberg, *Manet: A Retrospective* New York, Hugh Lauter Levin Associates Inc. (1988) p. 272.
45. Ross, op. cit., p. 8, citing Ramstedt op. cit.

46. Tabarant, op. cit. p. 414.
47. George Heard Hamilton, *Manet and His Critics* New York, Norton (1969) p. 249.
48. Compare Baudelaire's 'No doubt woman is sometimes a light, a glance, an invitation to happiness, sometimes she is just a word' from *The Painter of Modern Life* [1863] trans. Jonathan Mayne, London, Phaidon (1964) p. 30. See also Leon LeGrange, 'Du Rang des Femmes dans l'Art' *Gazette des Beaux-Arts* 1860, vol. 8, p. 39 for a famous analogy between women and flowers, where he concludes that women artists should confine themselves to painting flowers because they alone can compete with the grace and freshness of women themselves.
49. Tabarant, op. cit. p. 439 notes that, from varnishing day, there was a crowd around the painting.
50. I am grateful to Laura Mulvey for drawing my attention to this disjunction.
51. The special significance of the concept of masquerade for theories of femininity has been argued in feminist film theory by M. A. Doane, in feminist philosophy by Luce Irigaray, in art history by Tamar Garb, see particularly 'Unpicking the seams of her disguise: Self-representation in the case of Marie Bashkirtseff' *Block* no. 13 1987–8, p. 79–86. This paper is particularly relevant, but a full discussion of the psychoanalytical and later feminist thinking on this theme cannot be undertaken here.
52. P. Wollen, 'Manet: Modernism and Avant-garde' *Screen* 1981, vol. 21, no. 2, pp. 21–22.
53. L. Nochlin, *Realism* London, Penguin Books (1971) pp. 164–5.
54. This is the topic of another paper. It involves a series of differences between the gloved hands, the crossed in the lap hands, the expressive hand gesture, the tumescent exposed arm. These differences are precise inscriptions of stratifications of class and sexuality.
55. Devere's *Parisian Costumes for English Ladies* London, Empkin and Marshall, October 1880, illustrates a Plate (90) which compares directly with the costume of the barmaid. In editions of this guide for October 1881, the fashion is widespread.
56. T. J. Clark, op. cit. (1984), p. 253.
57. Richard Sennett, *The Fall of Public Man* Cambridge, Cambridge University Press (1976).
58. Cited Tabarant, op. cit., p. 440.
59. The classic instance of this eroticisation of working women's muscular arms, revealed by rolled up sleeves, comes from the Archive of Arthur Munby, now in Trinity College Cambridge. I look at this area of interaction between bourgeois men's fantasies and the working woman's body in a forthcoming book *Sexuality and Surveillance: Bourgeois Men and Working Women* London, Routledge (1995). See a fine study of this from the perspective of a working-class woman in Heather Dawkins, 'The diaries and photographs of Hannah Cullwick' *Art History* 1987, vol. 10, no. 2, pp. 154–187.
60. Clark, op. cit., p. 252.
61. Ross, op cit., illustrates a print (Fig. 46) of a man flirting with a *dame de comptoir* whose arms are folded neatly across her waist.
62. Illustrated in Ross, op. cit., Fig. 41.
63. J. Tagg, 'A democracy of the image: Photographic portraiture and commodity production' in *The Burden of Representation* London, MacMillan (1988) pp. 35–6.
64. Julie-Victoire Daubié *La Femme Pauvre au XIXième Siècle* Paris, Guillaumin (1866).
65. Paule Minck, op. cit., pp. 50–1.
66. G. H. Hamilton, op. cit., p. 252; Huysmans' comments were appended to his book on *L'Art Moderne* which appeared in 1883.
67. I am constantly indebted for this important formulation to T. J. Clark 'On the Social History of Art' in *The Image of the People* London, Thames and Hudson (1973).
68. S. Freud, *On Sexuality* London, Pelican Freud Library, vol. 7, p. 342.

69. We are all indebted to Carolyn Steedman and her book *Landscape for a Goodwoman: A Story of Two Lives* London, Virago (1986) for her critique of both feminist and left literatures on working-class lives which refuse to consider the complexity of working-class subjectivity and desire.

70. I am referring here to Laura Mulvey and Peter Wollen's film *Riddles of the Sphinx* London, British Film Institute (1976) script published in *Screen* 1977, vol. 18 no. 2, pp. 15–26.

2 Frida Kahlo's 'grotesque' bodies

KATE CHEDGZOY

> In a dark room she measures herself against a forgotten and idealised self-image. Her desire for wholeness is dislocated. Fragments of a former existence haunt her. Bound over to communicate an experience too uncomfortable to hear: expectations are unreliable.[1]

> As soon as one steps out of the classroom . . . the dangers rather than the benefits of academic feminism . . . become more insistent. Institutional changes against sexism here . . . may mean nothing or, indirectly, further harm for women in the Third World. This discontinuity ought to be recognised and worked at. Otherwise, the focus remains defined by the investigator as subject. . . . I see no way to avoid insisting that there has to be a simultaneous other focus: not merely who am I? But who is the other woman? How am I naming her? How does she name me? Is this part of the problematic I discuss?[2]

In 1925, when she was an eighteen-year-old pre-medical student at the elite National Preparatory School in Mexico City, Frida Kahlo suffered terrible injuries as a result of a crash involving the bus she was travelling on. According to an eye-witness account, as Frida lay in the road, her pelvis crushed, pierced through the womb and vagina by a metal rod, somehow all her clothes were torn off and her naked body was showered with gold pigment which a fellow-passenger on the bus had been carrying. Even at this moment of utter physical pain and abjection, her body was made into an object to be displayed and looked at. And if the objectivity of the account is questionable, it nevertheless testifies eloquently to the desire to convert Kahlo's lived existence into a sort of bizarre art object. In her own career, the visual recreation and reinterpretation of her body became the focus of her work as an artist, constantly transgressing and unfixing the possibility of a distinction between art and life. In her wide-ranging and provocative discussion of Kahlo's cultural status, Joan Borsa has warned that the critical preoccupation with Kahlo's representations of her body, particularly the body in pain, may have the effect of depoliticising the work by over-personalising it, reducing it to the status of solipsistic therapy, and thereby perpetuating a reactionary account of female artistic production:

> I am not interested in demonstrating that . . . her art is the result of a life filled with physical and emotional pain or that her work somehow speaks of a truly female space. These approaches which now surround Kahlo's work further

reinforce the myth of the artist as tortured genius and present the woman artist as victim – as if irreconcilably outside and other.[3]

During an interview recorded for a 1990 BBC *Omnibus* programme Madonna spoke of her intense emotional investment in Frida Kahlo's painting *My Birth*, which she said had come to fulfill the iconic function in her life to which the Catholic images of her childhood were no longer adequate. Later, a friend of mine who works with young women in crisis commented that a number of her clients lay claim to a similar fascination with this terrible yet haunting image, circulating reproductions of it among themsleves as amulets or fetishes. As Jean Borsa has demonstrated, commodified images of Kahlo proliferate in western culture, on posters, book covers, and fashion spreads.[4] Moreover, the tone of much critical discourse about Kahlo seems to indicate that in her case the problematic question of the relationship between the artist's life and her work has a special significance for her commentators. Kahlo's uniquely iconic role is particularly striking in the context of feminist art criticism, where, as a woman artist whose primary subject matter was her own body, she has come to occupy a central but contested position. In what follows, I ask why this should be so.

My aims here are to offer a theory which can account for the unique intensity of the feminist critical response to Kahlo, and to provide a way of interpreting the special fascinations which her self-portraits offer feminist spectators, without personalising and pathologising these representations to an extent which would deny Kahlo's political location and agency as the subject of her own artistic practice. I hope to show that Kahlo used intimate representations of her body to make highly politicised public statements. Drawing on Julia Kristeva's theory of abjection,[5] and the Bakhtinian concept of carnival,[6] I locate my reading as a white western feminist of Kahlo's work both in the context of recent attempts to theorise the female body – particularly that body which is in some way disfigured, hystericised, or rendered 'grotesque'[7] – and of the related project of constructing a critical language which can speak of emotional and physical pain. I am not presuming to offer a definitive or comprehensive account of Kahlo's work, and I recognise that there are other, equally productive and appropriate contexts in which to locate an analysis of it.[8] Nevertheless, it seems to speak very directly to these preoccupations, which clearly have their origins in women's emotional and political experience. It has been suggested to me that there are political problems with the appropriation of Kahlo's self-portraits by western feminists as a way into understanding their own experience; but I would argue that turning a critical gaze on these problems can itself further our understanding of the culturally specific ways in which the female body is represented and encoded.

Although I use psychoanalytic concepts in an attempt to understand what is at stake for the viewer of Kahlo's art, I am aware that merely to psychoanalyse the traces of subjectivity which the viewer perceives in her paintings risks reinstating the colonising gestures of the Surrealists' appropriation of her work and persona. André Breton, who championed Kahlo in the 1930s, has been described as nurturing a fantasy of Mexico as 'the Surrealist place *par excellence*',[9] and chose to represent her as a naive and spontaneous genius who had stumbled on the tenets and practices of Surrealism by a process of intuition. Kahlo herself rejected the label of 'Surrealist', while astutely using Surrealist contacts to further her career, asserting that

> I never knew I was a Surrealist till André Breton came to Mexico and told me. . . . And it is doubtless true that in many ways my painting is related to that of the Surrealists. But I never had the intention of creating a work that could be considered to fit in that classification.[10]

However, in the introduction to the brochure for her New York debut at Julien Levy's gallery in 1938, Breton wrote:

> My surprise and joy were unbounded when I discovered on my arrival in Mexico that her work had blossomed forth, in her latest paintings, into pure Surreality, despite the fact that it had been conceived without any prior knowledge whatsoever of the ideas motivating the activities of my friends and myself.[11]

Whitney Chadwick comments that Breton here detaches Kahlo's work from its Mexican cultural (and, she might have added, political) context, and places it as confirming the work and theories of male Surrealists without developing them. In a gesture which is at once misogynist and racist, Kahlo is constructed by Breton as the embodiment of femininity, the unconscious, and the exotic – all qualities which the Surrealist movement celebrated, but which nonetheless deny Kahlo agency as the subject of her own personal/political history and her artistic production. The danger that this gesture will be repeated in the western feminist movement's appropriation of Kahlo has already been noted:

> The emphasis given in her work to the body, to personal emotion and to motherhood provided a visual counterpart to a growing feminist art history. However . . . she has also come to represent an archetypal image of woman as victim. As an artist she has been ascribed an almost naive self-absorption, and her admittedly great emotional and physical traumas have been seen as the

major impetus of her art. Despite the laudable aims of such a reappraisal, it does little to address her active role in the formulation of a language of art which questioned neo-colonial cultural values. In fact her current status embodies both aspects of the modernist 'other', the feminine and the unconscious, which are consistently used to characterise Latin America itself.[12]

To use a concept like abjection, which has origins in psychoanalytic theory, to analyse Kahlo's work, may thus run the risk of confirming her association with the unconscious and the exotic, trapping her within an objectified identity constructed by the colonising discourses of western rationality. To avoid this, psychoanalytic theory can more profitably be used as a means of accounting for the fascination which Kahlo's paintings currently exert over the European female – or more precisely, feminist – viewer. Is this fascination merely an exploitative pleasure in the contemplation of an exotic, unconscious and narcissistic femininity, whose display compensates for the sensual deprivations of the puritan North? That is, are we using Kahlo's work to assuage our own lack? Or is it possible that, in the recognition of the other woman's subjectivity – be it suffering, self-absorbed, or revolutionary – which Kahlo's work offers us, a more truly liberating and intersubjective dynamic can come into being?

Jean Franco has noted that just such an intersubjective relation is already embodied by the artistic form of Kahlo's doubled self-portraits (for example *Tree of Hope* and *The Two Fridas* (Fig. 2.1)). These double portraits depict either a Tehuana[13] and a European Frida, or a naked and a clothed Frida. In their very form, these paintings undo the possibility of a facile identification of Frida Kahlo (as the subject of her own work) with a single unconscious, commodified object of the gaze. Franco's analysis undoes some of the easy assumptions the viewer might be tempted to make about the potential political meanings of conventional art forms; as she points out elsewhere in her book, one way in which Kahlo's self-portraits can be said to challenge the conventions of European art is that her 'mutilated body trespasses on the place of the female nude':[14]

> The unclothed body is not a 'self' but a socialised body, a body that is opened by instruments, technologised, wounded, its organs displayed to the outside world. The 'inner' Frida is controlled by modern society far more than the clothed Frida, who often marks her deviation from a norm by defiantly returning the gaze of the viewer. The naked Frida does not give the viewers what they want – the titillation of female nakedness – but a revelation of what the examining eye does to the female body.[15]

Franco's work is both persuasive and politically challenging. But one limitation of her argument here is that it does not do enough to displace

Fig. 2.1 *The Two Fridas* Frida Kahlo (1939)
Museo de Arte Moderno, INBA

the viewer – whose identity is not problematised – from a position as the
unique subject of this transaction. Although she makes a convincing argument for the paintings' resistance to the colonizing gaze, Franco seems to
imply that this gaze is exclusively male, although this is not made explicit.
For me, the most pressing question still is: what is the relationship
between Frida Kahlo's body and the multiplicities of the western
(European/North American) *female* gaze?

   To answer that question, I turn now to the theoretical concepts of
abjection and carnival. Julia Kristeva's theory of abjection offers a
psychoanalytic understanding of the process by which the norms of
embodied identity are disrupted. It gives an account of the construction
of desiring subjectivity which stresses the faultlines, tensions and

difficulties of achieving a stable identity as the embodied subject of an unproblematic desire. In *Powers of Horror*, Kristeva says:

> The non-distinctiveness of inside and outside is unnameable, a border passable in both directions by pleasure and pain. Naming the latter, hence differentiating them, amounts to introducing language, which just as it distinguishes pleasure from pain, as it does all other oppositions, founds the separation inside/outside. And yet, there would be witnesses to the perviousness of the limit, artisans after a fashion who try to tap that pre-verbal beginning within a word which is flush with pleasure and pain.[16]

Frida Kahlo may be understood as just such a witness, such an artisan. Her paintings represent the moment of abjection which institutes a flickering in and out of existence of the frail, permeable boundaries between inside and outside, pleasure and pain. Kristeva's own writing on abjection is often marked by a sense of the inadequacy of language to record the extremes of psychic and physical experience. In Kahlo's paintings, what eludes language in this fashion is made visible: the representation of the body becomes the material realisation of abjection, enabling the artist to become a user, not of words, but of colours and forms capable of embodying the physical and psychic distress which exceeds or negates the expressive capacity of language. The pictorial image of the agonised abject body thus takes on an ironic and carnivalesque beauty, so that the ability of Kahlo's paintings to fascinate the gaze is seen to be generated by the tension between the pain and horror of what they represent, and the luscious visual pleasure which they offer the spectator. Abjection offers a possible way of understanding this disjunction because it shows how embodied subjectivity is constructed through the differentiation of pleasure and pain, while stressing the impossibility of ever fully achieving such a differentiation. According to Jacqueline Rose,

> Abjection is a primordial fear situated at the point where the subject first splits from the body of the mother, finding at once in that body and in the terrifying gap that opens up between them the only space for the constitution of its own identity, the only distance which will allow it to become a user of words. . . . The body appears at the origin of language, not as idealisation, therefore, but as that which places both the subject and language most fundamentally at risk.[17]

The key themes in abjection are the construction of subjectivity over and against the desired and feared maternal body, which can never be fully repressed, but always returns to haunt the fragile, vulnerable subject; and the subject's experience, consequent on this inadequately achieved repression, of those liminal states in which the boundaries of the body, of the self, are blurred, transgressed, and refigured. The experience of abjection is also evoked by phenomena which inspire disgust or horror because of the threat which liminality poses to the attempt to stabilise – and thereby control – the categories we use to interpret meaning.[18] Both abjection and carnival (which I shall discuss in more detail below) share a tendency to take the body and subjectivity as ahistorical, transcendent givens, collapsing the feminine into the maternal, and taking the maternal body as the key image of embodiment as such. Reading this account against the grain, it becomes clear that abjection is a crucial component of the defensive fantasies which shape the body and the subjectivity of patriarchal masculinity. The female body is abjected as the Other of this masculine subjectivity, but can never be fully repressed or excluded. Abjection thus constitutes the theoretical embodiment of the way that patriarchal structures and subjects are always already infected by their worst fears.

While its psychoanalytic origins mean that abjection is primarily a theory of the formation of gendered and sexualised identity, its potential usefulness for analysing the construction of colonialist ideologies and racist subjectivities is clear.[19] Hence, while, as I suggested earlier, its use in this context entails political risks, it is also indispensable, in that it enables me, as an inescapably white and European subject, to become aware of and account for the dynamics of othering which may infect my fascination with Kahlo – that is, the process by which I ascribe to her work those aspects of my own identity which I experience as frightening and disruptive, but which I cannot bear to relinquish. Kristeva's work throughout the 1970s and in the early 1980s was preoccupied with precisely this question of the relationship between individual, subjective identity, and socio-political structures – including those which secure oppression on the grounds of racial or sexual difference. In *Powers of Horror*, she delineates the processes by which the maternally-connoted, pre-Oedipal realm of the semiotic and the symbolic law of patriarchal society are differentially constructed and maintained. Earlier, in *Revolution in Poetic Language*,[20] she had stressed that submission to the symbolic law of patriarchal society is essential, for it is the only means by which the infant can become socialised as a subject in language: the alternative of remaining in the pre-Oedipal semiotic realm precludes the possibility of social signification, and thus entails psychosis. Nevertheless, it is acknowledged that the semiotic can never be fully eliminated from subjectivity. It is conceived as an oppositional realm, associated with what is always alien, marginal, repressed, other; with those artistic practices and social instances which disrupt the symbolic by means of fragmentary, provisional, carnivalesque eruptions, thereby revealing the points of stress

Fig. 2.2 *My Nurse and I* Frida Kahlo (1937)
Courtesy Dolores Olmedo

and instability in the symbolic realm and undermining its claim to mastery. The maternal is placed firmly on the side of this potentially revolutionary semiotic, because the semiotic is associated with the primary processes of the pre-Oedipal mother-child dyad. Kristeva describes it as, 'a modality which bears the most archaic memories of our link with the maternal body – of the dependence that all of us have *vis-à-vis* the maternal body, and where a sort of self-eroticism is indissociable from the experience of the (m)other'.[21] For me, this is an apt diagnosis of what is most powerful and haunting about Kahlo's work. It describes the emotional intensity which saturates paintings like *My Nurse and I* (Fig. 2.2), or the dozens of self-portraits where so often this very eroticism is predicated on an acknowledgement of unassuageable loss and pain. In Kahlo's work, this narcissistic eroticism is inseparable from a sense of the loss of the (m)other and a constant yearning to recuperate it.

The necessary relationship of abjection to the maternal, which in Kristeva's work frequently stands as an image of femininity as such, means that the female body becomes the privileged signifier of abjection, emblem of the most agonising ambivalence of subjectivity: the desired and feared dissolution of identity which is associated with engulfment by the body of the mother, by sexual passion, or by the death drive. As Kristeva puts it, 'devotees of the abject, she as well as he, do not cease looking . . . for the desirable and terrifying, nourishing and murderous, fascinating and abject inside of the maternal body'.[22] The power of abjection lies precisely in this ambiguity; in the fact that what repels is also that which attracts most strongly. Hence its relevance to Kahlo's paintings: they body forth the experience of abjection which the subject normally excludes from its awareness, offering the viewer a temporary immersion in this horribly fascinating phase of the construction of subjectivity. Their troubling combination of beauty and horror enables the viewer to take pleasure in the lusciously depicted body and the returned gaze of the (m)other, while holding at bay – though only just – the loss of identity which normally accompanies this desired and feared fusion.

In a highly polemical critique of *Powers of Horror*, Jennifer Stone argues that the theory of abjection 'exchanges history for carnival and stamps on memory'.[23] However, a number of recent works have demonstrated that Kristeva's theories can usefully be deployed in the service of a more historically informed, materialist reading of culture, by means of a critical process which 'translocate[s] the issues of bodily exposure and containment, disguise and gender masquerade, abjection and marginality, parody and excess, to the field of the social, constituted as a symbolic system'.[24] The experience of embodiment and the workings of desire cannot be disentangled from social relations which are effects of hierarchical structures of power, gender, and wealth. The concept of carnival can be shown to expose the horror of abjection as a misogynist projection, and it provides a political and social framework for the ways in which women's bodies have been hystericised, idealised, or rendered grotesque. It is arguably this process which is explored in Kahlo's painting.

For Bakhtin, the carnival principle is embedded in the grotesque body, which is typified by events and activities – eating, defecation, birth, death, sex – in which the boundaries between bodies, and between bodies and the world, are obscured, eroded and displaced. He almost always speaks in very general, abstract terms of *the* body, regardless of factors like race and gender which we might see as important in contributing to differentiated constructions of embodiedness. And yet his descriptions of the grotesque body are replete with characteristics which have traditionally been coded as feminine, whereas the classical body to which it is opposed has certain conventionally masculine qualities:

> One of the fundamental tendencies of the grotesque image of the body is to show two bodies in one: the one giving birth and dying, the other conceived, generated, and born. This is the pregnant and begetting body, or at least a body ready for conception and fertilisation, the stress being laid on the phallus or the genital organs. From one body a new body always emerges in some form or other.[25]

The characteristics of the grotesque body are clearly sexualised here, without questions of gender or sexuality ever being allowed to affect the conceptual framework which is being constructed. In another passage, woman is described, in a classically misogynist gesture, as being 'essentially related' to the 'material bodily lower stratum', which is a crucial aspect of the principle of carnival:

> She is the incarnation of this stratum that degrades and regenerates simultaneously. She is ambivalent. She debases, brings down to earth, lends a bodily substance to things and destroys; but first of all, she is the principle that gives birth. She is the womb. (p. 240)

This would seem to indicate clearly that the female body has a special relation (albeit not one which appears to offer great advantages to women) to the grotesque body. Nevertheless, this does not lead Bakhtin to work with gender as a conceptual category in his analyses of culture.

One of Bakhtin's most vivid images of the grotesque body is his description of the Kerch terracotta figurines representing senile, pregnant hags:

> This is typical and very strongly expressed grotesque. It is ambivalent. It is pregnant death, a death that gives birth. There is nothing completed, nothing calm and stable in the bodies of these old hags. They combine senile, decaying and deformed flesh with the flesh of new life, conceived but as yet unformed. (pp. 25–6)

In some ways, Kahlo's work might seem to sanction this essentialist, biologically determined understanding of femininity. It has sometimes been claimed by feminist art critics as typifying a naively pictorial relationship to the external reality it supposedly represents, forming a celebratory testimonial to the unique power of female biology. I would argue, however, that Kahlo's paintings of birth, miscarriage, and the grotesque and suffering body, actually represent the process by which the female body is socialised, rendered abject by the technological gaze of patriarchal culture. These representations are surely linked with her own painful and ambivalent experiences of both the biological potential (thwarted in her case) for motherhood, and the practices of technologised medicine. But the

Fig. 2.3 *Broken Column* Frida Kahlo (1944)
Courtesy Dolores Olmedo

relationship between representation and experience in this context is less straightforward than many commentators have assumed. Discussing the 1944 painting *Broken Column* (Fig. 2.3), North American feminist art historians Karen Petersen and J. J. Wilson say, 'Frida wore this kind of brace and felt this kind of pain.'[26] No one, of course, can ever really know what another person's experience of pain is like; but this comment has a kind of distressing accuracy in so far as it testifies to the difficulty of finding an analytical language capable of dealing with the agony represented in *Broken Column*. It seems that words can only reiterate this pain, not account for it. The work of Petersen and Wilson played a vital historical role in the growth of feminist art criticism, but its drawback in this case is that it maps the artistic criteria of 1970s North American feminism (for example, the demand for a realistic representation of specifically female experience) onto Kahlo's work, erasing her agency as an artist and reducing her, in a somewhat colonialist move, to the naive and spontaneous illustrator of her own unproblematically self-present experience. In contrast, I would argue that Kahlo deployed the carnivalesque in order both to explore and problematise the relation between art and experience.

In an essay on Kahlo, Angela Carter has said that 'Women painters are often forced to make exhibitions of themselves in order to mount exhibitions . . . Fame is not an end in itself but a strategy.'[27] Kahlo used her unique status as a celebrated icon of *Mexicanidad* – deriving partly from her relationship with the publicly idolised Marxist painter, Diego Rivera, who depicted her in his murals as a revolutionary distributing both arms and the weapon of literacy to the oppressed masses; and partly from her self-presentation as an incarnation of folk tradition – to carve out a context in which she could shape an identity for herself as an artist. Mary Russo has shown how the female grotesque is associated with 'making a spectacle [or as Carter says, perhaps even more appositely, an exhibition] out of oneself', connoting a certain shameful inadvertency; an embarrassing loss of control, loss of boundaries.[28] Conversely, I would argue that Kahlo's work reinscribes the grotesque in order to make a spectacle of herself in ways which actually enhanced her control over her art and life. Her own bodily experience was the main subject of her artwork, and at the same time she put enormous care into decorating and displaying her body as an artwork in itself. For example, her identification with the Tehuantepec people functions as a strategic identification with the most matriarchal of indigenous Mexican cultures. Even when confined to bed by pain or illness, she dressed herself in their lavish traditional costume. This is not merely to reproduce the female body as exotic object of display as it recurs in patriarchal, colonialist culture, however. Kahlo chose this style of dress in order to affirm publicly the previously devalued Mexican side of her dual heritage: art critic Michael Newman has argued that this kind of affirmation of *Mexicanidad* was a political gesture of reaction against the Europeanising policies of the pre-revolutionary regime.[29]

Biographical accounts of Kahlo have often been inclined to attribute her fascination with the creation of an elaborately decorated appearance to mere vanity, but this is clearly inadequate to account for the particular, over-determined and politically charged form in which her supposed vanity expressed itself. Late in life, she would decorate the plaster corsets which supported her disintegrating spine: one of the most striking of these juxtaposes the hammer and sickle, emblem of the revolutionary politics to which she was committed throughout her adult life, with an unborn foetus which seems to prefigure the central image of her 1945 painting, *The Birth of Moses* (Fig. 2.4). Kahlo's interest in representing failed and frustrated maternity is often ascribed to a biographical origin in her own thwarted

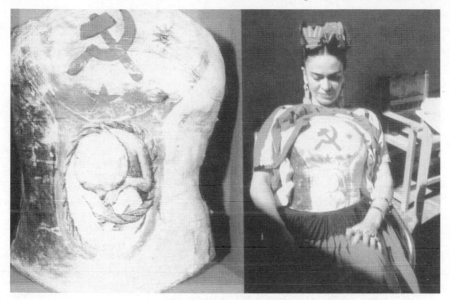

Fig. 2.4 *Corset with Hammer and Sickle* Frida Kahlo (1950)
Courtesy Redstone Press

desire for motherhood, but works like this make clear that such desires and disappointments are always experienced in a political context. As Mara R. Witzling has recently said, 'Kahlo took her own private vision and externalized it vividly, in a public language that could not be misunderstood. In do soing, she took a step in moving the experience of the female subject from its marginal cultural position toward the center.'[30] This is what brought the once culturally marginal body of work which Kahlo's art constitutes to occupy a paradoxically central position in feminist art criticism. Whilst this disconcerting centrality may sometimes have been achieved via a colonialist appropriation of the commodified figure of 'Frida Kahlo' as a symbol of exotic otherness, at its best her fascination for feminists has also enabled a salutary recognition of the subjectivity of the other woman; a subjectivity which western feminists must recognise as such if they are to resist their own personal and political abjection.

Notes

1.   Jacqui Duckworth, 'Coming out Twice', in Tessa Boffin and Jean Fraser, (eds), *Stolen Glances: Lesbians Take Photographs*, London, Pandora (1991) pp. 155–61.
2.   Gayatri Chakravorty Spivak, *In Other Worlds*, London, Methuen (1987) p. 150.

3. Joan Borsa, 'Frida Kahlo: Marginalization and the critical female subject', *Third Text* 3, 1990, pp. 21–40.
4. Ibid., p. 28.
5. Julia Kristeva, *Powers of Horror: An Essay on Abjection*, trans. Leon S. Roudiez, New York, Columbia University Press (1982).
6. Mikhail Mikhailovich Bakhtin, *Rabelais and his World*, trans. Helene Iswolsky, Cambridge, Mass., M.I.T. Press (1968).
7. Throughout this essay, I use the term 'grotesque' in the specifically Bakhtinian sense explained below, pp. 12–13. It should not be taken to imply an aesthetic evaluation of Kahlo's body.
8. Despite Kahlo's commodification, and the extensive interest in her life and work in recent years, there are few substantial studies. Those which do exist tend to situate her work in relation to some combination of Marxism, feminism, Surrealism, psychoanalysis, or the Mexican cultural context. In addition to the works cited elsewhere in this study, useful articles include Laura Mulvey, 'Frida Kahlo and Tina Modotti', in her *Visual and Other Pleasures*, London, Macmillan (1990), originally written with Peter Wollen for a 1982 exhibition at the Whitechapel Art Gallery, London; and Terry Smith, 'From the Margins: Modernity and the case of Frida Kahlo', *Block* 8, 1983. Hayden Herrera's massive and fascinating biography, *Frida*, London, Bloomsbury (1989) is indispensable, but marred by Herrera's lack of awareness of her own positioning.
9. Whitney Chadwick, *Women Artists and the Surrealist Movement*, London, Thames & Hudson (1985) p. 87.
10. Cited by Herrera, pp. 254–5.
11. Cited by Chadwick, p. 88.
12. Oriana Baddeley and Valerie Fraser, *Drawing the Line: Art and Cultural Identity in Contemporary Latin America*, London, Verso (1989) p. 92.
13. Kahlo frequently chose to wear – and to paint herself wearing – the flamboyant costume of the Tehuantepec region of Mexico. It served to affirm the Mexican peasant side of her *mestizo* identity; moreover, according to Hayden Herrera, 'Tehuantepec women are famous for being stately, beautiful, sensuous, intelligent, brave, and strong. Folklore has it that theirs is a matriarchal society.' op. cit. p. 109.
14. Jean Franco, *Plotting Women: Gender and Representation in Mexico*, London, Verso (1989) p. xxiii.
15. Ibid., p. 107.
16. Kristeva, *Powers of Horror*, p. 61.
17. Jacqueline Rose, *The Haunting of Sylvia Plath*, London, Virago (1991) pp. 33–4.
18. Examples offered by Kristeva of such abject phenomena, and the strategies used to render them manageable, include anything from the skin on milk, via the human corpse, to the entire edifice of Jewish dietary prohibitions.
19. In *Powers of Horror*, Kristeva takes the notoriously fascist and anti-semitic writer Louis Ferdinand Celine as an emblematic artist of abjection. To my surprise, I have not been able to find any work which uses the notion of abjection to explore constructs of racial otherness, but I am currently engaged on such a project myself, with particular reference to seventeenth-century representations of racial and sexual otherness, from Shakespeare's *Othello* (1604) to Aphra Behn's *Oroonoko* (1688).
20. Julia Kristeva, *Revolution in Poetic Language* New York, Columbia University Press (1984).
21. Julia Kristeva, 'A question of subjectivity'. Interview with Susan Sellers in *Women's Review* 12 1986, pp. 19–22.
22. Kristeva, *Powers of Horror*, p. 54.
23. Jennifer Stone, 'The horrors of power: A critique of "Kristeva"', Francis Barker *et al*,

(eds), *The Politics of Theory*, Colchester, University of Essex (1983) pp. 38–48. Stone argues that Kristeva's work is of questionable value to a radical political agenda, since her theory of abjection is elaborated primarily in relation to the anti-semitic, misogynist and fascist texts of Céline, and it is by no means clear in *Powers of Horror* whether she conceives of her writing as descriptive or prescriptive.

24. Mary Russo, 'Female grotesques: Carnival and theory', Teresa de Lauretis, (ed.) *Feminist Studies/Critical Studies*, London, Macmillan (1988) pp. 213–29.
25. Bakhtin, *Rabelais and his World*, p. 19.
26. Karen Petersen and J. J. Wilson, *Women Artists: Recognition and Reappraisal from the Early Middle Ages to the Twentieth Century*, London, Women's Press (1978) p. 134.
27. Angela Carter, *Frida Kahlo*, London, Redstone Press (1989).
28. Russo, 'Female Grotesques', p. 213.
29. Michael Newman, 'The Ribbon around the Bomb', *Art in America* April 1983, pp. 161–9.
30. Mara R. Witzling, *Voicing our Visions: Writings by Women Artists*, London, Women's Press (1992) p. 294.

3   Women and Surrealism

FRANCES PRESLEY

The poems which follow reflect the changing influence of Surrealism in my poetry. I first began studying Surrealism in the seventies. At that time, in European universities, the impact of feminism was not yet evident, and Surrealist studies were unselfconsciously male-dominated. My own feminism was hesitant, and usually confined to my non-academic writing. 'Free Union' was written in an unconscious attempt to eliminate the false divisions of subject and object in male Surrealist love poetry, and in my own *amour fou*.

In the eighties, I began to write poems about women's art, including that of Leonora Carrington and Meret Oppenheim. My discovery of invisible or undervalued women writers and artists was a more powerful method in affirming the female subject, both past and present, than the critique of male authors.

Free Union

With your hair of wire borrowed from no-man's land
of a forest at the onset of night
of a fakir's bed

with your nose of a cliff ridge
Striding Edge shaking off walkers

with your beard of burnt paper
ever curling away from its own expansion
with your beard that threatens your mouth of cherry liqueur
your mouth of dye water from a Grantham factory

with your back of a bus
moving out into city traffic

with your spine of perfectly spaced steps

with your waist of a beech tree
of a concrete column
of a letter box
of a profaned object
made of cold metal

made of ridged bark
leaning and upright
above the snow floor
above the concrete slabs

with your thoughts at telescopic range

with your fingers of gelignite
with your flannel fingers
in a static blanket
with your fingers of hooks
to suspend their own questions

with your balls of rag dolls
taking in the demand
of every child's hand
with your ripe gooseberry balls
inside a cluster of thorns

with your penis of an old maid
raised by salvation's kiss
the most grateful face I know
with your penis of rock candy
ready to be broken
by the first careless holidaymaker
with your coach tour wheel penis
ready to impress with tarmac facts
your penis a potholer's torch
finding the rock divide

with your eyes
lying at the bottom of a button tin
with your eyes of discarded pebbles
with your eyes
of an unforgiving projector reel
and the dust revolving in its shaft of light

After André Breton's 'L'Union Libre'. A surrealist idea reversed.

Leonora at the Serpentine
(Paintings 1940–1990)

saint Anthony recedes backwards
into himself
lowering his eyelids
as women often do

the patriarchs have stopped enumerating
or have they?
is the world of dreams nothing
but newer and busier patriarchs:
digital sequence under our feet?

the tall hats have gone
but the ties are still around their necks
and the hens between their legs
'O henny, henny penny
have a wee drop of whisky, hen'

Leonora is biting open   ·
pomegranates
she is not bitten
she bites with the snake

red is not the optic fibre monotony
of the new mandala
it is her shaped red
cabbage leaves

hiero nym
her sacred name
she is compared to Hieronymous
but not to saint Jerome

O saint Anthony she's got
your number

Imago

The stones of her body where it lies

feet

under

water

I stood on the shore of lake Neuchâtel, black water, black night
with my back to the lights of
                the natural history museum

Fig. 3.1 *Stone Woman* Meret Oppenheim
Courtesy Dr B. Wenger

My poem is to be superimposed on Oppenheim's *Femme-pierre* (Fig. 3.1),
a painting which dates from 1938, when she had left the Surrealist scene
in Paris and returned to Basel, entering a period of psychological and
artistic crisis that would last eighteen years. It shows a woman made of
stones, with her legs in the water. Of this painting Oppenheim said:

> A stone woman is prevented from action, but her legs are immersed in the
> stream . . . The stone is my inability to do any work, and the only really posi-
> tive thing is the feet, which represent a connection with the unconscious.

When I look at *Femme-pierre* I see silence and crisis, but also survival
and strength.

4 A credit to her mother

ANNETTE KUHN

Fig. 4.1

My family photograph collection includes two copies of the same studio portrait of myself at four months of age. The baby is naked, lying tummy-down on a blanket, facing camera but looking upwards to a point somewhere above camera level. This, as far as I know, is the earliest photograph taken of me; and one of my copies of it accordingly features on the very first page of the photograph album I began putting together when I was eight, in an effort to make both a family and a life history for myself.[1] The other copy, sent to me by my mother long after I had left home, grown up, and broken contact with her, bears a lengthy inscription on the reverse:

> Thought perhaps you might like this. You were a beautiful baby from the minute you were born. I loved you and you were always immaculate and well cared for. Your hair was very dark and there is a great resemblance to Marion and Samantha. Written in pencil, you may want to erase.

This inscription, pointing up a likeness between my infant self and my two nieces, the only daughters of my two much older half-brothers, was obviously written at the time the picture was sent to an adult and estranged daughter. The copy of the picture which carries this message – my mother's copy – has been trimmed, so that the area of the image which had been background and not baby is cut away.

Two copies of the 'same' photograph, then, but embodying very different uses and meanings at different moments for the various people with investments in it: the parents of the newborn baby, the child herself as a little girl, the mother of the adult daughter, the daughter as an adult. In itself, the image carries meanings outside these immediate contexts, too, revealing a great deal about how infancy is understood in a particular social and cultural formation.

The baby's nakedness, connoting newness, naturalness, innocence, is set within particular conventions of photographic portraiture, which in turn mimic high art conventions – notably, but not exclusively, those of the (adult, female) nude – suggesting that this is no mere snapshooter's effort, but a professional piece of work. In the process babyhood in general, a particular baby, and a specific image are elevated, made special, lifted out of the ordinary, the everyday. My photograph is in these respects no different from the thousands, the millions even, like it: it speaks volumes about the cultural meanings of infancy, the desires our culture invests in the figure of the newborn child. But while such meanings are certainly present in the specific contexts in which images like this are produced and used, every image is special, too: gesturing towards particular pasts, towards memories experienced as personal, it assumes inflections that are all its own. My photograph, then, is the same, but different.

On the surface, the family photograph functions primarily as a record: it stands as visible evidence that this family exists, that its members have gone through the passages conventionally produced in the family album as properly and necessarily familial. My photograph thus records the fact that a particular child was born and survived. But recording is the very least of it. Why should a moment be recorded, if not for its evanescence? The photograph's seizing of a moment always, even in that very moment, anticipates, assumes, loss. The record looks towards a future time when things will be different, anticipating a need to remember what will soon be past.

Even for outsiders, family photographs often have a poignant quality, perhaps because they speak all too unerringly of the insufficiency, the hopelessness, of the desire they embody. The image of the infant, innocent in its nakedness, naked as the day it was born, cannot so much fix that innocence as testify to the inevitability of its slipping away, of a slippage from grace. Hence the sadness, the sense of loss and longing, I read in my mother's words. 'You were beautiful', she says: beautiful, pristinely, 'from the minute you were born'. Her choice of the word 'immaculate' here is telling indeed: I was, she recalls, spotless, unsullied, free from sin or strain – precisely in a state of Edenic innocence.

Perhaps the mother's recollection speaks a degree of identification with the baby – a desire that she, the mother, might partake of the newborn's innocence; that in giving birth she too will have been reborn, granted the gift not just of innocence but of a fresh start. More specifically, the 'immaculate' may be read back to the baby's very conception; as an expression of my mother's wish (which might well have been retrospective – written into the past constructed in her inscription, that is) to have been my only begetter, for me to have been hers alone.[2] The reference to my nieces, my brothers' daughters (one of whom I have never met) – in effect negating the role in my conception of the man I knew as my father, who was not the father of my brothers – would certainly support this reading.

It seems, then, that the mother's love for her baby, not least in its retrospective assertion, is far from unambivalent. 'I loved you,' she tells the grown-up daughter who has left her. Loved me, that is, in my immaculate, unspoiled state: which suggests that this love had a hard time, and very likely failed, to survive the loss of innocence, to survive the baby's growing older and the mother's learning the hard lesson that life carries on much as before, except that now there is another mouth – and one that talks back, into the bargain – to feed.

In readings which shift back and forth across contexts – from the cultural to the familial to the individual to a specific constellation of family relations – the notion constantly re-emerges, in different shapes and forms, of infancy as spotlessness, innocence; and of the figure, the image, of the newborn child as embodying at once a desire for return to innocence and a knowledge of the absolute impossibility of such a return.

It is also apparent, though, that the naked and 'immaculate' body of the newborn Annette figured for my mother as *tabula rasa*, an empty slate, on which her own desires could be written – in an endeavour, perhaps, to repair lacks of her own. Born fourth in a family of seven, the fourth daughter of a man who desperately wanted a son, she felt she had never been wanted, loved, or cared for enough, certainly by her father (in her account a violent man and a poor provider) who despite – or perhaps because of – his absence at war figured overwhelmingly in her childhood memories.[3]

It seems clear to me today that my mother's love for the 'immaculate' baby Annette was marked very much by a quest to love the abandoned and unloved child she herself had been: in other words, that this maternal love involved a work of identification; identification then subjected to threat through that erosion of the ideal that comes with the inevitable loss of the innocence attaching to the figure of the baby. My mother's inscription on, and indeed within, the photograph, made when her baby had grown up and to all intents and purposes decisively separated herself, speaks with some eloquence of these investments, their failure, her disappointment.

In the Eden myth, the moment of the fall from primal innocence is marked by Adam and Eve's covering their nakedness; and, significantly, in the family album nakedness is admissable only in photographs of babies and very young children. My mother tells me that not only was I beautiful in my natural state, from the minute I was born, I was always well cared for as well. Well cared for, of course, by her: well turned out, in another favourite phrase of hers. 'Immaculate' here then partakes not only of the natural but also of the cultural: the newborn's primal innocence is overdetermined by – perhaps even subsumed to – the mother's labour of care for her child.

When my mother says I was well cared for, I know quite well that she is referring as much, if not more, to a public presentation of a 'well turned out' child ('a credit to her mother', she would often say of Marion, the niece who she maintains resembled me) as to any less outwardly apparent caring or 'maternal love' on her part. Or rather, perhaps, that for her the two things are inseparable: one loves one's baby, of course; and the evidence and the guarantee of that love lie in the labour of care evident in the child's appearance. But there is more to this than mere display. The baby's body is here quite literally a blank canvas, screen of the mother's desire – desire to make good the insufficiencies of her own childhood, desire to transcend these lacks by caring for her deprived self through a love for her baby that takes very particular cultural forms.

In my mother's account, her childhood was deprived materially as well as emotionally, and for her the two types of lack were inseparably intertwined. In this context, loving becomes synonymous with having – or rather with being given – enough to eat and decent clothes to wear. This perhaps explains the enormous investment, in all senses of the word, in my appearance: not just in my clothes, but in my hair; which for special occasions, and with huge effort on her part and much discomfort on mine, my mother would tie in rags to make the ringlets she herself had worn, or would have wanted, as a little girl. As I grew older, she took an interest in my body language as well, trying to get me to stand straight and not slouch: 'Back up, tummy in!' For if I failed to be 'well turned out', that failure would surely be hers, and she would be exposed as a bad person: not just an unloving mother, but – worse, perhaps – an unloved and unlovable little girl.

I am my mother's only daughter, and her youngest child, always to my irritation referred to as her 'baby'. My childhood was nonetheless punctuated by many births in the family, of the children of my two brothers and of numerous extraordinary fecund cousins; and babies and talk of babies were, it seemed, pervasive. Among the favourite topics of conversation, especially among girls and women in the family, was the sex of a forth-coming baby: Will it be a boy or a girl? Which would be preferable? There was a solid, perhaps an overwhelming, body of opinion that girl babies were on the whole the better deal, because 'you can dress a little girl up'.

On this conscious level, at least, a mother's attention to her baby's appearance has everything to do with gender: her love for a girl infant will be legitimately expressed in ways different from her love of a baby boy. Significantly, my mother's description of my niece Marion as 'a credit to her mother' was never applied to Marion's two younger brothers.

Fig. 4.2

In the summer before my fourth birthday, a photograph was taken (possibly by my father) of my mother and me on the front lawn of our groundfloor flat in Chiswick, West London. It is the only picture I have of myself as a small child with my mother. At this time, I believe, my father was working as a jobbing photographer. He was certainly a skilled amateur, at least; and photos of me as a small child are plentiful and of high quality for the period and for people of our class. In this one, I am seated on my mother's knee as she embraces me firmly in the crook of her right arm and rests her left hand across my ankles. We are both looking at camera; and I am clutching a doll and wearing a tartan dress with puffed sleeves and matching knickers, and a bow in my hair. On the back of this photograph my mother has written:

. . . Chiswick. She was nearly 4 years old. Dress and knicks by me.

Again the picture has been trimmed, and part of the inscription cut away as a consequence.

This picture disturbs me somewhat: a feeling, I think, which has much to do with my mother's uncharacteristic presence in the image. On the surface, it seems a commonplace and happy enough example of family photography. But beneath the sunny facade lurk shadows: the mother-father-daughter triad the picture (assuming it was made by my father) points to was not in fact a 'real' family. The child being held so tightly was an intrusion. If I put myself in the position of my mother as she was at the time this photo was taken, a little younger than I am now, all sorts of ambivalences surface.

She holds on firmly to the little girl who is hers, whom she will perhaps desire to be hers alone. But children are a drain and a drag: they cost money and, worse, they tie you down. When I came along, unintended, her younger son was thirteen and she thought she was finished with child-rearing. Life had not been easy with the boys and their father, and now in her late thirties she was hoping, at last, for a good time. If she did find a bit of fun with my father, though, she had been thrown back to square one by its consequence: me. Trapped in a situation she had not bargained for, my mother was tied for the foreseeable future to a child she had neither planned nor wanted to have, and (in days when the concept of the single-parent family had yet to be invented) to a man she would grow to despise.

But if the child was a mistake, she was not entirely a misfortune: she was a beautiful baby from the minute she was born, her mother's only daughter, who would always be her baby. The care and pride that have been lavished on the little girl's appearance are visible in this picture, which is readable – and, I would contend, was certainly read by my mother – as evidence, proof of that care. This is underlined in the statement, seemingly addressed to no one in particular, that the little girl's outfit was of her, the mother's, own making.

Children are a costly commodity: their upbringing calls for hard cash, as well as a good deal of labour of various kinds. This, though (we are told), ought to be a labour of love, entered into freely and without reservation. Counting the cost is not appropriate. Sure enough, the family as it is represented in family albums is characteristically produced as innocent of such material considerations, above price. To this extent, the family album constructs the world of the family as a utopia. And yet I feel sure my mother, whose own childhood had been so marked by poverty, must have known, or even calculated, the exact cost – to herself, at least – of having and keeping me. Perhaps in my earliest years her economic and her emotional investments measured up to each other, so that her identifications – of her baby with the unloved little girl in herself – could proceed unchecked. In these honeymoon years, being the mother of a well turned out baby must have provided enormous pleasure and emotional reward.

Keeping up appearances could not have been easy, though. From my earliest years, perhaps right from my infancy, both my parents worked outside the home. When I was very small, they shared responsibility for cleaning the public areas of the block of flats where we lived and of which my father was caretaker. They also worked together in my father's photography business, and both had jobs as bus conductors. While I do not know whether these jobs were simultaneous or consecutive, nor indeed whether there were any periods when my mother was actually at home full-time, it seems clear that a lot of hard work was being done to earn the means to keep the household going; and that there must have been little in the way of leisure time for my mother to pursue hobbies like dressmaking. Since, however, clothes were still 'on the ration', in common with many others during the years of postwar austerity she would simply have had to find the time to 'make do and mend'. In this climate, making clothes for herself and her baby was perhaps a necessity as much as a hobby.

Whatever the case, though, keeping the baby 'immaculate and well cared for', while a source of pride and pleasure, must still have cost a good deal of effort. Hence the ambivalent feelings of a mother whose life and circumstances had been, indeed remained, far from easy towards a baby born into a world which held out the promise of new opportunities for the children of ordinary working people; a baby, moreover, who seemed to be the object of all the love and attention that she herself had been denied; a baby, nonetheless, who would one day grow into a woman in a society still unkind to those of her sex.

Thus may a mother's investments in her baby daughter, inflected by particular circumstances of time, place, culture and class, incorporate the social with the psychic. This mother's ambivalent identification with her baby daughter already contains the seeds of overidentification, of difficulties of separation. If a daughter figures for her mother as the abandoned, unloved, child that she, the mother, once was, and in some ways remains, how can mother and daughter disengage themselves from these identifications without harm, without forfeiture of love? How can mother and daughter learn to acknowledge that they are separate people, to respect their differences from each other?

Any resolution, it seems, must come with very great difficulty: there will inevitably come a moment when it is no longer possible for the mother to sustain the fantasy of her daughter as *tabula rasa*, of the daughter's body as screen of her own fantasies of plenitude. The child will one day start answering back, refusing the mother's 'gifts', along with the vision of the perfect, immaculate, well turned out, little girl. At this point, matters of appearance, including clothes, may well cease to be a source of pleasure for the mother, and even become a site of struggle between mother and daughter.

'You can dress a little girl up' is one of those statements, certainly in the context in which I quote it here, whose truth is assumed to be perfectly self-evident. It points to one of the obvious and most important pluses of having (and not, it should be noted, of being) a baby girl. As a piece of conventional wisdom, it condenses a range of commonplace and generally unremarked cultural associations between dress and gender. But it also asserts a good deal more than that, say, there exist distinct forms and styles of dress which are very much tied to gender. It implies as well that the ways in which we actually relate to clothes and to matters of appearance generally are a ground, as much as an outcome, of sexual difference.

If, for infants themselves, sexual difference is hardly yet an issue, it certainly figures very importantly in adults' attachments to babies and very young children, often in unconscious and contradictory ways. 'Dressing a little girl up' is held to be an occasion of rightful and proper pleasure, and reward, for its mother; the unspoken corollary perhaps being that while a boy will obviously have to be clothed, this is more of a functional necessity, and that to dress him *up* would be inappropriate. In this particular social, historical and cultural context, at least, the investments in a mother dressing a boy baby and dressing up a girl baby are assumed to be quite distinct. In this context it may well be inadmissable for a mother to claim, by word or deed, any pleasure in dressing a little boy up, as opposed to merely dressing him. For this in effect would be a confession that she was disturbing the natural and proper order of gender difference: making a sissy of him.

But even such a forceful prohibition as this cannot account for the *positive* pleasure a mother may take in 'dressing up' her little girl. For the mother, the labour of attending to the appearance of a girl baby is surely of a very particular kind: it is caught up in that series of investments and identifications at play in general in her care of her little daughter. Dressing up a baby girl is a socially sanctioned opportunity for a woman, in caring for the little girl in herself, to love herself; while at the same time providing her with the opportunity to display, for the public gaze, the praiseworthy qualities of an adult who puts the needs of others above her own: a good mother, in other words, and therefore a good woman.

In a number of ways, therefore, having a baby girl she can dress up might be intensely rewarding for a mother. However, the distinctions between dressing and dressing up on the one hand, and between having and being a baby girl on the other, signal areas of potential contradiction, and so are perhaps worthy of further exploration. Dressing up as opposed to mere dressing implies, as has been suggested, a more than purely functional attitude towards clothes: it points to the element of display, of performance, inherent in certain relations to dress. Clothes are what you put on and take off, and consequently various identities may – sometimes quite consciously – be created across the surface of dress. This element of performance holds within it the potential of prising apart the gender/dress association, and this in turn can disturb the order of gender difference naturalised in certain clothing styles.[4]

The naturalised order of gender difference rests on more than just the forms and styles of dress, on differences as it were in the content of clothing: it is a question of forms of relation to personal appearance more generally, to the entire realm of bodily adornment. Dressing up – like its cognate activities *making* up and *doing* one's hair – suggests a relation of fabrication, construction, production. Herein lies an interesting paradox: dressing up a baby is possible, indeed socially acceptable, provided – and because – the baby is a girl; while (less consciously, perhaps) dressing up will also actually produce any baby, male or female, as feminine. As long as one baby in its clothes could look much like any other, outwardly visible marks of gender (the colour coding of baby clothes, for example) acquire a certain importance. In this context, dressing up participates in the production of gender, while at the same time gesturing towards the very artifice of that production.

A mother's attention to the clothing and general appearance of a baby girl, then, participates in the social, cultural, and undoubtedly also the psychical, construction of gender; specifically, of course, of femininity. It fabricates something we are supposed to believe is natural, already there; and so reminds us that femininity is not in fact a given, but is a product of labour. But in the specific instance of a mother dressing up a baby girl, the labour involved is also imbued with particular investments of desire, fantasy and identification; with the body of the baby figuring as pretext for what will be experienced as an enjoyable creativity. In this sense, the baby girl becomes its mother's muse, its body her canvas, the dressed up little girl her mother's very own work of art: to be looked at, admired, photographed, and hailed as a credit to her mother.

The often arduous and time-consuming work of producing a well turned out baby girl then becomes an end in itself, its results apparent, its use value palpable. This is visible and unalienated labour, whose product bears, for all the world to see, the signature of its maker: indeed, the most satisfying sort of work. The end-product becomes identified with, reflects back on, the worker herself, the mother, just as it constitutes the baby as a little girl. As, through this labour, femininity is produced in and through costume, through masquerade, so a mother's investment accrues to her credit. Clothes, as they make the little girl, also make the grown woman.

The mother's fantasy of identification (in which she cares for her little daughter as she would be cared for herself, and produces the baby in herself as a beautiful little girl worthy and deserving of love) rests upon a degree of projection, the baby its object, its screen. In the processes of projection and identification, the baby is fantasised as part of the mother – who can then simultaneously have, and be, the baby girl. In both senses, the baby becomes her mother's possession, and the play with femininity involved in dressing her up part of the mother's own involvement with femininity and its paradoxes, its ambiguities and its masquerades.

In this respect, the mother's pleasure in dressing up her baby girl may not be entirely unalloyed. Aside from the possibility that her care for the child could be an attempt to repair, to compensate for, deprivations in her own childhood – in its very nature a highly problematic project – the mother must on some level also be aware that the femininity she is calling forth in the masquerade of the dressed-up little girl is not without its complications and contradictions in the world beyond the mother-baby dyad.

Related to this must be the virtual inevitability of the mother's fantasy of oneness with her baby girl coming unravelled: for as the child grows older the fantasy of the baby as the screen of its mother's desire will become increasingly difficult to sustain. It is here that the distinction between having a baby girl and being a girl child comes into play. What happens when the child herself intervenes in the dressing-up process, perhaps to assert her own wishes about her appearance? How, in such a circumstance, can a mother protect her investment? How can the child continue to be a credit to her mother? And what sort of story might the little girl herself have to tell about all this?

Fig. 4.3

One of the manifestations of my own mother's involvement with her daughter's appearance was a passion for fancy dress. My photograph collection bears witness to the fact that, until I was around eight or nine years old, I regularly took part in fancy dress competitions. This was entirely my mother's idea: she entered me in the contests, made the costumes, and encouraged me to display them to best advantage. A frequently expressed conviction of hers had it that costumes she called 'original' (which for her meant conceptual as opposed to mimetic) stood the greatest chance of winning; and that if an 'original' costume did fail to net a prize, it was still far superior as fancy dress to the obvious, and perhaps more acceptable, sorts of costumes little girls might be dressed in for these occasions – nursery rhyme characters, fairies, princesses, brides, and suchlike. While I cannot in truth say I would have preferred any of the more conventionally little girlish costumes, in what I did wear I nevertheless did feel exhibited, exploited, embarrassed. Even if I won, there was little pleasure in competing in this way – in being put on display, scrutinised, weighed up, given points, judged. As I grew older, I grew less willing and no doubt decreasingly compliant.

A photograph of me wearing the costume for what I believe to be the last fancy dress competition I entered shows me, aged about nine, wearing a long shift to which are attached empty cigarette packets, drinks cartons, ice-cream containers, drinking straws, matchboxes; with a headdress comprised of one waxed Kia-Ora orange juice carton flanked by a pair of ice-cream tubs. On my right arm rests a placard explaining the costume – 'Cinema Litter'; and on my left a jigsaw puzzle, presumably my prize. It is difficult to put a precise date to this photograph, partly because, like the others, it has been trimmed down: the background is consequently minimal, offering no clues as to location; and whatever had been written on the back of the picture has been cut away.

I find myself extraordinarily, perhaps excessively, troubled by this habit of my mother's of cutting photographs down. The historian in me objects to the tampering with evidence; the critic to the lack of respect for image composition. But the strength of the feeling really has to do with the fact that these acts of my mother's seem to me to be gestures of power, at once both creating the evidence that fits in with her version of events and destroying what does not; and also negating the skills and aesthetic choices of the photographer, usually my father. This particular photograph certainly looks like one of my father's efforts: if so, it must be among the very last pictures of me he made, for at about this time he seems to have given up what was in any case by now no more than a hobby.

In the context of my own memories, I see this photograph, which I find very painful to look at, as a 'cusp' image, marking a transition. It must have been made at around the time of our move away from my first home in Chiswick to live in the house of my recently deceased Granny, my mother's mother. This move was highly traumatic for me, in large part (as I now construe it) because although they remained together, leaving

Chiswick marked some decisive rift between my parents. At stake in some way in this, I suspect, was the issue of my paternity.

Our new home was very much my mother's territory: it had been lived in not only by her mother, but before that by one of her brothers. Over the following few years she saw to it that both her sons moved with their families into other houses on the same street. In all this, I believe my father must have felt increasingly marginalised: illness – he suffered from bronchitis which later became emphysema – by now dominated his life and isolated him from those closest to him. This, along with his abandonment of the hobby of photography, which had been a source of such pride and pleasure, must surely be symptomatic. I, too, felt displaced. In my new school, corporal punishment – completely alien and shocking to me – was practiced; I was mocked by the other children for my 'posh' accent; I even caught head lice and had to have my plaits chopped off. Desperately unhappy, I started putting on weight.

It was around this time, too, that I started 'answering back', embarking on a lengthy and bitter struggle with my mother over issues of separation – issues which would never be resolved. I recall feeling very unhappy about being put into this particular costume and into the fancy dress competition, and had doubtless let my objections be known in the various overt and covert ways of the uncompliant child – whining, sulks, refusal to smile and a general 'slouching on parade'. If the photograph itself reveals nothing of all this, neither, though, does it seem to me to present an entirely smooth surface.

The girl looks neglected and slightly scruffy, a far cry from the 'immaculate' three-year old. Little effort seems to have been put into her hair, badly cut (could this have been soon after the head lice episode?) and all over the place; her smile seems slightly doubtful; her eyes are closed. The costume itself, though, is perhaps more illuminating. It is certainly a clever idea in itself: but rather more noteworthy is the fact that the child wearing it is being displayed as a figure for the detritus, the discarded byproducts, of a pursuit whose pleasures hold a distinctly erotic appeal. The implications scarcely need spelling out: it is fortunate, perhaps, that this was to be the last of my fancy dress costumes.

My mother's passion for fancy dress can be regarded in certain respects as an extension of her earlier investment in 'dressing up' her infant daughter: though there is undoubtedly more to it than that. As a cultural form, fancy dress gestures with some urgency towards the performance aspect of clothes. Indeed, it renders this aspect entirely overt: for the whole point of fancy dress is that the masquerade is there, self-evident, on the surface.

Fancy dress partakes of the carnivalesque, a turning upside-down of the everyday order of hierarchies of class, status, gender, ethnicity. A bus conductor's daughter can be queen for an hour – or even, indeed, king, for girls can be boys and boys girls, and either can be neither. A fracturing of the clothes/identity link is thus sanctioned – at once permitted and contained, that is – by the cultural conventions of fancy dress.

Also, and relatedly, there is clearly a fantasy component to fancy dress: after all, the word 'fancy' itself derives from a contraction of 'fantasy'. But whose fantasy? In the case of 'Cinema Litter', as of the other fancy dress costumes my mother made for me, certainly not the little girl's, certainly not the daughter's. Costume which presents itself so unequivocally as performance or masquerade will often – and certainly in the case of 'Cinema Litter' – virtually beg for a symptomatic reading. But while an interpretation of 'Cinema Litter' reveals meanings tied specifically to a particular costume and context, taken together with all the other fancy dress costumes my mother made for me (and certainly if it is accepted that one of the issues at stake here is a mother's identification with her daughter) this can be seen as expressive also of fantasies of a rather different nature: the desire of a working woman, no longer young, to be noticed – seen, applauded, rewarded – as someone special, different from the rest, out of the ordinary, precisely 'an original'. The daughter in fancy dress, attracting attention, winning a prize even, becomes a vehicle for the mother's fantasy of transcending the limitations, dissatisfactions and disappointments of her own everyday life.

But given the 'conceptual' and/or the androgynous quality of the costumes she favoured, it seems to me that at this point my mother's fantasy had little to do with femininity as a site of redemption, and much to do with overcoming the limitations femininity imposes. To this extent, the unconscious aspect of the fancy dress project either runs somewhat counter to the earlier project of producing a 'well turned out' little girl, or underscores the contradictions and ambivalences around femininity that were already, perhaps, lurking in the latter.

While all this might bespeak resistance, or signal the (limited?) liberatory potential of certain cultural practices for individuals and social groups who lack power in the world, it should not be forgotten whose fantasy it was that drove these particular practices of dressing up and the fancy dress. For the little Annette, her mother *was* all-powerful; and it seems never to have occurred to her, the mother, that her daughter could possibly harbour genuine feelings or wishes or hopes or ambitions that in any way diverged from her own, the mother's.

What, then, of the daughter's story: the daughter put on display, exhibited to the public gaze in a quest for rewards from strangers for costumes, for outward appearances, that by nature and intent cloak, occlude and subvert – as well as create – identities? What if the daughter was not entirely comfortable with such identities, with being the site of another's investments, the vehicle of another's fantasies? What of the daughter who refused to smile prettily at the judges, refused to want to be picked out from all the others as a winner, and yet who found utterly unbearable the humiliation of losing? What of her? That little girl got fat, looked terrible in everything she wore, and answered back. What a disappointment to her mother.

Notes

1.   This is discussed in Annette Kuhn, 'Remembrance', in Jo Spence and Patricia Holland (eds), *Family Snaps: The Meanings of Domestic Photography* London, Virago (1991), pp. 17–25. On photography and memory, see Roland Barthes, *Camera Lucida* London, Flamingo (1984) and Rosy Martin's and Jo Spence's notes for an exhibition, *Double Exposure: The Minefield of Memory* London, Photographers Gallery (1987). On the family album, see Jo Spence, 'Visual autobiography: beyond the family album', in *Putting Myself in the Picture* London, Camden Press (1986), pp. 82–97.

2.   Kuhn, 'Remembrance', pp. 20–21.

3.   In a book-length memoir written when she was in her late sixties, my mother recalls her father's first return on leave from the war:

> [It] was in 1915, and our Dad seemed to have been away for ever. But one day during the summer holidays when we were playing on Moor Mead, a girl came running up to us and said, 'I think your dad's come home. A soldier went in your house.' Without waiting to hear the last of what she was saying, I was on my way home, my bare feet hardly touching the warm pavement . . . There in the kitchen was my dad, sitting in an armchair near the fireplace. I wanted to climb all over him, but before I could reach him, he said in a very stern voice, 'Where's your shoes? Put them on at once!'

4.   For further discussion of clothes as performance, see Annette Kuhn, 'Sexual disguise and cinema', in *The Power of the Image: Essays on Representation and Sexuality*, London, Routledge and Kegan Paul (1985), pp. 48–73. Judith Butler discusses 'gender performatives' in her *Gender Trouble: Feminism and the Subversion of Identity* New York, Routledge (1990), ch. 3 (iv).

5 Keeping mum, or why did Manet paint over Morisot's mother in black? A video poem

PENNY FLORENCE

In 1869 the painter Edouard Manet painted in black over a figure in another artist's painting. The artist in question was Berthe Morisot. The figure was of her mother.

You have just heard me speak these words. There are more.

The mirror is not a mirror. It is an incomplete painting.

The room is darkened. You can pick out certain more brightly illuminated parts of my white body, in the same mirror as my video camera. In my hand. As I move back and forth, you wonder if it is the effect of my movement or that of the lens. Which I move. The mirror is in a gilt frame, like an oil painting, and there are brushes and paints beside it.

In vision, we explore my body. What is in your mind as your eye accompanies mine? I am thinking of my body through your eye. Another body. Through the sight that is touch. Our voices are not the same. But maybe you think some of the same thoughts as me, before the words, maybe the gap between us is in language, not in thought. I make the words all nouns in deference to language, smoothing the unevenness of their arrival. Maybe you also think that thought before words is possible.

My image flickers as I reach to pick up a paintbrush with my free hand. The one without the camera. The brush hovers, like the broom of the sorcerer's apprentice. It is loaded with black paint, and as I finally grab hold of it, the drops turn blood red. The movement of the image slows as I scream without sound. I smear the blood down my face, and speak my first direct words to you. Perhaps you have brought me them. They astonish me.

Murder. Matricide.

The word wakens another. Woman, that is. She is almost thirty years of age. As she gets out of bed, you see that her nightclothes are in the fashion of the last century. Despite having just got up, she looks elegant. She lights a candle and sits down to write. She seem ill-at-ease. You notice her name inscribed on her leather writing case, 'Berthe Morisot'. But, try as she may, the words will not come. She takes the candle and goes out.

I am walking down a corridor. She is following me, but when I turn, she is not there. In the mirror there are two reflections, however. Is it us? Her and me, I mean, but perhaps you. Are you alone?

Fig. 5.1 *The Mother and the Sister of the Artist*
National Gallery of Art, Washington

The mirror is not a mirror. It is an incomplete painting, still on the easel, showing two women, somewhat under lifesize. On the right in the foreground dressed in black there is an older woman, and just off-centre and slightly behind, framed by the first figure, is a young woman dressed in white. I sigh and Berthe looks around, startled. In the candlelight, you see that the room is the same as that depicted. So do I. I say:

Portrait of the Mother and Sister of the Artist.

Berthe goes up to her painting and looks at it very closely, scrutinising the figure of her sister.

Edme!

The word is breathed, almost, rather than spoken. She touches the skirt of her mother's dress, then smears the still wet black paint down the side of her face, already wet with unfelt tears. You hear her voice, clearer now. Her accent is upper class.

That is where the trouble started. Once he had begun, nothing could stop him. He went from the skirt to the bust to the head to the background.

Berthe is standing paintbrush and palette in hand looking intently at her painting. You realise, seeing what she sees, perhaps, that the image is suffused with light, quite different. What is it? It is the figure of Madame Morisot, who is depicted wearing a pale dress suggestive of subtle colour. She herself, Madame Morisot, is sitting posed in the same dress for the portrait, head slightly bowed, book open. You hear her voice, mature, warm and self-assured:

It breaks my heart to see each season's work tossed into dark corners. Men indeed have all the advantages, and make life comfortable for themselves. I am not spiteful, but I hope there will be a compensation.

Another voice, a man's, while you watch Madame Morisot watch her daughter from under her brows:

Madame Morisot, as your daughters' drawing master, I feel I have to tell you this. It concerns them all, Yves, Berthe and Edme, especially the last, yes, especially Edme.

(You look at the figure of Edme, for it is she, the sister in the painting, now Madame Pointillon, new wedding-ring a clear gold mark on her finger. You wonder where she is now, why she is not posing.)

You may speak freely, M. Guichard.

Thank you, Madame. Given their talents and inclinations, my teaching is not going to give them mere drawing-room accomplishments. They will become painters. Do you realise what this means? In your place in society, this will be revolutionary.

Berthe looks up from her work, Madame looks down at her book, unhurried – and not before catching the painter's eye.

Berthe walks to her desk, her back to the painting, to her mother. The words finally come to her. She can write now. You see the letter Berthe is writing as she writes it. Her handwriting moves rapidly across the paper and you hear her voice repeating the words:

That is where the trouble started. Once he had begun, nothing could stop him. He went from the skirt to the bust to the head to the background.

Something is happening. You wonder what it is. The page dissolves, shape-shifting like amoebae, into the form of a naked white woman, thin, but with strong arms and round breasts, lying back with feet crossed at the ankle. It is a painting, *Olympia*, by Edouard Manet.

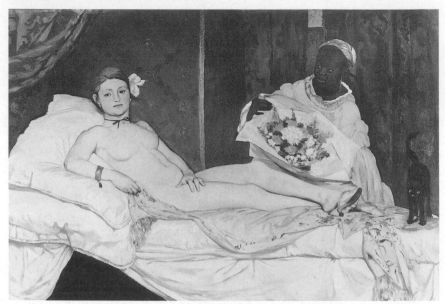

Fig. 5.2 *Olympia* Edouard Manet (1863)
Musée D'Orsay, Paris

The white woman is reclining on white cushions on a white daybed. Dressed in pinkish white, there is a black woman, holding a huge bouquet of white and blue flowers, with a touch of red, like the ostentatious bow in the white woman's hair, like the long earring in the black woman's ear. She leans forward, looking at the white woman. The white woman looks at you. So does the black cat at her feet. Who has sent the flowers? Does Olympia give flowers to her black sister? They are luscious, bright, see both women's hands, reach out! Berthe Morisot's writing continues over the body of the white woman, swelling over her slight curves, concentrating around her navel:

He kept on and on cracking jokes, laughing like a madman, passing me the palette and taking it back until at last by five o'clock we had made a total caricature.

The surface of *Olympia* distorts again, and you wonder what will appear this time. The image hesitates between *Olympia* and Berthe's *Portrait*, and you notice that the figure in white, the sister, has a bow in her hair, blue to Olympia's red.

You hear a man's voice speak the poet Baudelaire's words, first spoken for Jeanne Duval, his black mistress, a woman of mixed race. You look more carefully at the black woman with the flowers.

Strange goddess, dark as the night,
Whose scent intermingles musk and Havana,
The work of some shaman, Faust of the Savannah,
Black-bodied sorceress, child of blackest night.

But the black woman is disappearing. She is dissolving, becoming white, her dress becoming black. Ah, it is the image of the larger figure, the mother in Berthe's *Portrait* which now seems to be clearer. She, the mother, is white where the black woman is black, black where she is white. Is she, too – you see her in *Olympia* behind Olympia with the flowers in place of a book – a mother?

The man's voice continues, Baudelaire's words written for his white mistress, Madame Sabatier.

Your head, your ways, your grace
So fine, like the lie of the land;
Laughter plays in your face
Like a cool wind in a bright sky . . .

And so I want, one night,
At the sound of the sensuous hour,
Towards your body's delight
To slink, a silent coward,

To punish your happy flesh,
To bruise your shriven breast,
Your startled side to gash
With a wound, wide, deep . . .

The image that is *Olympia* suddenly bursts, and, through a hole that starts in the painted side of the white woman, the black woman and the white woman step out. The black woman is still holding her bouquet and wears a simple tunic. She picks up another tunic and gives it to the white woman. She slips it on; both are now dressed in Greek chitons and act as a chorus. The canvas surface is now blank. Or a mirror? They stand to the side of it, facing forward, arms folded. Words appear on the blank canvas. Their voices are flat as they speak the words without looking to read. They have urban working-class accents. The two women, as chorus, speak Berthe's words:

Quote: '*My mother finds the whole episode funny. But I find it agonising.*'
I say, my voice surprising you, perhaps:
Victorine!

The white woman, Victorine, turns, walks to the other side, turn back and says:

M. Manet has arrived. He is early for tea, as usual. Shall I show him in?

Edouard Manet comes in anyway, hands his hat and stick to Victorine, and ignores her long look. She goes out. He cuts a dash as a fashionable man in his prime, about thirty-eight. You notice his impassivity; he is a true dandy. Berthe is standing looking at her painting, which now fills the frame, in a preoccupied way.

Ah, Edouard. I am having such difficulties with Mama.

Edouard exchanges formal niceties with Madame Morisot, who is sitting in her pose. He turns his attention to the painting. As he looks at it, he starts to sigh and breathe erratically, becoming increasingly agitated. He begins to pace up and down while Berthe watches frozen in surprise, brush and palette in hand. Suddenly he takes the brush from her and begins to paint, quick, short strokes. As you watch him, you hear Berthe's voice reading from her letter.

He took the brushes and put in a few accents that looked good. Mother was in ecstasies. That's when the trouble started.

Madame Morisot leaves her pose to see what is happening, and you notice that her face in the painting has taken on a strange resemblance to mine. You hear my voice, you resist it, you want to know what is going to happen. I persuade you by saying:

If I stay with the feeling, it is clear. If there was an image about which nothing was known by any living person beyond its surface, would you be untroubled by the need to select facts? Or would you invent them? and why, how?
(Furtively, I open another book seeking other facts. Aha, I've caught you! Is that your voice or mine?)

Fact: Berthe modelled for Edouard at this time. Like Jeanne and Victorine before her. Like them? Fact: Berthe married Edouard's brother five years later. Fact: she founded, the following year, with six men, an artistic group Manet never joined. The Impressionists. Fact: she fought his influence. Fact: the Impressionists, first called the Intransigeants (how similar, how different!), were radicals.

Edouard, now frantic, grabs the palette from Berthe, and with a new brush poised, looks to choose another colour. He cannot find it. He looks exasperatedly among the jars and paintpots.

Once I begin to grapple with the facts, I need more of them. I need to anchor myself against this inrush of detail and impressions. I do so with my body. You, too, women, are part of that anchor. You, to whom I speak, are possessed of female bodies. No. Are embodied in femaleness. No. Body forth the feminine. No. Are women. Ah! I wonder if you assume I mean contemporary, white and of my class.

You hear Edouard's voice, speaking with a slight laugh:

The Morisot girls are charming. It's a pity they are not men. They could do a lot for art as women by marrying an academician each and stirring up trouble in the establishment.

Edouard eventually finds what he is looking for, pushed to the back, relatively unused. Black.

You hear the voices of Victorine and Jeanne in chorus.

Fact: last year, 1869. Edouard Manet has just finished The Balcony, *with Berthe prominent in the foreground. Fact: a lithograph from his topical political painting* The Execution of the Emperor Maximilien, *itself unexhibited, is suppressed.*

My voice interrupts as I blurt out:

Hearing you say that, I have just realised something. Berthe was not the only one who had problems with composition. Edouard did. The Execution of the Emperor Maximilien *was among the most difficult. He actually tore it up – it's huge – and recombined parts of it. I often do this with sketches.*

Edouard's brush is coming at me in the painting, you see it too, it feels suffocating. Despite its attack I have to speak:

But this is how I relate to my camera. Is it aggression? It's something like it. But once you, I mean me, once I actually record aggression towards the camera – a wave crashing into it, a paintbrush jabbing towards it – it appears as an attack on you, or whoever watches. It isn't against the lens any more. The lens is no longer a barrier. The lens – changes.

Manic now, Edouard is frantically going over the figure of Berthe's mother in her painting. She still looks like me. You hear me say:

The real Mme. Morisot speaks.

You hear her say:

Oh, Edouard, that's marvellous! Yes, I think that's much better now, don't you, Berthe, my dear?

Jeanne and Victorine, standing aside from the others, speak as chorus.

Fact: France 1869, the Second Empire, prosperity on the surface. 1869. The Workers' International begins to support strikes and the right of women not to be confined to the home. The eve of the Franco-Prussian war and the Third Republic. Fact: The siege of Paris will be next year. Edouard Manet, Morisot family friend, will join the National Guard. Does he remember Baudelaire's hatred of his military father? Fact: Barely two years on, the Paris Commune will last a few months and end in carnage.

Berthe is walking up an impressive flight of steps. You see them stretch far up ahead of her. She moves on through vast galleries, paintings covering the walls. You hear her voice:

1869. Dearest Edme, I am going to the Salon to see what the Jury have selected this year. Manet begged me to look for his painting, since he didn't dare himself. He laughed in a strange way and blurted out that his painting was extremely bad and would be a great success.

Berthe is looking for the painting. Jeanne and Victorine speak:

Edme, would she have been a great painter? Like Yves, the eldest Morisot sister, she has just got married. Like Yves, she will never paint again. Except for a portrait of her husband.

Berthe is aloof from the crowds, the only unaccompanied woman. A new voice, a woman's, speaks. You hear her.

My dearest Berthe, I am often with you in my thoughts. I follow you everywhere in your studio and I wish that I could escape, if only for a quarter of an hour, to breathe again the air we once breathed. Your loving sister. Edme.

There is a scuffle. Some incident is taking place near one of the paintings on display. Berthe goes to see.

Jeanne and Victorine speak as a chorus.

Fact: Five years later Berthe will marry Eugene Manet, Edouard's brother. He will support her in her work. He will challenge a man to duel for saying the Impressionists were 'six lunatics, one of whom is a woman'. Fact: Edouard was against her joining them.

Berthe catches sight of one of Edouard's paintings, *The Balcony*, and sees herself prominent in the foreground. She looks hard at her painted self. Her image.

Well! I look, not exactly ugly. Strange, perhaps.

You hear Berthe speak from her letter:

Dearest Edme, This painting, this work you mourn for, is the cause of so much grief and trouble . . . You have a serious attachment and a man's heart totally devoted to you.

A man is waving his walking stick at Manet's painting. Two uniformed attendants are restraining him. I wonder if you assume, without thinking about it, that they are men. As they would have been. Berthe manages to see enough to reassure herself that the painting is all right, and begins to walk back along the corridors. Occasionally she looks behind her. I am among those who follow her. We find ourselves back in the same room as before. But the only painting on the wall is *Olympia*. Victorine and Jeanne stand beside it in attendants' uniforms. A queue of people in modern dress files past with their guidebooks, some hardly giving the painting more attention than the books. They totally ignore Jeanne and Victorine. And Berthe and me, who are stock still.

I say:

Olympia caused an uproar when it was first shown. They say that the reason was that the public were 'unused to pure painting. They failed to understand the meaning of those graduated tones of white. A symphony in white.'

Jeanne speaks, for the first time alone:

And you? Do you understand the meaning of a symphony in white?

She is proud and angry. Victorine, Berthe and I look at her, as if for the first time. Indeed, she has changed. She now wears African-inspired clothes.

The people filing past are now predominantly women.

Victorine clears her throat. And speaks. To me:

She's right. Why should I be chorus to your story?

Jeanne to Victorine:

What have I been, if not chorus to your story?

I to Jeanne, perhaps, or mainly:

Chorus to Manet's. Or rather to Baudelaire's.

Jeanne picks the bouquet out of *Olympia* and holds it in front of Victorine's face. As she takes it from Jeanne it turns into a mask in the form of a white woman's torso; the eyes are breasts and the mouth pubic hair. Victorine's face becomes the mask.

The man's voice is once again heard. He says:

Berthe Morisot, in the words of a contemporary critic, paints 'a world which excludes Man and his desires, a paradise in which there is only Eve and no Adam'.

You realise that *Olympia* is now on the easel in Berthe's drawing room in place of her *Portrait of the Mother and Sister of the Artist.*

Jeanne in her fine costume is examining Berthe's palette and brushes.

Victorine, now fully clothed in working woman's costume of the 1860s, swaggers in.

Jeanne points a brush at the figure of *Olympia* and describes a much larger shape in the air. You hear me say:

Until the 1980s most histories of their time did not mention feminism. Or take much account of women at all.

You hear Victorine exclaim:

No! But it's true, nobody was much interested in my drawings.

She starts looking intensely through a frame formed by her fingers, as if devising a shot.

You hear Jeanne reply:

I didn't know you were an artist. Maybe a lot of models were. Probably still are. Berthe sat for Manet several times.

Victorine to Jeanne:

Yes, but we've got nothing in common with her. Berthe. I mean, she had private lessons. Sometimes with Corot. And wasn't she the great-granddaughter of some-body?

Jeanne to Victorine, while tracing Olympia's outline with a dry brush:
We all are.

Victorine to Jeanne:
A painter. Fragonard, that's it. Fragonard. Ladies on swings and all that. I wonder who her great-grandmother was.

Jeanne continues to examine the painting minutely.
I want to understand more about him.

I say to you:
But I find he's in the way. He seems to make it hard to reach her, the spell goes wrong, conjures him. I don't want to accept that this is the way.

Victorine:
Who?

Jeanne:
Manet. Edouard. That painting The Execution of the Emperor Maximilien. *The soldiers are wearing French uniforms. But it was in Mexico, after the French pulled out. That interests me. It's politics.*

Victorine:
But Berthe. Berthe's mum!

Jeanne suddenly pushes the brush she is holding into the palette and then, tentatively at first, on to *Olympia*'s body.

Victorine:
Hey, I'm the painter.

Jeanne:
How do you know I'm not?

Then she begins to paint in earnest, emphasising Olympia's slight curves, making her fuller, darker. As she begins to focus on her stomach, you see that she is turning her into a pregnant black woman.
You want portraits of mothers, well, here's one, in the flesh.

Olympia's rounded and luscious black belly starts to give birth. The bow in her hair comes undone. The figures in the painting, you realise, are both now of black women. They begin to swirl round, the red ribbon streaming, and the newborn is cradled in Jeanne's arms, dark and furious. The umbilical cord snakes between the ribbon and the women.

Madame Morisot, too, holds a baby. She puts her into a pram and the cord coils across your vision. With difficulty, she begins to walk with the pram up an impressive flight of steps. You see them stretch far up ahead of her. Berthe is at the top with Edouard. He is blindfolded with a blood-red ribbon. She runs her hands down her face, leaving a smear of black paint. Manet is trying to reach out to her, but he cannot. His image multiplies and then becomes a crowd of men in nineteenth-century costume, some of them soldiers in French uniforms.

Madame Morisot struggles up the steps. The crowd is increasing as it merges into a modern crowd of men. She loses hold of the pram, and just snatches the child out before it bounces down the steps. The men are milling about before the doors of the gallery, indifferent, barring the way. Berthe stands on the threshold with Jeanne and Victorine. Some of the men try unsuccessfully to make room for Madame Morisot and her baby. She just manages to pass her to Berthe, who gets jostled away. The cord uncoils. The movement of the crowd prevents Mme Morisot from following. The cord is stretched between them. There is blood on her stomach, and she falls. The crowd trample over her. Berthe sees Edouard among the men. His blindfold is about his neck. They look at each other for a long moment.

You hear Berthe's toneless words.

Have you seen Mama?

THE END

Notes

The following notes are unnumbered because numbers in a text like this might be obtrusive. They are arranged in sequence following the text in the order in which they seem most likely to be useful.

The painting by Morisot with which Manet interfered is *Mme Morisot and Her Daughter Mme Pontillon (The Mother and Sister of the Artist)* 1869–70. Oil on canvas 101×81.8 cm. National Gallery of Art, Washington D.C., Chester Dale Collection (Fig 5 1)

The incident was recounted by Morisot in her letters. See Rouart (ed.) *The Correspondence of Berthe Morisot*, London, Lund Humphries (1957). Most of the words Morisot speaks above are either translations or close paraphrases. The same is true of Mme Morisot and the drawing master, M. Guichard. In *Women Artists. Recognition and Reappraisal from the Early Middle Ages to the Twentieth Century*, London, (The Womens Press 1979, p. 92) Petersen and Wilson refer to the story. For broader commentary see also Parker and Pollock *Old Mistresses: Women Art and Ideology*, London, Pandora (1988) p. 43; Pollock *Vision and Difference*, London, Routledge (1988) p. 56ff; Garb *Women Impressionists*, Oxford, Phaidon (1986) and Adler and Garb *Berthe Morisot*, Oxford, Phaidon (1987). In *Berthe Morisot's Images of Women* (Cambridge, Mass., Yale University Press 1992) A. Higgonet points out that the painting is exceptional in relation to the rest of Morisot's oeuvre (p. 67).

On matricide, see Irigaray in Whitford (ed.) *The Irigaray Reader*, Oxford, Blackwell (1991) pp. 34–52, 'The bodily encounter with the mother' and 'Women-mothers, the silent sub-stratum of the social order'. Also relevant is Lacan on women and the mother: see Mitchell and Rose *Jacques Lacan and the Ecole Freudienne*, London, MacMillan (1990) for example pp. 123–36. For feminist commentary on Lacan see Grosz *Jacques Lacan. A*

Feminist Introduction, Routledge (1990), esp. Chapter 6. In *In Search of Our Mother's Gardens*, London, The Women's Press (1983). Alice Walker asks what it meant 'for a black woman to be an artist in our great-grandmothers' day?' (p. 233ff.)

Full details of the painting by Manet which is most important in the piece above are: *Olympia*, 1863, Oil on canvas 51×73¾ in. Museum of Impressionism, The Louvre (Fig. 5.2). Others referred to, but not illustrated are: *The Balcony*, 1868, Museum of Impressionism, The Louvre. *The Execution of the Emperor Maximilien*, 1867, Stadtische Kunsthalle, Mannheim. (Other versions may be seen in the Museum of Fine Arts, Boston, Ny Carlsberg Glyptotek, Copenhagen and the National Gallery, London. These are all illustrated in Hanson's *Manet and the Modern Tradition*, New Haven, Yale University Press, (1979), (Figs 77–81), and so is the lithograph referred to above (Fig. 82). See also pp. 111–14, and Sandblad (1954).

The year before *Olympia*, Manet painted a portrait, now in Budapest, of Jeanne Duval, famous as the poet Baudelaire's mistress and the inspiration for some of the poems in his *Les Fleurs du Mal*. (Illustrated in Florence, *Mallarmé, Manet and Redon*, Cambridge, CUP (1986), Fig. 72, alongside *Olympia* and a portrait of Morisot, Figs 71 and 73). I would agree with Reff in his detailed study of *Olympia* that there was no single model, either in person or in paint, for the Black Woman in *Olympia*, but Manet was close to Baudelaire at the time (Reff 1976 p. 89ff.); Hanson states that there was one model (Hanson 1979 p. 99), and that it was Laure, whose portrait he also painted. Certainly, Laure's rounded eyes and features in the portrait resemble those of the black woman in *Olympia*, and their headdresses are similar.

The white woman who posed for *Olympia* was known by name to some of the people who would have seen it when it was first exhibited. She was Victorine Meurend, who often posed for Manet, and was herself an artist. Manet had painted her portrait in 1862. (Unluckily, Eunice Lipton's fascinating book based on her life *Alias Olympia* came out after this piece was written.)

The poems by Baudelaire quoted above are: 'Sed non satiata' and 'A celle qui est trop gaie', both published in *Les Fleurs du Mal*, 1857, though written in c.1842 and 1852 respectively. *Les Fleurs du Mal* was immensely influential, and among its contents were two cycles of poems dedicated to Baudelaire's mistresses, Jeanne Duval and Madame Sabatier. Their blackness and whiteness are thematically important and, while complex, tainted with stereotypes. The translations are mine. The originals are, respectively:

> Bizarre déité, brune comme les nuits,
> Au parfum mélangé de musc et de havane,
> Oeuvre de quelque obi, le Faust de la savane,
> Sorcière au flanc d'ébène, enfant des noirs minuits . . .

and

> Ta tête, ton geste, ton air
> Sont beaux comme un beau paysage;
> Le rire joue en ton visage
> Comme un vent frais dans un ciel clair . . .
>
> Ainsi je voudrais, une nuit,
> Quand l'heure des voluptés sonne,
> Vers les trésors de ta personne,
> Comme un lâche, ramper sans bruit,
>
> Pour châtier ta chair joyeuse,
> Pour meurtrir ton sein pardonné,
> Et faire à ton flanc etonné
> Une blessure large et creuse . . .

The quotations from critics are actual. See, for example, Courthion in his undated *Manet* (Library of Great Painters): 'It shocked by its luminosity. It is one of the finest symphonies in white in the whole of art.' (p. 76) The idea of a 'symphony in white' goes back to a poem by Théophile Gautier, 'Symphonie en blanc majeur', and it connects with Baudelaire's theory of Correspondences in his poem of that name. In turn, this derives from the mystic Swedenborg. The American painter James McNeill Whistler, who lived mainly in London and Paris, painted three 'Symphony in White' paintings between 1862 and 1867, all of girls in white. There is thus a whole cultural and philosophical frame of reference being evoked (see my own *Mallarmé, Manet and Redon*, Cambridge, Cambridge University Press, 1986 pp. 523), but in such a way as to obscure both how the painting and the ideas may be connected with the realities of Victorine's and Jeanne's lives. Of Victorine herself as she appears in Manet's portrait, Courthion observes, 'She played the guitar and sketched . . . Manet shows her as thoughtful, if a trifle limited' (ibid, p. 72).

The politics of production/performance

6 *Thelma and Louise*: on the road to feminism?

JANE ARTHURS

The film *Thelma and Louise* (dir. Ridley Scott, 1991) attracted a great deal of attention in both the daily press and in more specialist film journals after its release, particularly in the United States where it was considered important enough as a cultural event to make the front cover of *Time* magazine:

> Academics, psychologists and lesser pundits have all weighed in with opinions on a movie that is rapidly being seen as pivotal in the battle of the sexes, as well as the unhappy history of women in the cinema as second class citizens.[1]

The press response was extensive and formulated in terms easily assimilated into feminism. It thus provides an insight into popular understandings of what the label 'feminist' means, particularly in relation to film. I have analysed a selection of mainly British and American reviews of *Thelma and Louise* as well as some feature articles written in response to the controversy aroused by the film in the United States in order to establish what made the film popular despite its perceived feminism, why it was popularly thought to be a feminist film and what arguments were made against its being seen as feminist. In the process I discuss the theoretical and political assumptions underpinning these evaluations.

Among the issues raised is the way in which the institutional positioning of the film and its mode of address affected the critical response, both in terms of making it more accessible to popular enjoyment and also of casting doubts on its 'authenticity' as a feminist film for some critics. A recurring theme is that of the ways in which popular feminism was differentiated from a stereotypical image of 'professional feminism' which emerges as a negative standard against which the popular success of *Thelma and Louise* was measured. Is female authorship seen as an essential component of such 'authenticity' and how far might this impact on the male-dominated Hollywood industry? The extent to which academic theories of feminist representation and aesthetics have infiltrated the discourses of mainstream reviewing is uneven and the debate in the reviews was conducted predominantly in terms of whether it afforded a positive representation of women.[2] It did, however, touch on how far the film deconstructs the patriarchal codes of Hollywood cinema, and the reviewers responses to the film as pleasurable fantasy for female audiences has implications for the ways in which the politics of popular pleasures are debated within film and cultural studies.

As an approach to considering the ways in which the institutional positioning of the film as a Hollywood product has affected the critical response, I want to contrast *Thelma and Louise* with a Dutch feminist film *A Question of Silence* (dir. Marleen Gorris 1982) which did well on the independent and art house circuit but which did not receive the kind of popular critical acclaim of *Thelma and Louise*.[3] Textually and thematically, *A Question of Silence* is comparable to *Thelma and Louise* in its use of role reversal within a popular genre (the crime thriller and the road/buddy movie) and in both films women murder a man and are then called to account by the law. Although they both attracted press criticism on the specific issue of their representation of women as violent, the pattern of the critical response to the two films was quite different. *A Question of Silence* received almost entirely negative reviews from the mainstream press and enthusiastic response from feminist and specialist film periodicals. By contrast, the majority of the mainstream press celebrated *Thelma and Louise* for its successful incorporation of feminist themes within a popular format, while the response from the feminist press was mixed. The difference cannot be explained by any change in the proportion of female reviewers; they remain almost exclusively male except in the more specialist film or left-wing press. Changes in the cultural and social context within which the films entered into circulation must play some part in creating the differences: in the nine years between the two films feminist discourses have been assimilated into cultural criticism in so far as there is a much wider understanding and acceptance of the problematics surrounding gender representation. Changes in perception of women's roles in work and in the family have brought about a shift in popularly accepted ideals of feminine identity that could well have made audiences more receptive to *A Question of Silence*, and I do not underestimate the more radical implications of factors such as the random nature of the murder. But it is the difference between the two films in their sources and mode of address that I think is crucial in understanding the wider popularity of *Thelma and Louise*. It is worth considering how far *A Question of Silence* was perceived by the mainstream press as feminist propaganda because of its origination as a European film financed by the Dutch government as being of 'cultural value', scripted and directed by a woman described as 'a forthright feminist'[4] by *The Times* (a right-of-centre broadsheet newspaper) and distributed in Britain by a feminist collective called Cinema of Women. *Thelma and Louise* was released as just another

Hollywood film whose main function is to entertain as many people as possible. It was not marketed as a feminist film; the press pack information avoided any mention of feminism, concentrating instead on details such as the number of Thunderbird cars used in production. It was directed by Ridley Scott, an established Hollywood name, who was keen in the publicity to emphasise the comedy rather than the violence in the film. This means that it cannot be positioned as propaganda made by and for the politically committed, or as a film addressed exclusively to women. It is therefore much more acceptable to the mainstream press who maintain a deep suspicion and antagonism towards what has been termed 'professional feminism'. Even Peter Cox of Britain's most reactionary populist tabloid, *The Sun* (which has had a running battle with feminists over its misogynist editorial policies), called it 'a little gem of a film' and referred to its feminism in a positive, if chirpily patronising, way: 'There's overtones of women's rights and the girls regularly score over the moronic men.'[5]

The film also conforms to general expectations of cinematic entertainment in a variety of ways which were actually defined by contrast with the popular perception of feminist films as dogmatic and tedious propaganda.[6] Negative reviews of *A Question of Silence* warn of the 'horrid dangers of using polemic as a vehicle to carry drama',[7] accuse it of 'simplistic didacticism'[8] and describe its address as strident, shrill, heavy, rigid, militant, humourless, over-stated and wooden. Such elements of this terminology as appeared in the reviews of *Thelma and Louise* were used to mark the film's difference from other feminist films for those reviewers whose antipathy to feminism was based on the dominant negative stereotype. They are thus turned against feminism as such. For these commentators, the capacity of *Thelma and Louise* to produce pleasure precluded it from being a feminist film. 'It's too commercial, not to mention funny and exciting for a mere sermon.'[9] 'It never allows the drag factor of feminist dogma to slow it down for an instant.'[10] Christopher Tookey, film reviewer in the right-wing *Sunday Telegraph*, admitted that he approached the world's first feminist road movie with some dread: 'I anticipated a humourless and man-hating tract . . . my fears were groundless: this is one of the best films of the year and the most entertaining road movie since *Bonnie and Clyde*.'[11] *Thelma and Louise* was described as funny, sexy, exciting, entertaining. Above all, Thelma and Louise were fun to be with. In an explicit comparison with *A Question of Silence* (of whose dark humour he was seemingly unaware) Philip French, the film reviewer of the Sunday broadsheet *Observer* newspaper, commented: 'The vivacity and good-humour of Davis and Sarandon prevent us from viewing them as a pair of psychopaths or like the glum heroines of Marleen Gorris's dogged revenge sagas.'[12] Similarly, Marsha Kinder in the US film journal, *Film Quarterly*, compared *Thelma and Louise* favourably with *Messidor* (dir. Tanner 1979), a European feminist road movie which explores 'the repression of women in the context of larger issues of history and class conflict', and whose tone she described as 'uncompromising and grim'.[13] *Thelma and Louise*, with its glamorous heroines, was in her view more likely to be politically effective than the style of films produced by feminist film makers in the 1970s, which tend to appeal to the already committed feminist.

The reviews suggest that the style and image of a stereotyped 1970s feminism is perceived as irrelevant and unattractive to the majority. This is contrasted to a more popular version of feminism in which a changed mode of address is crucial. This is not just a historical shift caused by, as Kinder argued, the loss of a 'widespread belief that incisive political analysis can help one control the process of rapid restructuring that the world is undergoing'[14] but is also a shift in class address. The broadening of feminism from an arguably marginal and predominantly middle-class politics to a more diffused current within society necessitates a mode of address that connects with popular forms of culture. 'Identification' in *A Question of Silence* depends to an extent on an intellectual alignment with a middle-class professional's growing realisation of her own oppression, through a rational process of investigation that reveals the institutionalised forms of patriarchal power. *Thelma and Louise*, by contrast, works with images that are sufficiently contradictory and ambiguous to make the women available as objects of desire and narcissistic identification for a wide spectrum of women and men, the majority of whom would not think of themselves as committed feminists, but whose expectations of gender roles have been modified as the result of two decades of feminist activism.

It is just such a feminist address that the women's magazines have done much to construct and which has contributed to the fact that in media terms 'feminism is sexy again' (as recently asserted in a supplement produced by *The Guardian*, a left-of-centre broadsheet newspaper, in conjunction with *Elle*, a magazine for 'the new woman'). Popular feminism foregrounds emotional identification with 'attractive' images, whereas the academic and political discourses of professional feminism, which have their roots in the feminist movement of the 1970s, engage with their audiences primarily on the levels of logic and argument. From a popular perspective, this is boring didactic 'professional feminism', associated with middle-class, middle-aged professionals working in, for example, the law,

education, academia, local government, politics, the media. These feminists purportedly decry popular feminism as a product of the 1980s' preoccupation with individualism, pleasure and style. To younger women,
who take many of the changes fought for by these older women for
granted, the professional feminists can seem puritanical and authoritar-
ian. This division is to some extent a product of the dominant stereotypical representations of the 'women's libber' which grossly simplify and
distort the complex political identities that make up the feminist movement. But this should not be allowed to lessen the urgency of the construction of more attractive images of women's struggle for independence
and power.

How far was it perceived in the reviews of *Thelma and Louise* that such
'attractive' images of feminism should be self-determined? Certainly it
was generally assumed that authorial identity and intentions were perti-
nent to the discussion of the film as feminist, and the extent to which
Thelma and Louise is female authored was one of the issues affecting the
critical response to the film. Khouri's motivation for writing *Thelma and
Louise* was reportedly that she was, as an ex-actress, fed up with the
paucity of good roles for women in Hollywood films. Clearly in agreement, *Time* magazine's analysis of the film's impact included the assertion
that 'everyone was complaining there were not enough good parts for
women'.[15] Going further still, it was also assumed that the commercial
success of *Thelma and Louise* would affect the industry in ways consistent
with feminism by changing the balance of power between the sexes in
what is acknowledged to be a male-dominated industry. 'Ten years from
now it will be seen as a turning point.'[18] It was thus argued, for example,
that the film's commercial success would not only encourage a rash of
similar movies in which women would play the main roles, but it would
also provide more chances for women as writers, producers and directors.
In general there was a sense of welcoming excitement at the prospect of
the male domination of Hollywood being challenged.

Susan Sarandon and Geena Davis, who play the two lead roles, also fea-
tured in the discussion of the film's authorship. Sarandon was quoted as
having had an influence on the way the film was finally shot in order to
make more space for the women characters amongst Scott's penchant for
screen pyrotechnics. The political significance of the women's performance was often taken to be determined by the extent of the actresses'
commitment to feminism in real life. Saradon was described as a 'woman
who lives life entirely on her own terms as a campaigner for feminist and
environmental causes'.[17] Davies was quoted as saying 'I'm on the same

journey as the characters I play . . . I was too dependent on men in particular.'[18] Yet these assertions of the congruence between their own feminism and their role in the film were contradicted by Davis asking: 'Why,
because this film stars women is it suddenly a feminist treatise, given the
burden of representing all women?'[19] Sarandon also observed 'It's not a
feminist movie. These two women still talk about men and still want to
be with them just like Geena and me.'[20] These disclaimers could be part
of a marketing strategy to try to distance the film from any negative
stereotypes popularly held about 'radical' feminists and ideologically
motivated feminist films. Instead the film was associated with the 'acceptable face of feminism' in which women's right to equal opportunities at
work and their aspirations for personal growth are generally accepted in
liberal culture.

Definitions of feminism and feminist film clearly also inflected assess-
ments of Scott's position as director. For some, it threw doubt on the film's
feminism, and the *Daily Telegraph* reviewer described the film as having
produced 'tedious post-mortems about whether it should have been
directed by a woman'.[21] Scott's fame and previous success as a Hollywood
director mean that the film can quite easily be understood not as a feminist
film but as a 'Ridley Scott film', with its trademark of visual gloss and
postmodern knowingness in relation to genre conventions. His use of
women in the lead-roles added to his reputation for liberalism but was also
viewed as a commerical gimmick to renew the popularity of a genre by
injecting some innovation into a previously successful format, a tactic
already used by Scott in *Alien* (1979). The series of three 'Alien' films
(*Alien* 1979, *Aliens* 1986 and *Aliens 3* 1992), like *Thelma and Louise*, occupy
a controversial space between feminist and mainstream film that is variously read as progressive or as recuperating feminism.

In this latter view, the success of this film will do nothing to enhance
women's chances within the industry. It merely serves to consolidate male
dominance through the appropriation of feminist themes into a context
that defuses any potential threat to the patriarchal power relations in the
industry. Suspicion of 'man-made women's films,' as De Lauretis calls
them,[22] is an issue in feminist criticism because it is regarded by many as
axiomatic that feminist culture arises out of an 'authentic' expression of
women's experience, or at the very least must, by definition, be female-
authored. In this perspective an important part of the feminist project is
to challenge male dominance of cultural production which enables male
subjectivity to be accepted as the universal norm. However, in film production the issue is complicated because although the film director is des-

ignated the author of a film for marketing and evaluative purposes, the truth is that there are a multiplicity of 'authors', all of whom will have some influence on the final text. The emphasis should be on the level of female participation in the collaborative process rather than focusing on the director as sole author. And although it would have been preferable on many levels for the film to have been directed by a woman, I share De Lauretis's view in defining a feminist understanding of 'women's cinema' which is not 'too liberally or literally any cinema made by and for women'. The category should accommodate films made by men if 'they directly address questions of gender and sexual difference'.[23]

It is clearly a matter of debate whether an institution like Hollywood can 'author' a feminist film or not. The arguments are part of a wider strategic question for feminist politics, namely whether to work for change within the mainstream, or to build feminist alternatives. The alternative institutions of independent film, relying as they do on grant aid or artisanal modes of production, are considered by many feminist filmmakers as the only possible context within which to make a feminist film, because compromises forced by profit-seeking do not have to be made. It is also more likely that women will be able to take on the key decision-making roles in independent contexts of production. Doubt about Hollywood's potential as an institution within which feminist films can be made also arises from the way in which established textual conventions and production practices are likely to impinge on any attempt by an individual to produce a feminist film. As Christine Gledhill points out:

> Textual meanings are not fixed entities to be deployed at the will of a communicator but are produced by textual interactions shaped by a range of economic, aesthetic and ideological factors that often operate unconsciously and are unpredictable and difficult to control.[24]

This problematises the notion of the 'authentic' expression of women's experience when they are inevitably working within an already established patriarchal culture. These arguments have been used to dismiss the relevance to feminism of initiatives to increase the numbers of women making films in Hollywood. But I would argue that although the presence of more women in positions of power in Hollywood does not in itself guarantee the production of feminist films, it does make it more likely that conditions more favourable to their production will be generated. Besides, feminism is about economic equality as well as cultural issues and women should have a fair share of the well-paid jobs and lavish budgets available in Hollywood rather than having to scrape together inadequate funding from independent sources. Such deprivation of resources limits formal possibilities. What forms would emerge from a mature, well-funded feminist film culture is a question for the future.

Debates about the feminist nature of *Thelma and Louise* referred to its formal characteristics. The terms in which these debates were constructed can be related to parallel debates within feminist film theory. During the 1970s, oppositional feminist film practices and debates in academic film theory challenged mainstream narrative for reproducing patriarchal ideology both through the function that 'woman' has conventionally played in narrative and through the positioning of the spectator as masculine via the relay of looks that structure the spectator's relation to the narrative events portrayed.[25] These theories drew on radical critiques of cinematic realism and complex Lacanian psychoanalytic theory for the development of a feminist counter-cinema. This cinema refused the pleasures of narrative in favour of the use of formal experimentation, in order to disrupt the reproduction of an unproblematic gendered identity. It is significant that there was little evidence of these discourses in the mainstream critical evaluation of *Thelma and Louise*, not because of the complexity of the concepts and language used, which do not translate easily into a short review, but rather because the use of realist narrative is so fundamental to entertainment cinema that it is simply not on the agenda to criticise a film for using this form. It is also the case that more recent feminist film theory has challenged the argument that narrative cinema has the power to position the spectator in one relation to the narrative and thus reproduce patriarchal ideology in an unproblematic way. Now there is more emphasis on the ways in which narrative offers a variety of points of identification which differentially position spectators, and on the importance of contextual factors in determining what readings are made.[26] There is more interest in finding ways to subvert the conventions of Hollywood without abandoning the popular appeal of the form. Kinder, for example, argues that postmodern cultural politics includes a 'growing confidence in making endless revisions in the basic paradigms and in the case of the cinema and the mass media the prevailing paradigms are Hollywood genres'.[27]

One of the earliest studies of the representation of women in Hollywood cinema was Molly Haskell's *From Reverence to Rape*, which was influential in drawing attention to the dominance of demeaning and negative roles for women in contemporary Hollywood films. This, Haskell maintained, was a backlash against the women's liberation movement.[28] The notion of 'positive images' which, it is argued, can function as role models for women in the real world has infiltrated mainstream reviewing practices to the extent that evaluation of *Thelma and Louise* as a feminist film was conducted in the popular press almost always with reference to the question of whether the two female protagonists offered positive role models for women. The fact that women are in the central roles and it is the men who are reduced to bit-part caricatures was widely perceived as a feminist strategy. 'It sweeps away the outrageous stereotyping that has haunted female characters in major films,' says Sue Heal in *Today*, a popular tabloid newspaper with a large female readership.[29] The performances of the two lead actresses, Susan Sarandon and Geena Davis, were cited by all the reviews as the main reason for the film's power and attractiveness. The strength, humour, vivacity and likeability of the two women was argued to be a positive role model for women viewers. The significant feature of the images they portray was their ambiguity, which was interpreted as going beyond the fixity of response elicited by the simplified stereotype of a feminist. These women may be angry, but they are also funny; they may be struggling for freedom and independence, but not at the cost of losing their desire for men and their desirability to men; they may be strong, powerful, even violent, but they remain vulnerable. They stumble into their feminism through the emotional consequences of their actions rather than as an intellectual choice. They are thus an image that could be contrasted to the popular stereotype of a feminist as a tub thumping, threatening, puritanical, dungaree-clad harridan. According to Christopher Tookey in the *Sunday Telegraph*:

> It contains at least one timely social insight: namely that feminism can be sexy . . . Geena Davis . . . will undoubtedly influence more women to re-evaluate their lives than the entire works of Andrea Dworkin.[30]

A heterosexual image of feminism that does not exclude aspects of traditional femininity was how the mainstream reviewers read the film's 'positive images', thus ignoring the potential lesbian reading of the women's rejection of traditional feminine roles, their outsider status and the final on-the-lips kiss before their ambivalent yet triumphant escape from patriarchal society.

Categorising films as feminist on the basis of their provision of positive role models presupposes a homogeneous audience who share the same political and moral values. It denies the many differences and divisions of identity, belief and goals amongst women in general but also within the feminist movement itself. Negative reviews of the film also discussed it in terms of its provision of role models for women but condemned it for having a potentially harmful effect on women either, because it distorted what it means to be a feminist, or, from an anti-feminist perspective, because it revealed what is wrong with feminist ideology. For example, the use of role reversal, in which women take over the roles more usually assigned to men, has the agreed advantage that women are in a position of power, and act as subjects rather than objects of desire. But in doing so they can be seen to be taking on masculine characteristics such as the use of violence to achieve what they want. Sheila Benson, the *Los Angeles Times* film critic, considered it a 'betrayal of feminism . . . concerned with revenge, retribution and sadistic behaviour'.[31] The film was criticised for simply reproducing a masculine revenge fantasy. The fact that it is women in the driving seat and with their finger on the trigger does not challenge the violent patriarchal values on which the narrative is based. From this perspective the film has nothing to do with a feminist politics whose goals are the transformation of social reality rather than equal access to men's places in the social hierarchy regardless of ethical or any other considerations.

The 'role model' line of argument assumes a direct relationship between representations and behaviour. Differences in evaluation can, however, stem from whether the reviewer is using a discursive rather than realist reading strategy. It is useful to differentiate between spectators who assume that film representations are mimetic and to be read as if the events were happening in real life, and those who understand film representations as meaningful in their relationship to other representational discourses rather than in direct relationship to social reality. Negative responses to *Thelma and Louise* in the press were more likely to take a realist approach and be written by general features journalists rather than specialist film reviewers. Pleasurable fantasy can be regarded as an irrelevant distraction from political action or, even worse, as an incitement to inappropriate and undesirable strategies of resistance. A case in point was Nigella Lawson's comment on the film's ending in the *Guardian* women's page (addressed to left of centre, public sector professionals sympathetic to feminism):

> I'd rather die may be an understandable reaction. It is hardly, however, the feminist option. How about 'I can't go back so I'll leave him, get a job, a place of my own and lead my own life.'[32]

In another article on the same page, Joan Smith discussed the violent events in the film as if they had really happened. The shooting of the would-be rapist was 'unjustifiable in law and morality' and the blowing up of the petrol tanker was 'a wanton piece of environmental pollution'.[33] From a moralist rather than feminist perspective, Lynette Burrows in the

Daily Telegraph, a right-wing paper addressed to middle-class business people, described the film as 'pernicious . . . beneath the glamorous appearance of the two girls in the film is the moral character of Attila the Hun'.[34] What these writers shared was a conviction that violent behaviour in film leads to the same behaviour in real life and violence is inappropriate for women; it is neither feminist nor feminine. Women were seen as morally superior to men and should not be encouraged to sink to their level.

It is argued that mainstream narrative conventionally functions to contain the threat posed by women's sexuality. Whether *Thelma and Louise* does in fact disrupt and subvert these patriarchal codes of narrative is a matter of contention. The women's sexual relationships with men function as important narrative turning points. But there were differences of opinion in the reviews as to whether the ideological implications of the narrative events were feminist. For example, the feminist magazine *Spare Rib* argued that the women were punished for sexual transgression as in so many other Hollywood films. Although Thelma's escape from her husband is presented as totally justified, it has extreme consequences for both women. Thelma's loose and drunken behaviour could be read as inviting the attempted rape which sets the plot in motion. The next day she picks up a good-looking young hitchhiker; that this scene follows so closely on the rape is further evidence of Thelma's culpability: 'Just 24 hours later she is seen cavorting with another stranger, whom she consents to sleep with. This reaction totally negates the previous trauma and offensively trivialises the seriousness of the rape and its effects.'[35] A further consequence of that night of passion is that she loses all of their money and turns to armed robbery as a means to survive. From this point there is no turning back; her transgression can only end in imprisonment or death. In contrast, an extended review in the British Film Institute monthly magazine, *Sight and Sound*, provided a feminist reading which argued that the women's sexuality was what makes the narrative radical; if the road movie is 'the pleasure principle on wheels', having female protagonists is transgressive in showing women seeking pleasure and seizing control of their own bodies.[36]

For those reviewers who were concerned to analyse and place the film generically, *Thelma and Louise* was variously characterised as a road movie, a western, a buddy movie, an outlaw movie, all of which are recognised as 'masculine genres' that have particular resonance as popular myths of a specifically American identity. The film uses the iconography characteristic of these genres but there was a difference of opinion in the reviews over whether the film deconstructed or merely reproduced that imagery. It was argued in a glowing review by Mick Brown, the film columnist of the right-wing *Daily Telegraph*, that the women's journey across a landscape which has accrued generic connotations of freedom and independence drew attention to the gendered exclusivity of the imagery: 'The breathtaking expanses of the American south-west, and the open road as a symbol of newly discovered freedom, take on a new meaning in the discovery of feminine power.'[37] The women were appropriating a masculine dream of what it means to be American as expressed in popular myth. The women's suicide leap into the Grand Canyon has been interpreted as an embracing of the feminine principle to escape from the insistantly phallic landscape and technology with which they had been surrounded. Conversely the visual pleasures constructed by 'Scott's muscle flexing *mise-en-scène*[38] – the phallic imagery, the fetishisation of technological hardware, the wide open spaces characteristic of the western and the road movie – have been seen as appealing to conventional masculine pleasures of film spectatorship. It is argued that the imagery provides a recognisable and comfortable masculine visual context within which cross-gendered identification with the two women is made less problematic, while at the same time the sexiness of the two women retains the pleasures of erotic contemplation of the female body: 'the camera lingers on Davis and Sarandon as if it couldn't get enough of them' according to Terence Rafferty of the *New Yorker*.[39]

The contradictory responses to the film demonstrate the inconclusiveness and complexity of the issues involved and the impossibility of determining the question of the film's feminism solely from the text in isolation from the conditions of its production and reception. The interpretive frameworks brought to bear on the film arise out of its insertion in a political and cultural context in which the meaning of the term 'feminist' as applied to culture is a matter of contestation. The public debate over *Thelma and Louise* drew on the construction and circulation of popular understandings of 'what feminism is', and is a contribution to it.

There is a crucial difference between those reviewers who reduced the film to a précis of the narrative events and then argued the consequences of its logic for feminist politics in the real world, and those who acknowledged film's function in relation to fantasy which may have no simple correspondence to people's actual behaviour or political allegiances. Read as fantasy, the majority of reviewers were in no doubt that *Thelma and Louise* is a feminist film. Focusing on the key narrative events (the shooting of the rapist, Thelma's transformation from oppressed housewife to irrepressible outlaw, the women's suicide at the finale) the reviewers argued its feminism in terms of fantasy, pleasure and female desire. The shooting was 'the perfect fantasy of revenge for all those times women have had to stand by silently taking insult and abuse'.[40] The women are active protagonists whose desires propel the narrative: 'They seize control of their bodies . . . Here the female body is not a landscape to be mapped, a frontier under conquest. This is the liberated body.'[41] Their death was a moment of exhilaration, not defeat: 'It's hard to find anyone who thinks the women should have turned themselves in.'[42] It is a fantasy of escape from life under patriarchy: 'The ending contains a central truth about feminism: there is no return to dependency on men.'[43] These pleasurable fantasies are feminist in that they make women feel powerful and capable of achieving autonomy and freedom.

The reviews often commented on the vocal response the film elicited from audiences. Women cheered when Louise shot Thelma's attacker, they laughed at the absurdities of the other men in the film and shouted encouragement to the women when they took assertive action. There were 'whoops of delighted recognition among ordinary female cinema goers'.[44] Men were not excluded from enjoying the film (the audience profile in the United States was initially 70 per cent women though this later dropped to 60 per cent) but women had claimed it for their own. The pleasure signalled by this response from women was taken as evidence of the film's feminism. It generated a sense of group solidarity which enhanced the experience of the film as a fantasy of power. The word most commonly used in the reviews to express this emotion was 'delight' and part of that delight was the unexpectedness of the experience. As Louise says to Thelma: 'This is just the first chance you have had to express yourself' – a line that 'drew applause from New York audiences packed with women'.[45]

The question of the political implications of pleasure has played a large part in recent debates within feminism. Media studies theorists have been concerned to re-evaluate popular 'women's genres' such as soap opera and melodrama in a way that enables feminism to validate the pleasures taken in these forms by large numbers of women. Attention has been given to the role of fantasy in narratives addressed to women, and arguments for their subversive potential have largely superseded the previously held view that popular forms reproduce dominant ideologies. There is greater recognition of their polysemic potential and the possibility of negotiating progressive readings of popular forms. The act of consumption itself has been theorised as potentially subversive in relation to women carving out a space for their own pleasure in lives devoted to pleasing others.[46] More recently it has been argued that the pleasures that audiences take in main-stream cinema 'aren't dictated by any rules of same sex identification or by heterosexual understandings of desire', and that the division of genres into masculine and feminine on the basis of the pleasures they offer are rooted in common sense understandings of gender which need to be challenged.[47]

A recurring term in these debates is 'empowerment'. It is argued that a precursor to political emancipation for women is the recognition of their shared experience of oppression, a recognition that can be generated through the communal consumption of popular culture. This identification with other women can generate a sense of strength through solidarity, even where what is being shared is the masochistic pleasures of melodrama. How much more potentially empowering then, are utopian fantasies in which a different and more powerful role for women is imagined, giving a sense of future possibilities beyond the experience of contemporary realities. The aim here is to redefine what it means to be a woman, while recognising that this is never a fixed or undifferentiated category.

A contrary viewpoint evident both in the reviews of *Thelma and Louise* and in academic film criticism is that the pleasures experienced by audiences of mainstream film are politically contradictory and may be of no great significance in furthering the cause of feminism. To some reviewers the fact that the film is enjoyed by so many men was confirmation that it is sufficiently open to a range of interpretations to render a feminist reading inappropriate. An influential strand within feminist film theory argues that Hollywood films with strong independent women in the lead roles are merely examples of the 'incorporation' of feminist ideology.[48] By this it is meant that patriarchal capitalism defuses potential threats to its continuing dominance by allowing spaces for the expression of opposition in contexts where it can be contained. From this perspective, the pleasure that a cinema audience feels in identifying with subversive desires enacted on the screen is actually a way of ensuring that they take no further action on a more political level. De Lauretis argues that this depoliticisation is the result of the conversion of radical feminism into a more acceptable and less threatening liberal feminism in which the feminist assertion that 'the personal is political' is transformed into the personal *instead* of the political. The profit motive ensures that important differences between women are minimised, particularly in relation to race and sexuality, to retain the broadest appeal without alienating the white heterosexual market. To maintain cross-gender appeal, elements are retained that allow for male, masculine and patriarchal identifications. For De Lauretis, for example, a feminist women's cinema is one that addresses its audience 'as a woman' which is to say that all points of identification are female, feminine or feminist.[49]

In response to these contradictory viewpoints on the popular success of *Thelma and Louise* and what significance it may have for a feminist cultural politics, I want to emphasise that what is distinctive and important about *Thelma and Louise* is that, in general, mainstream reviewers did not regard its perceived feminism as a negative attribute. This was not only because the institutional positioning, mode of address and ambiguity of the film differentiated it from unpopular tendentious films regarded as typical of feminism, but also because its text is open to interpretations that mesh easily with the type of liberal feminism that has gained widespread acceptance in the United States and Britain. This is why for some feminist theorists this film is not really feminist at all; it is merely an incorporation of those aspects of feminism that do not radically challenge the status quo either in political or aesthetic terms. But the mere fact that the challenge is not 'radical' does not, I would argue, mean that it has no value to feminism at all. Cultural politics needs to take account of what is achievable within existing structures at the centre as well as the margins. In terms of a direct political impact, although the film produced fears in a few right-wing moralists that it would cause an outbreak of violent conflict between the sexes, it is in fact the case that *Thelma and Louise* has not had any immediate measurable influence on behaviour beyond reports of women wearing T-shirts claiming 'Thelma and Louise Live Forever!' or holding up two fingers to truck drivers and shouting 'bang, bang!'.[50] The belief that popular culture can act as a form of resistance which has important long-term consequences for the power relations in society is based on the argument that mass cultural forms can be used to construct an oppositional understanding of a group's sense of actual and potential identities.[51] Only by making connections with the popular imagination can any political ideology achieve ascendency, and it is that process which makes the analysis of the forms of understanding and pleasure offered by popular feminism so important. Where *Thelma and Louise* succeeds is in inviting a critique of patriarchal society, albeit in liberal rather than radical terms, in combination with an address that engages the spectator's desire. It is experienced by many as liberating in that it is a freer, more powerful representation of what it means to be a woman than is available in the mainstream overall. Yet it retains its acceptability to a wide audience and thus its commercial viability, an achievement whose significance should not be missed, fulfilling as it does the need faced by any political movement to find a way to speak to the uncommitted in terms that are understandable and pleasurable. *Thelma and Louise* does not offer a radical alternative to patriarchal cinema but rather moves inside it to disrupt the codes of gender in Hollywood film. Incremental change in filmic conventions can come about if the ground rules can be shifted in a gradual way so as not to alienate the mass audience. It is possible that in the future we will have a popular cinema that does not rely on masculine fantasies of power for audience gratification but which instead constructs new and more varied ways of experiencing and representing our gendered identities.

Notes

1. Richard Goodall, *The Sunday Times*, 7 July 1991, p. 35.
2. Meaghan Morris, in 'The practice of reviewing', *Framework* 22/23, 1983, p. 58, comments that constraints of space in daily newspapers encourage an 'abrasive, assertive mode of discourse', so that the assumptions on which the reviewer's evaluations have been made are rarely made explicit.
3. See Jane Arthurs *Reading a Feminist Film: Responses to A Question of Silence* unpublished MA dissertation. Institute of Education, London University, 1984, for an analysis of the reviews and of responses to this film collected through audience research. The ethnographic evidence was useful in providing access to a wider range of readings than those made by the mainly male reviewers, in circumstances free of the constraints exerted by the review as a signifying practice. This approach was, however, beyond the scope of the present study.
4. George Brown, *The Times*, 18 February 1983, p. 11.
5. Peter Cox, *The Sun*, 12 July 1991.
6. See Steve Neale, 'Propaganda', *Screen*, XVIII:3, Autumn 1977, p. 10, for an analysis of the way that propaganda is predominantly discussed from a liberal humanist perspective in which 'all ideologies are ideological except liberal humanism. This is the basis for a seemingly non-ideological dismissal of partisan art.'
7. Lindsay Mackie, *Glasgow Herald*, 4 September 1982, p. 8.
8. Paul Jackson, *Western Mail*, 14 May 1983, p. 10.
9. Shaun Usher, *Daily Mail*, 12 July 1991, p. 31.
10. Hugo Davenport, *Daily Telegraph*, 11 July 1991, p. 14.
11. Christopher Tookey, *Sunday Telegraph*, 14 July 1991, p. xiv.
12. Philip French, *Observer*, 14 July 1991.
13. Marsha Kinder '*Thelma and Louise* and *Messidor* as feminist road movies', *Film Quarterly*, 45:2, Winter 1991–2, pp. 30–1.
14. Ibid., p. 30.
15. Richard Schnickel, *Time*, 24 June 1991, pp. 52–6.
16. Peter Keough, *Boston Phoenix*, quoted in Schnickel, p. 53.
17. Terence Rafferty, *New Yorker*, 3 June 1991, p. 86–7.
18. Anna Stewart, *Daily Mail*, 24 May 1991, p. 38–9.
19. Geena Davis, quoted in *The Guardian*, 17 July 1991, p. 17.
20. Susan Sarandon quoted in Stewart, *Daily Mail*, 24 May 1991 p. 38.
21. Hugo Davenport, *Daily Telegraph*, 11 July 1991 p. 14.

22. Teresa de Lauretis, 'Aesthetic and feminist theory: rethinking women's cinema', E. Deidre Pribram (ed.) *Female Spectators*, London Verso, (1988) pp. 174–96.
23. Teresa De Lauretis, 'Guerrilla in the midst: women's cinema in the 80s', *Screen*, XXI: 1, Spring 1990, pp. 6–25.
24. Christine Gledhill, 'Pleasurable negotiations' in Pribram, *Female Spectators*, pp. 64–89.
25. See Annette Kuhn, *Women's Pictures* London, Routledge, (1982) for a full account of these theoretical approaches.
26. See Jackie Stacey 'Desperately seeking difference', *Screen*, XXVII: 1, Winter 1987, pp. 48–61, for example.
27. Kinder, 1991, '*Thelma and Louise* and *Messidor*', pp. 30–31.
28. Molly Haskell, *From Reverence to Rape: The Treatment of Women in the Movies*, London, New English Library, (1975).
29. Sue Heal, *Today*, 12 July 1991, p. 34.
30. Christopher Tookey, *Sunday Telegraph*, 14 July 1991, p. xiv.
31. Quoted by Richard Schnickel, *Time*, p. 52.
32. Nigella Lawson, *Guardian*, 17 July 1991, p. 17.
33. Joan Smith, *Guardian*, 17 July 1991, p. 17.
34. Lynette Burrows, *Sunday Telegraph*, 28 July 1991, p. 20.
35. Eleanor Blader, *Spare Rib*, July 91, p. 19–20.
36. Manohla Dargis, *Sight and Sound*, July 1991, p. 14–18.
37. Mick Brown, *Daily Telegraph*, 5 July 1991, p. 15.
38. J. Hoberman, *Village Voice*, 28 May 1991, p. 51.
39. Terence Rafferty, *New Yorker*, 3 June 1991, p. 86–7.
40. Mick Brown, *Daily Telegraph*, 5 July 1991, p. 15.
41. Manohla Dargis, *Sight and Sound*, p. 18.
42. Richard Schnickel, *Time*, p. 56.
43. Christopher Tookey, *Sunday Telegraph*, p. xiv.
44. Hugo Davenport, *Daily Telegraph*, 11 July 1991, p. 14.
45. Charles Bremner, *Times Saturday Review*, 29 June 1991, p. 6.
46. Charlotte Brunsdon provides a thorough critical account of this work in 'Pedagogies of the feminine: feminist teaching and women's genres', *Screen*, 32: 4, Winter 1991.
47. Yvonne Tasker, *Criminal Women: Thelma and Louise and Other Offenders*, Unpublished paper delivered at AMFIT conference, London, 1992.
48. See, for example, Annette Kuhn, 1982, pp. 134–140.
49. Teresa De Lauretis, 1988, p. 180.
50. Reported by Charles Bremner in *Times Saturday Review*, 29 June 1991, p. 6.
51. Christine Gledhill applied this argument to feminism and film in 'Recent developments in feminist film criticism' *Quarterly Review of Film Studies*, 3: 4, Fall 1978. A full account and critique of this 'culturalist' approach can be found in Jim McGuigan, *Cultural Populism*, London, Routledge, (1992).

7 *Carmen,* or the undoing of women

JEAN ANDREWS

Feminist criticism

In an innovative, personal and often passionate study, *L'opéra ou la défaite des femmes* (1979), Catherine Clément takes her version of post-Lacanian feminist critical philosophy to the opera.[1] Hers is one of very few feminist readings of opera and therefore, although rather idiosyncratic, extremely important. The feminist musicologist, Susan McClary, recognises as much in her introduction to Betsy Wing's 1989 translation of Clément's book.[2] She cites Jeremy Tambling's *Opera, Ideology and Film* (1987) as the only existing major full-length study of opera available in English which attempts to consider opera in the context of feminist criticism.[3] In a more recent book on politics in opera, *Viva la Libertà* (1992), the political scientist Anthony Arblaster acknowledges the same lack.[4] Sally Potter's film *Thriller,* made in 1979, coincidentally the year Clément's work appeared in France, offers, within a performance framework, a critique of the portrayal of women in opera which is in many respects very close to Clément's theoretical approach. Her film investigates the story of Mimì in Puccini's *La Bohème* in search of an explanation of the oppression of women apparently built into operatic convention. Using a montage of dance and mime, stills from Covent Garden productions, photographs of real seamstresses from the late-nineteenth century, excerpts from the Gigli/Albanese 1938 recording of *La Bohème* and from the soundtrack of Hitchcock's *Psycho,* and a voiceover by an actress whose first language is French, her black Mimì interrogates the received version of her life and death and a range of patriarchal philosophies in search of clues which would enable her to understand what happened to her and why she was silenced.[5] Clément provides an answer to this question which is as beautifully damning of masculinist culture, as intellectually rigourous and yet as elusive as Potter's film:

> Rodolfo's love is rhetoric.
> No rhetoric exists which does not foretell destiny; and Mimì's is drawn in the words of Rodolfo. Poetry, already she is no longer a woman, she will never be one. A young girl dedicated to her flowers, she will not have another life. There she is held in the poet's images. Muse, inspiration, she joins the cohort of young girls sacrificed by the seducer, in order to let him live in suspended

time: an instant of poetry, yet another, a last winter's day, yet another, and life
stops. Then only Rodolfo will wake up, who has seen nothing. He did not do
it on purpose.[6]

Arblaster, in his relatively short chapter on 'Women in Opera',
acknowledges the prominence of Clément's work in feminist criticism of
opera but takes issue with her for concentrating too much on opera's
tragic heroines and ignoring both the equally tragic fates of many heroes
and the 'success' of heroines such as Beethoven's Leonore/Fidelio and the
women of the Mozart/Da Ponte trilogy. Although he appears to challenge the substance of her argument, one cannot help suspecting that he
is somewhat discomfited by the subjective way in which she presents it.
So, when Clément sees opera as the victimisation of women, Arblaster has
little patience with her, claiming that 'the balance of sympathy is weighted
more towards women in opera than it usually is in the real world'.[7] In fact,
there is little meeting of minds between Clément and Arblaster despite
the pains he takes to recognise the importance of feminism as a political
issue in opera.

Clément is probably better known for her earlier collaboration with
Hélène Cixous on *La Jeune née [The Newly-Born Woman]*, and indeed the
influence of Cixous's thought on her work is not to be underestimated.
Clément looks carefully at the words in opera, the libretto, exclusively the
work of men, which have been unjustly, but understandably, overshad-
owed by the music. In Clément's reading, opera heroines must die because
they are a danger to what is and must remain a man's world: their aspirations to independence are intolerable. She confirms Arblaster's reading,
but from the feminist perspective. Opera is, at least from the age of Mozart
to that of Puccini, a ritual enactment of the torture, subjugation and
putting to death of women by men. Clément argues that the threat is
rooted in the fact that opera heroines are morally and emotionally better
than their male adversaries in spite of a set of textual and theatrical conventions which demand that they should be the weaker vessels. Tosca and
Carmen, for example, possess superior knowledge and experience to their
lovers; Lucy Ashton (*Lucia di Lammermoor*) or Gilda (*Rigoletto*) are
endowed with almost unworldly innocence and idealism; and Violetta (*La
Traviata*) and Norma show deeper love and greater unselfishness than any
of the men who surround them. For her:

> Opera is about women. No, not a feminist version; no, not a liberation. On the
> contrary: they suffer, they cry out, they die, that is called singing. They expose
> themselves, their dresses cut away to the heart, glistening with tears, to those
> who come in order to take pleasure in their feigned agonies.[8]

There are more profound philosophical problems in Clément's analysis than the sins of omission highlighted by Arblaster, however. Her argument appears to accept that the formulaic representations of suffering women in nineteenth-century opera are more concentrated versions of Romantic literary stereotypes. Indeed, her classifications are remarkably similar to those identified over sixty years ago, in a very different intellectual climate, by the Italian critic, Mario Praz.[9] He famously isolated a series of female stereotypes in Romantic literature, most notably the Medusa figure and *la belle dame sans merci*, two images of rapacious femininity set to devour the unsuspecting male Romantic hero. Unfortuntely, there are times in Clément's study when she appears to come dangerously close to taking similar stereotypes for granted. Even when she does so from an earnest desire to rehabilitate the virago, as she does very beautifully in the case of Turandot, for example, it seems a pity to accept the categories laid down by masculinist criticism without some questioning.[10] Why employ these classifications, even for the purpose of subversion, when it would be so much better to evolve a new set from feminist principles? The answer to this seems to be that Clément's criticism, like the myth criticism of Praz, is grounded first and foremost in Romanticism and that although a feminist critic, she has built a considerable element of her reinterpretation of opera on an acceptance of masculinist readings of Romanticism.

Praz was perhaps the most influential critic to trace the roots of the darker side of Romanticism to the late-eighteenth century, a period he describes as both 'polite and effeminate' and fascinated by the 'dark and lugubrious'.[11] As the late-eighteenth century gave priority to emotion and sensibility over reason and order, the more 'masculine' values of the Enlightenment, so Romanticism grew out of essentially 'feminine' qualities. This well-worn argument proves too seductive for Clément. In her endeavour to reappropriate Romantic opera for feminism she takes it much further by distinguishing hysteria as the strongest force in opera; hysteria being an extreme manifestation of emotion and sensibility which, in Freudian psychoanalysis, is particularly associated with women. In Clément's ingenious diagnosis, hysteria, naturally, becomes a positive force. The problem is that it is hard to tell if this very clever manoeuvring of masculinist criticism succeeds or not; whether Clément is radically re-reading and refashioning the classifications pioneered by Praz, or whether she is to some extent succumbing to them, simply because opera offers these virgin/whore, goddess/demon stereotypes of feminity in such an apparently unambiguous manner that it is extremely difficult to break opera out of the moulds which seem to fit it so well.

This is compounded by the way in which Clément chooses to write. *Opera or the Undoing of Women* is couched in the same sort of quasi-poetic, quasi-mystical language as *The Newly Born Woman.* As such, it consistently avoids overt theoretical discussion and instead elaborates an emotional, visceral reaction to the portrayal of women in opera.[12] Acceptance of and challenges to Romantic stereotyping of women and femininity are intermingled and the argument is ultimately, and perhaps deliberately, ambiguous.

Because Clément's argument derives so ambiguously from masculinist criticism of Romanticism, her work has a great deal in common with another relatively recent non-feminist work on opera: Peter Conrad's *A Song of Love and Death: The Meaning of Opera.*[13] Like Clément, Conrad embraces myth criticism and Freud and the entire Praz legacy. Indeed, he might just as well have dedicated his book to Lévi-Strauss, as Clément did, such is the coincidence of their approach and interpretations. Nevertheless, they are written in two very different styles and, in many ways, Conrad's book can be used as a commentary on Clément's, since he deduces and supports all his arguments logically and she sweeps into hers intuitively. Clément's approach demands much more of her reader but since it does not distinguish very clearly between 'masculinist' stereotypes of Romanticism and feminist reinterpretation, it is very useful to set her arguments against Conrad's in order to see exactly where she departs from 'masculinist' Romantic tradition.

Clément begins to appropriate myth criticism and Freudianism for feminism by placing hysteria at the heart of opera. By a very deft, audacious exploitation of Freud, Clément manoeuvres the two most prominent masculine symbols in opera into the female realm: the great seducer himself, Don Giovanni, and Orpheus. Her argument is ingenious. After treating countless hysterical women whose neuroses appeared to be due to rape by the father or a father figure, Freud was forced to conclude that either all the fathers were rapists or all the daughters liars. Because he could not avoid being on the side of the patriarchs, he had to brand the hysterical women liars. Following this model, Elvira, Anna and Zerlina, in *Don Giovanni,* are hysterical women, whose condition forces them falsely to accuse Giovanni, a brother-figure rather than a father-figure, of sexual violations, past, present and to come. There are no seductions, so, Giovanni, a proven liar and proud of it, must acquiesce in the lies of an army of hysterical Elviras, Annas and Zerlinas to maintain an empty reputation. Clément concludes:

> The lie is truly shared; and Don Giovanni, beyond the mythical difference of the sexes, joins by a subtle ellipse his female accomplices. An hysteric, like them.[14]

For Clément, Orpheus, too, belongs with the female hysterics:

> Don Giovanni is not far from Orpheus, torn apart by the Bacchantes, jealously guarding their secrets, jealous of this man too close to them, too far away from them, and violent, because he also wanted it.[15]

Orpheus is an hysteric because he desired and shared in the violence of the Bacchantes just as Elvira, Anna and Zerlina desired the pain of Giovanni's non-seductions. Arguing Orpheus and Giovanni into the female realm is a spectacular coup but it also exposes Clément's reading at its most ambiguous. Is her embrace of what she identifies as the masochism of the female hysterics and her absorption of male hysterics into that group a triumph of what in *The Newly-Born Woman* would be the feminine realm of the gift over the masculine realm of the proper; giving over possessing, desiring violence rather than perpetrating it, the hysterical over reason? Or does it imply a less than questioning acceptance of Freud's diagnosis of hysteria in women and an admission that opera heroines are more or less accurate representations of this? Clément never makes it clear.

For his part, Conrad also sees Giovanni and Orpheus as being of fundamental importance in opera: Giovanni as a standard-bearer of heterosexual masculinity; Orpheus because he is the symbolic founder of opera, the great patriarch, in the words of Conrad, 'a singer who was also an ancient mystagogue'.[16] Conrad dates the beginning of opera to Monteverdi's *Orfeo*, first performed in 1607 in Mantua, and sees it as a 'revival of pagan worship, in seditious opposition to Christianity'. For him, the songs of the classical Orpheus, beloved of Renaissance mythographers, which celebrate the conjunction of death and the erotic, are in direct opposition to the values of reason and ethical responsibility enshrined both in Renaissance Christianity and humanism. Thus, Orfeo and his music lay the foundations for an art form that is rooted in the sensual, the Dionysian.

> [Opera] is the song of our irrationality, of the instinctual savagery which our jobs and routines and our non-singing voices belie, of the music our bodies make. It is an art devoted to love and death (and especially to the cryptic alliance between them); to the definition and the interchangeability of the sexes; to madness and devilment, to drink when Don Giovanni sings his so-called champagne aria, to eating when Carmen invites Don José to gobble up everything in the tavern; and to blasphemy against a Christian religion that reproves this bodily glory and chastens the organism in which the voice is warmly housed.[17]

When he speaks comfortably of 'our rationality', 'our jobs and routines' and 'our non-singing voices', he makes no distinction between male and

female. When he speaks of 'the definition and interchangeability of the
sexes' he is merely acknowledging the opera convention of mezzo-
soprano 'trouser roles' rather than probing the roots of female-to-male
cross-dressing. For him both sexes are equal as they take their pleasure
and suffer in an erotic dance of death. The only enemy is a common one:
reason and responsibility. For Clément, on the other hand, the erotic is a
political, psychological mechanism which permits the domination of one
sex by another. However, taking this essential divergence into account,
Conrad's claim that opera is about irrationality and instinctual savagery
might actually be used to support Clément's attempt to place the hysterical at the heart of opera. The difference is that she has chosen to use a
term first used by Freud to describe, then by many others to condemn, the
irrational as manifested in women, whereas he has opted for words, such
as 'instinctual savagery' and 'Dionysian', which have a much more positive value. Both writers speak of irrational excess, but her vocabulary
comes from the pathology of a supposedly predominantly female disorder
and his from that most positive source for all western artistic endeavour,
classical antiquity.

It is no coincidence that Conrad mentions Don Giovanni and Carmen
in his opening remarks. If Orpheus is the father of opera, then Giovanni
and Carmen are its twin deities, erotic demon-gods:

> The two most dangerous and scandalous operatic characters are a pair for
> whom existence is an erotic career – Don Giovanni and Carmen. Don
> Giovanni is dedicated to pursuit and research, the imperial and universal
> adventure of sensuous experience. Carmen's more feminine concern is
> evasion, escape from the monopolistic men who presume to own her. . . .
> Neither of them is interested in love as an emotional unison. The erotic imper-
> ative dismisses such stability. They must remain in motion forever – pursuing
> in Giovanni's case, manoeuvering free in Carmen's – and can be satiated only
> in death. They are complementary . . . as eternal antagonists not marital part-
> ners: Giovanni seeks to know all the women in the world . . . Carmen seeks to
> keep all the men in the world from knowing her.[18]

Conrad accepts Giovanni as the archetypal male erotic adventurer.
Carmen is the archetypal *femme fatale*, the difficult, impossible to understand, spell-binding woman of so much male fantasy. Unwittingly,
perhaps, Conrad's views of Carmen and Giovanni also fall nicely into the
categorisations of *The Newly-Born Woman:* Giovanni always seeking possession in his realm of the proper or property and Carmen always evading
possession because hers is the realm of the gift, freely given. For Conrad
one of the keys to Carmen is found in the gypsy song at Lillas Pastia's.
Invoking Kierkegaard's opinion of *Don Giovanni,* he believes her to be a

'sensuous genius' who can only find true expression in music, the more irrational the better:

> The gypsy song comes from nowhere, for no reason – and its very gratu-itousness is what makes it such a revelation about Carmen. For it is a song about music, and about what Kierkegaard calls its demonism. . . .
>
>   The musical cacophony begets a whirling motion, as the bodies of the gypsy girls silently sing . . . At its most intense, it passes beyond articulacy. Its climax is Carmen's triumphant, shouted 'Tra-la-la-la'.[19]

Kierkegaard's idea of 'demonism' comes from his 1843 treatise *Either/Or* in which two sides of a persona argue in turn in favour of ethical rectitude and aesthetic hedonism.[20] The proponent of aesthetic hedonism bases his argument around Giovanni, claiming that the only way in which he can achieve his constant goal of immediate satisfaction is through music which transcends linguistic prevarication.[21]

Conrad takes Kierkegaard's argument to imply erotic satisfaction. Reading Kierkegaard a different way would of course align Giovanni once more with the feminine, making him a participant in pre-linguistic dis-course and making his music a sort of *écriture féminine*, and confirming Clément's appropriation. The very fact that this possibility does not intrude into Conrad's line of thought shows the gap between his work and Clément's. She too considers the gypsy song to be very revealing about Carmen, whom she terms her best friend and favourite, the most feminist, the most independent-minded of opera's doomed women.[22] For Clément, Carmen is a perpetual outsider, a woman assuming the freedoms of a man in a traditional society, a gypsy, a daughter of Egypt (the gypsies speak of their smuggling as *'les affairs d'Egypte'* ['Egyptian business']) among the settled people of Seville. The gypsy song is a celebration of her difference and her power:

> *Les tringles des sistres tintaient*
> *Avec un éclat métallique,*
> *Et sur cette étrange musique*
> *Les Zingarellas se levaient. . . .*
>
> *Les Bohémiens à tour de bras*
> *De leurs instruments faisaient rage,*
> *Et cet éblouissant tapage*
> *Ensorcelait les Zingaras.*
> *Sous le rhythme de la chanson,*
> *Ardentes, folles, enfiévrées,*
> *Elles se laissaient, enivrées,*
> *Emporter par le tourbillon!*
> *Tra la la la Tra la la la.*

The rings of the sistrums chimed
With a metallic splendour
And at this strange music
The gypsy girls arose. . . .

The gypsy men swung their arms
To make their instruments rage,
And this bedazzling commotion
Bewitched the gypsy girls.
To the rhythm of the song,
Burning, maddened, fevered,
They let themselves, drunk,
Be carried off by the whirl.[23]

In this song Carmen sings of orgiastic movement and music: the music provided by the gypsy men on their sistrums, guitars and tambourines, the movement by the gypsy girls who surrender themselves totally to the marriage of song and dance. Carmen remembers a lost gypsy paradise and her song recreates the music and movement of this memory on stage. It is the one time in the opera when Carmen is truly singing for herself and for joy. While the image of gypsy women intoxicated and frenzied by music controlled by masculine hands would seem to reinforce the usual clichés about sexual licence among gypsy women, Conrad appears to circumnavigate this difficulty by making no distinction throughout his work between male and female sexuality.

For him, the most important aspect of the song is its retrospective description and actual stimulation of movement. This is because it denotes 'demonism', a return to basic instincts, to the Dionysian values of Orpheus. Carmen represents not so much the irrational as the hedonistic and her song is a hymn to unfettered sensuality. For Clément, too, movement is the central image in this song, but for a very different reason. Conrad mentions that the sistrum she sings of was an instrument associated with Isis. However, while he notes it merely for serendipity, for Clément the link is of supreme importance. She explains that Isis one day found Osiris unable to walk because his legs had become stuck together. She parted them, he got up and walked and ever since the festival of Isis has been celebrated as one of movement, symbolised in the ever-moving sistrum. According to Clément, however, this is really a means of commemorating the sovereignty of the realm of the gift, the realm of the feminine. The association of Carmen with the sistrum makes her a daughter and sacred priestess of Isis. Isis, who gave her brother the gift of walking after he had lost it, is the superior deity; Carmen among the smugglers and gypsies, in the feminine night, is a reigning queen. The gypsy song is therefore a celebration of her power.

For Clément, Carmen dies because she refuses to surrender her freedom to the will of another, least of all a *payllo*, or settled man. Hers is a majestic act of female defiance. For Conrad, on the other hand, Carmen must die because of her demonic dynamism, because she has too much energy, because, like Giovanni, she is an existential gambler, 'risking everything on a dare or a jest or a practical joke'.[24] Whereas Clément's reading comes from an overtly feminist perspective, for Conrad the issues identified by feminism do not arise.

Interpretation and performance

Our heroine is indeed Carmen. She first sees the light of day in Prosper Mérimée's novella.[25] The tale is then adapted by Henri Meilhac and Ludovic Halévy, an experienced team of librettists, for Georges Bizet and although the opera is not an unqualified success on its first performance, it soon establishes itself as the only French nineteenth-century opera to remain in the standard repertoire. It is arguable, indeed, with the success of George Gershwin's black musical version, *Carmen Jones*, as supporting evidence, that Carmen is the most popular opera of all time.[26] How ironic, that an opera which had the female chorus in revolt during rehearsals for the first production because they were expected to 'smoke' and indeed move about on stage, an opera which offended against every tenet of nine-teenth-century bourgeois propriety by having as heroine a lawless gypsy who is neither prepared to make sacrifices for her honest, upright lover, nor to repent as she meets her end, should achieve such popularity.[27] In the past it was perhaps incumbent on an audience to see *Carmen* as a sort of fable where the wicked heroine is justly punished by Don José. Certainly, Mérimée expressed the wish, in a letter to his friend Señora de Montijo, that *Carmen* should be a good moral example to the fine ladies of France, but not without a certain amount of irony.[28] This tradition is implicitly recognised in Anthony Arblaster's assessment of *Carmen* in the light of feminism:

> *Carmen* seems to me one of the operas we understand much better in the wake of modern feminism. We appreciate better Carmen's qualities, her extraordi-nary independence and control over her own life; and we understand better why she dies: such independence is more than many men can tolerate. 'She acts like a man, that is all.' Precisely, and that is what men find so hard to accept.[29]

There is no way in which a radical feminist interpretation would be allowed in mainstream productions of *Carmen*, of course, since the means of financing such productions still rest largely in the hands of those for whom feminism is a peripheral matter. Two films entitled *Carmen* were made concurrently in Spain in the mid-1980s. The Italian director Francesco Rosi filmed his version of Bizet's opera entirely on location in Andalusia in the summer of 1983, a project that had previously been offered to the Spanish director Carlos Saura. The flamenco dancer Antonio Gades chorcographed Rosi's film and the same year played the male lead in a film he co-wrote with its director Carlos Saura about the staging of a flamenco ballet based on the opera and Mérimée's novella. In 1991, the Spanish actress and theatre director Nuria Espert produced Covent Garden's first new *Carmen* in twenty years, and it was subsequently released on video, directed for the camera by Barrie Gavin. Of the many *Carmens* available in the late-twentieth century, I have chosen to concentrate on these three productions, because their strong and deliberate Spanish influence gives them a point of cohesion and because they have reached a very wide audience through cinema, video and television.

The scene in which Carmen dances for Don José on his release from prison and the way it is told are of pivotal importance in the novella and in the opera. Mérimée's *Carmen* is narrated by a French archaeologist on a tour of Spain in 1830. Having met the infamous bandit José Navarro in the mountains near Cordoba, he finds him some months later in gaol in Seville awaiting execution the next day. Don José, on his last night, then tells his visitor the story of his love for Carmen. He describes how Carmen persuaded him to let her escape as he was escorting her to prison after the fight in the tobacco factory, how he went to prison instead, was stripped of his rank and put on humiliating guard duty and how she then took him to a room in the house of an old procuress, Dorothée, as his reward. She gaily buys lots of provisions and sweetmeats with the two piastres in gold she smuggled to him with a file while he was incarcerated and he, still mindful of his soldier's honour, refused to use.

While the bewildered José stands in the room laden down with all the purchases she dances around him and laughs madly, telling him he is her *rom* and she his *romi,* the romany words for husband and wife. Then she scatters everything on the floor, flings her arms around his neck and tells him that she pays her debts because that is the law of the gypsies. It is at this point in his narrative that José is obliged to pause.

> 'Ah! monsieur, cette journée-là! cette journée-là! . . . quand j'y pense, j'oublie celle de demain.'
>   Le bandit se tut un instant; puis, après avoir rallumé son cigare, il reprit:
> 'nous passâmes ensemble toute la journée, mangeant, buvant, et le reste.'[30]

'Oh, sir, that day, that day . . . when I think of it I can forget tomorrow.'
The bandit was silent an instant; then, after relighting his cigar, he continued:
'We spent the whole day together, eating, drinking and the rest.'

It seems that the memory is too powerful for him, that he is incapable of putting it into words. When he resumes the story his mood has changed. Unable to describe what happened at the heart of his encounter with Carmen he resorts to enumerating the trivia, with the effect that Carmen remains a mystery. He recites a whole catalogue of silly things she did during their day together: dissolving handfuls of sweets in a jug of water, throwing caramelised egg-yolks against the wall, breaking the only plate in the house to make castanets so that she could dance for him. Carmen is frivolous and childish in the extreme, but she is also shown to be an adulteress, a prostitute, an habitual liar, a thief, a sorceress and an accomplice, perhaps many times over, to murder. She easily persuades José not to go back to barracks when he hears the retreat sounded and just as easily dismisses him in an off-hand manner the next morning. At first, she laughs as riotously as she did the night before, but then, more seriously, warns José that he has encountered the devil. The testimony of the French archaeologist, whose chiming pocket watch Carmen stole from him one evening in Cordoba, and the tragic history of Don José, provide ample evidence to support her warning.

Mérimée's Carmen frightens and fascinates. In the libretto of Meilhac and Halévy, she becomes an untamable free spirit, tied to nothing and no one. Very little of the background information on Carmen provided in the novella is retained in the libretto. Carmen tells her own story in her own words and the only concrete information the opera offers is that she is a gypsy who occasionally consorts with a band of smugglers. In the first act, in her *habanera* and *seguidilla* (arias which evoke the Hispanic traditional dances of the same name), she declares that love and her heart are alike: capricious, passionate, self-willed. In the second-act duet with Don José she proclaims her ideal: the liberty of a smuggler's life in the open air. In the final act, even in the face of death, she asserts her right to complete freedom and informs José that she will not and never has compromised on this. When Carmen dances for José in Lillas Pastia's tavern she is at her most self-contained, just as she is at her most mysterious in Mérimée's story. She provides her own accompaniment and the song she sings as she dances has no words. Like the pause in Mérimée, it is the part of the opera most open to interpretation. Any producer or director's view of Carmen, any singer, dancer or actress's portrayal must hinge on the way producer or director and performer collaborate to present this dance.

In the Saura/Gades film, Antonio the choreographer reads an excerpt from the Mérimée novella to his cast as a way of explaining to them his interpretation of Carmen, before they rehearse the scene at the old procuress's house.

> '*Elle mentait, monsieur, elle a toujours menti. Je ne sais pas si dans la vie cette fille-là a jamais dit un mot de verité; mais quand elle parlait, je la croyais: c'était plus fort que moi'.*[31]

> She was lying, sir, she has always lied. I don't know if that girl has ever told a word of truth in her life; but when she spoke I believed her; it was stronger than I.'

He sees Don José as a powerless victim of Carmen's diabolical charms and reinforces this in the ensuing rehearsal. When Carmen the dancer's representation of Carmen's sexuality does not live up to his expectations, he proceeds to give her a demonstration of what, in his opinion, Carmen's feminine wiles should look like and she is forced to reproduce his exaggerated gestures in the full run-through. This scene, intentionally or not, is a pointed example of the problems encountered by female performers in a male-dominated artistic environment: they have to reproduce femininity as imagined by the male. Antonio's Carmen is the product of several male imaginations, in order: the flamenco José, Antonio the choreographer, Antonio Gades and Carlos Saura, Bizet, Meilhac and Halévy, Don José el Navarés, the French archaeologist, Mérimée. The one female imagination present, and one of the most important in any performance, is denied any input whatsoever.

The Carmen of Francesco Rosi's film of the opera has a similar pedigree; Francesco Rosi, the director, and Tonino Guerra, who worked on the adaptation, intervene after Bizet/Meilhac/Halévy. Rosi's film is very much directed by and for the male gaze. This is made clear at the beginning of the first act when the lieutenant in command of the dragoons, Zuñiga, looks through his binoculars at Carmen and her friends splashing about in their underwear in a pool. What he sees is shared with the audience. Indeed, the whole of the first act is built around images of men eyeing-up women, whether it be the soldiers surrounding the timid Micaëla as she goes to the barracks to enquire for Don José, or the soldiers and village men looking appraisingly at the tobacco-factory women coming out from work scantily dressed. When Julia Migenes' Carmen makes her first singing entrance, her every movement seems to be directed to and by the male gaze. The male chorus asks where Carmen is. In answer the lame village buffoon points to the wall behind which Carmen is splashing in a pool. The men rush over and climb up to look over the wall. Carmen hears them as they ask: '*Dis-nous quelle jour tu nous aimeras?* [Carmen, what day will you love us?] then looks up and leaves the pool to answer them with her *habanera*. She dances up the slope from the pool and appears framed in a doorway in a vampish pose, gathering her skirts up around her thighs, grinding her pelvis and then holding her skirts bunched in her left fist which she rubs sensuously over her abdomen as she sings '*L'amour est un oiseau rebelle*' ['Love is a rebel bird']. Then she moves into the square and around the men and women gathered there like a nightclub singer performing a risqué routine, all prominent cleavage, suggestive looks, exposed thighs and churning hips. These gestures are concentrated when she dances in a room at Lillas Pastia's for Don José. Here, after some passionate kissing, Carmen moves to a mirror to prepare herself, all the while keeping Plácido Domingo's Don José in view.

Julia Migenes' Carmen gazes, as indeed does Laura del Sol's Carmen in the Saura/Gades film, into a mirror before she performs her seduction dance. Following the indication of Sally Potter's film, in which the dead Mimì spends a great deal of her time gazing into a mirror, seeking to reconstruct and recover her ego, this could quite plausibly be read as a time in both films when Carmen is in touch with herself, but, unlike Potter's amnesiac Mimì, confidently so. She recharges her batteries before she launches into her seduction of José. In both films, Carmen's gaze as she is filmed from behind looking into the mirror is confident and self-possessed. However, it is equally possible to read the mirror scene in both films as stereotypical female narcissism, an image of the female preparing herself for the consumption of the male, a reading which would be more consonant with the predominant male gaze of these films.[32]

Julia Migenes is all energy, expression and movement as she erupts into her dance in Lillas Pastia's; Domingo's Don José seems barely to respond. Throughout the dance the camera is most often positioned behind his back, at his eye-level, placing the audience tacitly in the position of Don José. Her dance for him amounts to a striptease as she casts off her blouse and her overskirt. Then as she teases him for wanting to answer the summons back to barracks she lies back on the mattress in a parody of intercourse, her skirts up around her pelvis. Yet, Domingo's Don José does not respond, not even when she rubs her foot into his chest. Instead he ignores her sensuality, and moves away from her to sing of the pure love he cherished for her during his long month in prison. At the end of his Flower Song he holds her, her knees tucked under her chin in a foetal position, her head against his chest, in an almost fatherly embrace. It is as if Carmen's sexuality is on open display for the man in the audience and the man behind the camera but at the same time, Don José is implicitly disapproving. Carmen is not worthy of the idealised love of the Flower Song and he is tortured by this knowledge. In the third act, the spoken dialogue is altered to allow José to accuse Carmen of being a whore, an accusation that is not present in the original.[33] It is the old problem, of course, honest, salt-of-the-earth young men like Don José are supposed to sleep with women like Carmen, but not to fall in love with them and there is a loaded ambiguity in the way in which such women are treated by the male gaze. Don José is a salutary example of the way such a woman can make a victim of a man, but the implied male gaze, at the safe distance of the voyeur, can luxuriate in it all.

It is striking how closely the first section of Carmen's dance in the full rehearsal in the Saura/Gades film resembles what happens in the Rosi film. (In fact, Gades choreographed both films.) Here, too, Carmen first looks at herself in a mirror as she adjusts her dress. Then, she seats José on a chair and prepares to dance. With the camera positioned behind José, slightly above and to the right of his eye-level, Carmen dances towards him and back from him, lifting her skirts up her thighs like Julia Migenes, albeit in a more restrained and stylised manner, performing the movements that Antonio the choreographer taught her. Carmen moves and invites, José remains still. Her invitation extended, Carmen returns to her chair and wills José onto his feet and over to her. He then dances in front of her but the camera remains behind his back until she gets up and they dance together over towards the prop that stands in for the bed. Throughout this scene the camera remains loyal to the male gaze.

The Saura/Gades film is much more complex, however, than the positioning of the camera in this scene would suggest. While on the surface it appears that Carmen the dancer's 'feminine' movements are being orchestrated for the male gaze of Antonio the choreographer – who discovered her and is grooming her to embody his version of Carmen, and also that of the male audience he must be presumed to represent – this is subverted in various ways. The first is the documentary style of the film, which, by moving in and out of the two planes of reality with increasingly less warning as the film progresses, allows a distance to develop between the audience and every other character except Antonio, whose point of view the audience is permitted to share from time to time. Carmen, therefore, remains a complete mystery to both Antonio and the audience and, as such, she cannot be said to wholly satisfy any gaze, male or female. The second is the scene which immediately follows the full rehearsal of the dance in Lillas Pastia's (the old procuress's). Carmen goes back to the rehearsal room at night to find Antonio, in front of the mirror, practising his secret, intimate dance, *la farruca*. Here, perhaps, is a scene which is the equivalent of Carmen's gazing into the mirror before she performs her seduction dance, a time when Antonio's own gaze is, for once, directed inwards.

When she comes in, she rejects his caresses and sits down, demanding something to drink. He gives her some *manzanilla* sherry and she then commands him to dance *la farruca* for her, for love, something he has never done before. He complies and she interrupts his dance, mimicking the aggressive instructions, '¡*Venga, cómeme ahora*! '[Come on, devour me now!]' he had been giving her in rehearsal, and then they embrace passionately and make love. Although she had allowed Antonio to dictate the way in which she would dance as Carmen and how she would express femininity, in this scene she is the dominant one, borrowing some of his masculine behaviour in order to perform her seduction and violating his secret world while not allowing him to know anything about her. When Carmen gets up and leaves him in the middle of the night and refuses to give any explanation, he dresses and goes once more to the mirror. He performs a few movements of his *farruca* and then stops, confused. Carmen the dancer has just fulfilled his, probably masochistic, fantasy of Carmen, leaving him as the fictional Carmen would have left José. He looks in the mirror, interrogating, not himself this time, but his interpretation of Carmen. He decides, in his bitterness, to develop his version to include all the clichés: the comb, the fan, the flower, the mantilla. As he does so, Carmen appears dressed in this way, taunting him as he continues to gaze into the mirror.

Yet, in this second seduction scene the placing of the camera reinforces the very male gaze that the action might seem to undermine. When Carmen and Antonio sit down to drink sherry together, the first image is of Carmen's extended foot in a stiletto-heeled shoe. The camera lingers and then moves slowly up her crossed legs to the table, where the full sherry glasses are placed, before cutting to Carmen's face. When Antonio gets up to dance the *farruca* for her the camera is placed roughly where her gaze would be but she is excluded from the shot. As Antonio dances it is framed like a masterclass or a public exhibition by a renowned maestro rather than a dance for Carmen alone. Antonio's status is reinforced by the comment he makes to Carmen that he has been dancing since he was fifteen years old. His gaze is directed boldly towards his public as he dances, not just at Carmen. When she decides to come up on stage and interrupt, the camera moves around behind Antonio's back and the gaze is once more his as Carmen first taunts him and then rushes into his arms. This Carmen is probably closer to Mérimée than to Bizet, Meilhac and Halévy, but, more significantly, this José is different from the others in that he deliberately goes in search of his Carmen and sets up a kind of masochistic fantasy for himself.

In Nuria Espert's production for Covent Garden, the tables are turned, almost symmetrically. Espert puts a great deal of authentic Spanish detail into her production, as indeed does Rosi, but, as might be expected from a Spanish director and a feminist actress, she manipulates it in a very different way. In the gypsy song at Lillas Pastia's, for example, she sets the tone for the rest of the Second Act with an ingenious reversal. As the music starts but before Carmen begins her song, a male flamenco dancer takes centre stage, surrounded by a semi-circle of men and women. Carmen remains languidly seated, holding a cigarette, while she sings and looks on. When she begins her song, the flamenco dancer is joined by one and then more female dancers but he remains the centre of attention, the object of Carmen's and everybody else's gaze. Carmen may sing of gypsy girls abandoning themselves to the intoxication of the dance but, in contrast, the strongest visual image is of a man absorbed in the music. Only when she has finished her song does Carmen join the display, dancing with a certain conscious irony and distance with the male dancer in the final flourish.

Then, in the scene with Don José in Lillas Pastia's, Carmen is equally languorous, equally distant. Here, it is once more the male who is on exhibition. Luis Lima's Don José has the rapidly changing facial expressions, the energetic movement around a relatively stationary figure, the fire and the passion that was Julia Migenes' in the Rosi film and, to a lesser extent, Laura del Sol's in the Saura/Gades collaboration. Maria Ewing, whose enigmatic portrayal of Carmen is renowned, stands on top of the table to greet José when he enters and then gets on the table again to perform her dance. She looks down on José from her elevated position on the table, subordinates him further by making him play her makeshift castanets and then barely bothers to move, swaying almost absent-mindedly where Julia Migenes swooped and swirled. He becomes so intent on providing her accompaniment that he hardly looks at her as she dances. He is soon distracted further by the retreat call. She remains self-absorbed; her face expressionless or mocking. She sings her wordless song carelessly and appears oblivious of José as he rushes about the tavern when he hears the retreat sounded. All he can do is kiss her foot as she continues to sway gently and try to make his exit. There seems always to be a physical distance between them. Unlike Migenes and Domingo they do not kiss and every time Lima's José tries to put his arms around Carmen, she moves away like a wary cat. She gives no impression that she is interested in José, physically or otherwise. Indeed she hardly responds to Gino Quilico's Escamillo either when he makes his grand entrance to Lillas Pastia's.

This Carmen appears to be much more concerned with her own secret business. The libretto, of course, does not dictate that any such thing exists, but Maria Ewing manages, by her body language and her detached singing, to give that impression and to let the audience know that these men are really just a vaguely inconvenient interruption.

In sharp contrast to the Rosi version then, this Carmen seems to be directed more for a female gaze: the inward, introverted gaze of Maria Ewing's Carmen who keeps her own counsel; and the implied female gaze of the audience which sees a male dancer instead of gypsy girls take centre stage in Carmen's gypsy song and sees José provide all the movement, energy and emotion lacking in Carmen's dance in the tavern. It is he and not Carmen who is on display and it is her gaze, the female gaze, which dominates.

In the Saura/Gades version, Carmen the dancer's portrayal of passion is moulded by the choreographer who discovered her, then directed in performance at his Don José exclusively; in the Rosi adaptation, Julia Migenes' Carmen is photographed in such a way that her frank carnality is projected towards the cameraman, the director, the audience behind Don José's back. In the Saura/Gades film the Carmen of the dance in the procuress's house is explicitly the product of masculine desire; in the Rosi film her all too obvious sexuality is implicitly aimed at an audience of men. In the Nuria Espert/Maria Ewing collaboration, however, Carmen keeps all her secrets. Whatever emotions she feels are turned inwards, she slips constantly out of the ardent José's grasp and she is unknowable.

An interpretation, like that of Maria Ewing, where Carmen is the voyeur: mocking, undermining, overplaying and, yet, consistently refusing to play the role of the difficult, impossible to understand, spellbinding *femme fatale* of male fantasy performs the difficult task of making what is essentially a male fantasy into a feminist icon; just as Clément's classification of Don Giovanni as an hysteric turns the great seducer, at least momentarily, into an ironic victim of macho agression.

Clément begins with an assertion that opera is about women, heroines who are crushed by a masculine order which fears them for having a power of which it cannot divest them without first destroying them. Then, almost in a volte-face, she invades the masculine camp and proceeds to absorb the great male figures of opera into the female realm. What she postulates with her ingenious manipulation of Freud is that because all the great figures of opera, irrespective of sex, are possessed of strongly feminine characteristics, opera is not simply about the victimisation of women: it is centred on the feminine; not only that, it is about the transcendence of the feminine. In part, Clément argues that opera is about the oppression of the feminine values of chaos, intuition, passion, and instinct by a masculine code founded on order and reason and, indeed, this element of her thesis coincides exactly with Conrad's argument, but what she has to say is far more complex.

Her interpretation deals both with the oppression of the feminine and with the oppression of women as women in a socio-political sense. The great anthem of her book is that opera is about the subjugation of women, and she begins by asserting this in terms which preclude any attempt to reinterpret the politics within opera in a way that would place the role of women in a positive light: 'Opera is about women. No, not a feminist version; no, not a liberation. On the contrary: they suffer, they cry out, they die.' However, by grafting her exploration of the persecution of the feminine by the masculine onto what she considers to be the misogynistic plots of opera, she moves beyond analysis of the political power of male over female within those structures. While firmly maintaining that opera is about the oppression of women on one level, she can demonstrate that it is also about the transcendence of the feminine on another. Moreover, the ambiguities of Clément's approach discussed at the outset of this study, which mean that it is not exclusively feminist, are a tribute to the inherent generosity of *écriture féminine* as well as a recognition of the complexity of art in both theory and performance.

A production, however, is, above all, an interpretation which must negotiate these ambiguities to provide a specific reading in a given time and place. A production like the Espert/Ewing collaboration shows that it is possible, in practice, to equate the feminine with the female and concentrate the interests and concerns of the female and the feminine exclusively in the female characters on stage. Because, according to Clément and Conrad, opera is centred on the feminine, women inevitably become the focus of attention and the male characters and the masculine order are relegated to a secondary position, almost in spite of the plot. In the Espert/Ewing collaboration this generates a performance which portrays not only the victory in death of the feminine over the masculine but of female over male, a truly feminist as well as a Romantic ending.[34] Maria Ewing coasts through her performance and pays scant attention to either José or Escamillo, because the balance of power is centred in Carmen and not in the men who surround her, gaol her, try to command her and finally murder her. On the surface it would appear to be a travesty of the text, but Conrad's argument justifies it on high Romantic grounds and Clément's on feminist grounds as well.

It is, nevertheless, inevitable that interpretations like those of Rosi and of Saura and Gades will continue to be produced and will probably constitute the mainstream for some time to come, since the funding for opera is largely controlled by traditionalists. Peter Conrad believes that 'Carmen can tolerate these inconsistent accounts of herself because her secret is her non-entity.'[35] His is an enlightened point, but as usual Clément gives the same point a much more imaginative gloss. She sees the shade of the powerful Isis rising, in triumph and approbation, over the prostrate body of the singer as the curtain falls at the end of the last act.[36] Carmen can tolerate these inconsistent accounts of herself because she is Isis, who freely gave her brother the gift of movement, whose being is not affected by how much she gives, who does not have to hold on to any particular identity because she can give something of herself to any interpretation and still retain her power. Isis rises as the curtain falls, presumably for those, like Clément, who have eyes to see her.

Notes

1. In their different ways, French feminist theorists such as Luce Irigaray and Julia Kristeva base some of their work on a reconstructive re-reading of Freud and Lacan. This is also true to some extent of Hélène Cixous. Clément was Cixous's collaborator on *La jeune née*, and so must also be described under this heading, although, in fact, post-Freudian is a term that describes *L'opéra ou la défaite des femmes* more accurately. Indeed, the book is dedicated to Lévi-Strauss and it is Lévi-Strauss and Freud rather than Lacan who are being used as a basis for her reading of opera.
2. *Opera or the Undoing of Women* London, Virago (1989).
3. Jeremy Tambling, *Opera, Ideology and Film* Manchester, Manchester University Press (1987). Tambling provides a very interesting survey of the various cinematic treatments of Carmen in the chapter entitled 'Rewriting Carmen' (pp. 13–39).
4. *Viva la Libertà!: Politics in Opera* London, Verso (1992), 'Women in Opera', pp. 225–44.
5. *Thriller*, 1979 (UK independent).
6. 'La verité passe comme un souffle d'air frais; l'amour de Rodolfo est rhétorique.
    Il n'existe pas de rhétorique qui ne dise le destin; et celui de Mimi se dessine dans les mots de Rodolfo. Poésie, elle n'est déjà plus femme, elle ne le sera pas. Jeune fille à ses fleurs vouée, elle n'aura pas d'autre vie. La voici prise aux images du poète. Muse, inspiratrice, elle rejoint la cohorte des jeunes filles sacrifiées par le séducteur, pour le

faire vivre dans un temps suspendu: un instant de poésie, encore un autre, un dernier jour d'hiver, encore un autre, at la vie s'arrête. Alors seulement s'éveillera Rodolfo, qui n'a rien vu. Il ne l'a pas fait exprès.' *L'opéra ou la défaite des femmes* Paris, Grasset (1979), p. 165.

7. *Viva la Libertà!*, p. 227.
8. 'L'opéra est affaire des femmes. Non, pas une version feministe; non, pas une libération. Tout au contraire: elles souffrent, elles crient, elles meurent, c'est là aussi ce que on appelle chanter. Elles s'exposent, décolletées jusqu'au coeur, luisantes de larmes, au regard de ceux qui viennent jouir de leurs supplices feints.' p. 24.
9. Mario Praz, *The Romantic Agony* Oxford, Oxford University Press, (1970). The original title of Praz's study of the dark side of Romanticism, which was first published in 1930, is *La morte, la carne e il diavolo nella litteratura romantica*. In it, he identifies the flesh, death and the devil as the nexus which inspires most of Romantic literature.
10. Op. cit., pp. 186–96. In Clément's analysis Turandot is not the capriciously cruel princess who has heartlessly caused all her previous suitors to be put to death and who urges the torture of the innocent Liù, but a creature of the feminine moon oppressed by the masculine world of the sun and daylight who, in rejecting all her suitors, is fighting for her very survival in a hostile world.
11. Mario Praz, (ed.) *Three Gothick Novels* Harmondsworth, Penguin (1968), *introduction*.
12. *Ecriture féminine* is identified in *La jeune née* as an anti-rational, alogical, unstructured and intuitive way of writing which may express the feminine much more adequately than the everyday structured, logical, rational discourse of patriarchy.
13. Peter Conrad *A Song of Love and Death: The Meaning of Opera*, London, Chatto and Windus (1987). Conrad has also published *Romantic Opera and Literary Form* Berkeley, University of California Press (1977).
14. 'Le mensonge est bien partagé; et Don Giovanni, au-delà de la mythique différence des sexes, rejoint par une subtile ellipse ses complices féminines. Hystérique, comme elles.' p. 71.
15. 'Don Giovanni n'est pas loin d'Orphée, dépecé par les Bacchantes, jalouses de leurs sccrets, jalouses de cet homme trop près d'elles, trop loin d'elles, et violentes, parce que lui aussi le désire.' p. 72.
16. Peter Conrad, 1987, p. 19.
17. Ibid., p. 11.
18. Ibid., pp. 42–3.
19. Ibid. pp. 44–5, p. 45.
20. Søren Kierkegaard, *Either/Or*, (trans. and ed. Alastair Hannay). Harmondsworth, Penguin (1992).
21. Ibid., pp. 43–4.
22. Clément, 1979, pp. 94–104, p. 94.
23. *Carmen* Erato, ECD 880 373, pp. 109–10.
24. Conrad, 1987, p. 49.
25. *Carmen* Paris, Livre de Poche (1983) p. 177. Mérimée wrote the novella in a week. It was based on a true story related to him fifteen years earlier on his first visit to Spain by his Spanish friend Señora de Montijo. In a sense, since a woman is perhaps the first teller of the story of Carmen it is only right that she should at last be returned to female creativity.
26. See Tambling, 1987, 'Rewriting *Carmen*'.
27. See Susan McClary, *Georges Bizet: Carmen*, Cambridge, Cambridge University Press (1992) pp. 23–8, for an account of the troubles surrounding the original production of *Carmen*.
28. *Carmen*, 1983 p. 178. 'Après Arsène Guillot, je n'ai rien trouvé de plus moral à offrir à nos belles dames.'

29. *Viva la Libertà!*, p. 233.

30. *Carmen*, p. 215.

31. Ibid., p. 208.

32. The gazing into the mirror could be seen as a return to the Lacanian mirror stage. It is certainly the one time when these Carmens approach the introspection of Maria Ewing's Carmen. It is also important to remember that mirrors are omnipresent in the rehearsal room in which the Saura/Gades *Carmen* is mainly located; it would be unwise to read too much into the deployment of mirrors throughout the film, since they are a practical necessity for a rehearsing dancer.

33. It is not indeed present in the amended libretto that accompanies the recording of the opera conducted by Lorin Maazel, but appears to have been added during the making of the film.

34. This ending is not, however, an empowering one in terms of real women's lives. (See the discussion of the ending of 'Thelma and Louise' in this volume, p. 98.) The same Espert production put on at the Teatro de la Maestranza in Seville in 1992 with Teresa Berganza in the title role produced a much more traditional *Carmen* since Berganza's interpretation of the role is far less overtly feminist and less controversial. Much more than straight theatre, opera productions depend on and vary with the personalities of the principal singers. Ewing could probably get away with her idiosyncratic Carmen in any production since the producer could not exert the degree of control over the singers that a director can in theatre, but conversely would not be a likely choice for a big budget cinema production such as the Rosi *Carmen*. That Julia Migenes was chosen as much for her looks as her singing in this film is indisputable; *Carmen* is still the only full opera she has recorded and she would not, before the film, have been, vocally, a likely choice for the role which is normally the preserve of mezzo-sopranos.

35. Conrad, op. cit., p. 335.

36. Clément, op. cit., p. 104.

All translations are my own.

8   Towards a feminist critique of television
     natural history programmes

BARBARA CROWTHER

For most people in the developed world, natural history programmes on television are the main source of reference about biological science outside school, and so must be recognised as an influential area of popular culture. But while several studies have been made of science on television, wildlife programmes have largely evaded the cultural scrutineers. Recognising that 'the current ideology of science on TV is a material force in reinforcing current priorities and practices in society'[1] media academics have, understandably enough, dealt with 'hard' science, the kind that might be concerned with nuclear expansion, microchips or genetic engineering.[2] Natural history might well be thought a low priority beside this, but its ideologies, and the version of science and the 'natural' that it promotes, have a particular and powerful bearing on the politics of gender in contemporary society.

Wildlife programmes are a mainstay of the television schedules in Britain and other western countries, consistently attracting high ratings; the BBC Natural History Unit's international reputation and the success of international co-productions ensure the genre considerable stability. They pride themselves – to quote from a BBC job advertisement in November 1991 – on their 'compelling subjects, well-structured stories, and state-of-the-art photography'. These features are certainly part of their longstanding popularity, a popularity which has lasted more than forty years since the BBC first transmitted *Zoo Quest* in 1954.[3]

The aim of this study is threefold: first, to examine the implications of the genre's success primarily from a feminist viewpoint, by considering how the appeal of this genre, and its patriarchal underpinning, may be illuminated through academic approaches associated with three different fields – literary studies, science, and media studies; second, to see how a range of methodologies brought to the service of the feminist project may provide an entry into an academically hybrid subject whose cultural status makes it seem both unquestionable and impregnable; and finally to speculate, tentatively, on how changes within the genre might enable it to challenge the patriarchal order.

Four texts will provide the main examples: *Continuing the Line*, episode 12 of 'The Trials of Life' (BBC, Bristol, 1990); *Queen of the Beasts* ('Survival Special', Anglia, first transmitted 17 March 1989); *Quest in the Flooded Forest* ('Survival Special', Anglia, 1981) and '*The Tale of the Pregnant Male*' ('Wildlife on One', BBC Bristol, first transmitted 1 March 1988).

Perspective 1: literary studies

'Compelling subjects, well-structured stories' – this formulation acknowledges that narrative is structurally central to natural history programmes in their mode of mediating scientific research. This has significant implications for the representation of science, but for television it is both a convenience and a rhetorical technique.[4] The centrality of the narrative element makes it both appropriate and fruitful to study these programmes through analytic techniques generally practised on literary texts, techniques that focus particularly on the narrative and the linguistic elements, or combine both in the study of a text's rhetoric, the various devices by which it attracts and persuades.[5] The rhetorical approach allows the formal (morphological) arrangement of a text to be studied alongside features of its linguistic behaviour (such as quotation, metaphor and narration) as part of a multi-faceted and complex 'utterance', whose address – the relationship between the 'voice' of the text and the reader – is also crucial.

Language

It is easy enough to identify in the language of wildlife scripts the conventional patriarchal concepts that underlie them – and indeed underlie natural history itself. Besides the obvious markers, like references to the animal 'kingdom' and to 'Man', there are significant distinctions made along gender lines. 'Competitive' behaviour and 'territorial aggression' are repeatedly attributed to male animals, while females have 'mothering instincts' and 'protect their young'. Moreover, animal groups are frequently perceived as consisting of a leader and his 'harem'.

This common descriptive language is part of the genre's use of anthropomorphism, which, by describing animal behaviour in terms that play on assumptions specific to the writer's culture, in turn validates these assumptions as 'natural' in human culture by 'finding' them in animal groups. Gendered behaviour is one of its favourite themes. Blatant examples (like Mrs Badger cleaning out the bedding) cover a more insidious drip-drip of metaphors around mothering and fathering roles, jilted lovers, jealousy, grooming and coyness. Some anthropomorphism is, of course, inevitable when speaking of animals, and it offers scope for considerable play in a text, with high entertainment value – an important rhetorical dimension. The substitution of a feminist anthropomorphism, offering an alternative commentary on a sequence of filmed animal behaviour, could be instructive in pointing up how value-laden the discourse is, but is itself no solution. The issue is more fundamental, the politics of anthropomorphic discourse much more complex.

Biologists and scientific journalists who have been brought up in the linguistic and cognitive tradition of patriarchy (e.g. using 'he' to refer to female animals) will, not surprisingly, perceive their primary material – the subjects of their research – in patriarchal terms. As Ruth Bleier explains:

> Necessarily incorporated into [our] world view is the patriarchal ordering of external reality, both natural and social. The language and relationships of dominance and subordinance, control and submission, male and female, become a part of our consciousness that orders and interprets the external world.[6]

It is not surprising, then, that the scripts of wildlife films reflect the perceptual world of the researcher and carry assumptions of male dominance.

A typical example comes from the film *Queen of the Beasts*: 'The overwhelming driving force in nature is to reproduce. It is not enough just to sire a lot of cubs.' David Attenborough, the pre-eminent British wildlife broadcaster and naturalist, is susceptible too, both in his books – 'When tricks like this can be played, it is not surprising that many animals go to great lengths to seize a female at the very first moment that she becomes sexually available'[7] – and broadcasts:

> This is a male Heleconius butterfly and he's settled on a pupa which he knows contains a female. He's waiting for that moment when the female will emerge, a virgin, and then in the first few seconds of her adult life he'll mate with her. And so intent is he on achieving that that he won't move even if I touch him with my fingers. But watch what happens if I take this, which is an adult female which is newly mated. What happens if I brush him lightly with her? [The male flies off.]
>
> The reason he left is because this female, when she was mated, was given a particular smell, which even I can detect – a smell that all other males find very repugnant. So if I let her fly away that male may return to complete his business.
>
> And even before the newly-emerged female's wings have expanded he mates with her, dabbing her with his smell which will repel other males for weeks. No rival will displace *his* sperm. (*Continuing the Line*)

In this example, the use of the passive voice in the phrase 'when she was mated' and the source of the active agency in 'he mates with her', give an indication of Attenborough's attitude to the sexual act, as perhaps does his gratuitous inclusion of the appositional phrase, 'a virgin'.

The tendency of scientific practice to betray its patriarchal leanings appears routinely in the discourse of scientific books and papers, not just on television, as Emily Martin demonstrates in analysing a large number of popular and scientific texts concerning human reproduction. She finds significant discrepancies between how the male and female components and functions of the human reproductive process are described. 'It is remarkable how "femininely" the egg behaves and how "masculinely" the sperm.' The process, she notes, is described in several sources through fairytale imagery, even, in one case

> liken[ing] the egg's role to that of Sleeping Beauty: 'a dormant bride await-ing her mate's magic kiss, which instills the spirit that brings her to life'. Sperm, by contrast, have a 'mission' which is to 'move through the female genital tract in quest of the ovum'.[8]

There is ample evidence that biological discourse is powerfully impreg-nated with 'commonsense' anthropomorphism emanating from an unre-flective patriarchal world view.

Narrative format

The linguistic practices of wildlife programmes, moreover, interact with the programme form itself, which is almost always a narrative one. Despite the versatility of natural history film footage – it can be edited to serve a number of different scripts – the types of story used to structure it are relatively few in number. Though each programme constructs a dif-ferent 'plot', a handful of core structures are found to recur constantly. These story-types themselves tend to reflect androcentrism and patriar-chal relationships. Three of the most characteristic are the life-cycle story, the quest narrative and the triumph of science (culture) over nature – mastery over mystery.

The terms of the life-cycle format, a familiar convention of traditional nature-study, need to be examined. It is not, as we might expect, a birth-to-death narrative, but a birth-to-parenthood one. This orthodox repro-ductive model of animal life nurtures the kind of biological determinism that feminists have long been campaigning against. What about life beyond reproduction? What about infertile and post-reproductive animals? How do animals cope with the aging process? These are not matters wildlife programmes tend to address.

The life-cycle structure was – ultimately – behind BBC television's recent wildlife blockbuster, David Attenborough's *The Trials of Life*

(1990). This was a sociobiological treatise covering twelve stages in the lives of diverse species throughout the world. Each episode showed them undergoing these 'trials' – 'home-making', 'hunting and escaping' and so on; but while episode 1 was *Arriving*, episode 12 wasn't 'Dying', but *Continuing the Line*. The 'line' in question was, self-evidently, the male line, another aspect of this conventional reproductive model. There is a hidden presumption that the female's line is assured; the interest is provided by the males' struggles against each other to continue their line – the enactment of the Darwinist imperative of competition. Survival of the fittest is, almost every time, about the fittest male.

> A female wolf who's just become sexually receptive joins her howling pack in the Canadian north. All the males are interested in her but there's a ranking system in the pack and the senior male has priority in mating. Others who try their luck have to be reminded who's boss. And he claims his rights. [The male and female wolf copulate.] . . . His genitals have swollen so greatly inside her that the pair are locked together. This is no unfortunate accident. It's an important part of the male's breeding strategy. . . . The aftermath of such a genital lock may be slightly painful, but the process has virtually guaranteed him his paternity. (*Continuing the Line*)

The privileging of males, and the preoccupation with the strong male in particular, underlies another typical wildlife television story, the naturalist as hero, a man with a quest. There is a long tradition of quest narratives in western folklore which encourages identification with this male figure who abandons his home comforts to 'do what a man's gotta do'.[9] Motifs of danger and discomfort are woven into the stories, but the drive of the narrative is always the urge for discovery, the golden fleece – in the example below, the elusive Hoatzin bird of the Amazonian forests:

> At first sight the Hoatzin looks like a link between the earliest birds and their reptile ancestors: it's a most appropriate denizen of this lost world . . . But where in this vast watery wilderness do you start to look for an undisturbed area where these birds nest? . . .
> Eventually there was nothing for it but to get out [of the canoe] and walk. It was only a few miles but it was through the flooded forest, the Igapo itself. It took Friedman [Koester] eight hours to hike to his camp while carrying over 75 lbs of film and food. To shift all the stores from this one canoe trip required three journeys, 24 hours of practically non-stop carrying. (*Quest in the Flooded Forest*)

Often, to heighten tension, the hero-scientist is working against a deadline, like extinction or seasonal weather. As in the folk-tale, the male seeker is often 'helped' by a woman (who, in the field, often serves as his photographer and note-taker).[10]

The third story which characteristically shapes television wildlife pro-grammes is that of the triumph of science over nature's mysteries. Here an enigma or puzzle from the animal world is presented, and after a series of false trails it is explained or resolved by the rational processes of science. *Queen of the Beasts* is framed in this structure. It is introduced in these words:

> For centuries lions with their awesome size and power have played a large part in human history, art and folklore. We learn at an early age that the lion is king of the beasts, and that a group of lions is a pride. For many years scientists have been wondering about those prides. Why, of all the wild cats in the world, is it only the lion that lives in groups?

In the film, two field researchers test out three hypotheses that have been proposed in answer to this question. The first two are found unsat-isfactory, though they offer partial explanations; the third is presented as solving the mystery. The framing validates certain lines of inquiry, but leaves important absences, as shall be seen later.[11] Indeed, the type of story chosen to structure any script is bound to affect its subject, setting up spe-cific terms for narrative satisfaction.

A significant feature of all three of these key narratives is that they are markedly end-oriented. Whether cyclical or climactic, they demonstrate an allegiance to linearity and cohesion in the stories themselves and through the single-strandedness of their structure. These features of textual unity and linearity have been identified by certain feminist theo-rists of language as the structures of discourse most highly valued in western culture, and characterised as phallocentric.[12] Perhaps all end-oriented narratives could, by this model, be seen as inherently phallocen-tric, and to some extent this tidy packaging is dictated by television convention, the half-hour or one-hour slot. However, the point is that there are other popular televisual forms which could no doubt accommo-date wildlife subjects successfully, above all the magazine format, a form consistently used for 'daytime' programmes (whose audiences are pre-sumed to be largely female); indeed, some science programmes already use it. Questioning the conventional format might help to expand the scope of the genre, to privilege other viewpoints, and to validate the process as much as the end-product of scientific investigation. It might also alter the relationship between filmmaker and audience.

Narrative positioning
The manner in which a text addresses its audience – the speaking and receiving positions it constructs – is a crucial area of rhetoric. Although

address operates in television through visual as well as linguistic strategies, and even through scheduling, an examination of the linguistic
dimension alone can throw considerable light on the way both women and
men in the audience may find themselves positioned in relation to natural
history television.

The voice fronting these films – the narrator – is almost always male:
in the British product, when it's not David Attenborough (a BBC figure),
it is usually a distinguished actor with a sonorous RP (received pronun-
ciation) accent. It is a voice that carries considerable authority. Its discursive mode is to present scientific knowledge as empirical truth,
supported by a smattering of scientific terms and Latin names, and an
impressive and unfaltering barrage of details and figures, serving as signifiers of knowledge.

The relationship of the verbal script to the images is important to its
revelatory style: the photography appears to reinforce the words, providing 'ocular proof' of their veracity. The realist editing mode (rendering
invisible the techniques and processes of production) obscures the fact
that the script is composed in conjunction with, and largely as a function
of, the available pictures. When the authorial voice thus 'captions' the
images we see on screen, viewers are not positioned to challenge its interpretations, and its authority is reinforced.

The interpellative force of the address is stronger when a presenter is
physically there on screen, in the field. His clear status as expert
(enhanced by the invisible autocue) is modified, personalised by manner-
isms – in Attenborough's case contorted postures, childish enthusiasm,
awe, whispered intimacy. His look to camera not only speaks directly to
each of us, but it becomes part of an invitation to share his experience, and
indeed his responses.

This combining of the factual with the experiential is part of the
rhetoric of wildlife television: sharing the immediacy of the filmic experience pulls us into an ideological position in which we go along with the
attitudes and responses signalled by the narration, which constitutes, as
it were, the 'preferred reading'. The address encourages us to indulge
certain feelings, and deny others.[13] We are, for instance, following the
example of the authoritative narrator, licensed to enjoy voyeuristic close-
ups of creatures following their basic urges, and to wallow unashamedly
in the cuddly and cute, but are expected to show stiff-upper-lip detachment at scenes of animal 'cruelty'.

Sometimes when the 'preferred' reading is at odds with our own
response – if we don't delight in watching the brilliant mechanics of the

spider trapping the fly, or if we feel we are being excessively prurient – we can feel quite uncomfortable. The objective, rational tone and the male-dominated narration tend to construct what we can call a 'masculine' reading position, and the more 'feminine' (emotional, subjective) our response, the more likely we are to feel marginal to the address.[14] The following example of this raises interesting issues too about gendered voice. The film *Queen of the Beasts* is about the social behaviour of lions. Its narrator is the actress Rula Lenska. The choice of a woman narrator must in some portion have been related to the film's recognition that male lions play an extremely marginal role in the life of a pride, their main role being to father cubs. (This angle allowed the programme to be trailered as somehow feminist, despite the fact that a large amount of the film still concentrates on the males' behaviour.) The famous sequence of lion infanticide in this film is worth close attention.

A pair of males from outside the pride have routed the senior male and 'the new masters of the pride have come for the females'. No intimation is given of what is to come. The following commentary, delivered in a pleasant, measured tone, is dubbed over film of a single male loping through the grass or standing looking around him, intercut with three brief shots of cubs hidden under a bush:

> Wary of these new and strange males, the females have wisely gone into hiding. But in this hide-and-seek game of life there is another and more immediate problem for these males. They cannot mate until the lionesses come into season. But the females already have cubs and so will not be ready to mate for another year or more. The new males simply cannot wait that long for their chance to father some cubs of their own. They are in their prime now and may only have possession of the females for two years – just two years in which to ensure their genetic patrimony. They cannot afford to look after another male's cubs; they cannot spend their short time at the top protecting another lion's young whilst waiting for their turn to mate. They have done their waiting out there on the plains where they wandered for years in search of this opportunity; they can wait no longer. [The male starts to run, gathering speed.] If the females lose their cubs they will come into season within days. The imperative for the new males is overwhelming: they must kill the cubs.

The commentary falls silent now as, in one continuous shot, the lion attacks one cub while a second runs off, and picks up and drops its limp body before moving off towards the second cub; this cub rears up in defence before being attacked and killed; the lion runs on to a third, savages it, and picks up its body. Then there is a long-shot of the lion carrying the cub's body as the camera zooms out to a vista of the whole savannah. The scene is emotionally very powerful; however, the script's immediate concern is to acknowledge something else, the skill of the camera crew: 'Despite all the years of research into lion behaviour infanticide has rarely been seen and *never* before filmed.' The commentary goes on:

> For all its apparent ferocity, the killing is only an expression of the urgent demands of the situation. But if the male's behaviour seems harshly pragmatic, perhaps the female's is even more surprising. Bereft of their cubs, the females now have exactly the same drives as the new males. They can expect around two years of stability. If they are to raise cubs they must start immediately. Within as little as 24 hours after losing their cubs the females come into season and start flirting outrageously with the new males.

This flirting consists of a female whipping with her tail the heads of male lions who are lying at the water's edge, and settling down near them, her hind-quarters nearest them. She is then mounted by a male.

> The females are nervous at first, a bit scared of the new males; but the orgies in the first few months after a takeover are [amused tone] a good ice-breaker, and soon strong bonds are formed.

There is something unsettling about a female voice delivering this script, which undoubtedly bears the signs of a 'masculine' text in its narration (the way it tells the story) and its address (the attitudes it assumes or wants us to share). Female viewers may, unconsciously or consciously, be aware of absences, not only in the content (why did the females leave the cubs unprotected?) but in the area of emotional address, and aware too of patriarchal language, imagery and attitudes. Rula Lenska speaks from within the classic male orientation of prime-time television, and indeed of science.

Wildlife issues could be handled differently. The narration could be more accommodating of different responses among the audience. Instead of the single (normally male) authorial voice of scientific truth, we could have many more, divergent voices. More open, multiplex scripts could replace the so-called phallocentric structures, with less reliance being placed on narrative as a controlling form, a form which demands closure. The scripts could be based around uncertainties in interpreting animal behaviour and debates about the status of scientific knowledge; above all, the programmes could validate lines of enquiry which have historically been silenced by the male domination of science, and which natural history programmes have consistently skirted round.

Perspective 2: the scientific context
The appropriateness of some of these alternatives is evident in the considerable body of scholarship which has now emerged to challenge patriarchal science. Research into animal behaviour based on practices or

hypotheses – or producing findings – that counter the orthodoxies of male science has until recently been denied serious attention.

A great deal of feminist biological research is in the field of primatology. The attraction for women of studying those animals closest in evolutionary terms to human beings may be the necessity of confronting there, in close-up, questions about what it means to be human. Donna Haraway's description of primatology as 'a complex scientific construction of self and other, culture and nature, gender and sex, human and animal, purpose and resource, actor and acted upon'[15] identifies crucial distinctions, and these have always been determined and controlled by men. Women may see them differently. Indeed, different women may see them differently again. According to Haraway: 'Field primatologists are particularly aware of and troubled by the patent differences in the primatologies authored by men or women, Japanese or Dutch nationals, British ethologists, or North American physical anthropologists.'[16]

Many radical scientists want to dismantle the myth of objectivity and neutrality on which 'rational' science is based, stressing instead the interactive nature of ethological study. Observers of animal behaviour carry personal and cultural histories and assumptions (a point traditional scientists tend to disregard); how far these may affect their interpretations is an open and salient issue. Furthermore, terms and labels used to describe and differentiate scientific subjects, and the knowledges on which these depend, may themselves be pre-emptive. The concept of a stable 'truth' is seen as increasingly problematic. Michel Foucault's claim that truth is produced through discourse is discussed in relation to science by Ruth Bleier: discourses, she explains, develop 'rules of exclusion' which 'determine who speaks, what is and is not discussed, how it is discussed, what questions may be asked, and what is "true" or "false"'.[17] The rules of orthodox scientific discourse can be traced to the earliest forms of training and thought, and are played out in the structures through which that discourse is sustained.

Epistemology and scientific convention

Schoolchildren, according to Lynda Birke, undergo a process of 'desensitisation' in biology courses, with the result that many girls, already socialised to be more sensitive than boys, are put off advanced biological training. This process is exacerbated by the procedures and ethos of experimental laboratories where it is considered important 'not to let your emotions get in the way': 'Objective detachment is . . . stereotypically masculine in our culture . . . To identify with your animals (a more 'feminine' position) is to cease to be objective.'[18] Birke argues that feminist science must engage with ethical as well as academic debates in science, the procedures as well as the product of research, because the way animals are treated by science 'calls into question beliefs about scientific objectivity and neutrality, which rest on assumptions about the 'otherness' of the subject-matter of science.'[19]

At the core of patriarchal rationality, in its preoccupation with constructing and controlling the Other, lies the nature/culture dualism. Women's place in the nature/culture opposition is ambiguous, being subsumed in the term 'Man' yet included as the opposite of man. Masculine culture, of which science is a part, situates women on the side of nature, conventionally representing us as closer to nature than men are, because of 'female instinct' or 'irrationality' for example. The nature/culture opposition overlaps conceptually with the male/female opposition. These symbolic divisions, in anthropology as much as in science, depend on perceiving the behaviour of the Other as inferior, as well as homogeneous and invariable.

Sexual dualism has become a 'naturalised' epistemological paradigm in our culture. Its reductivism, in encouraging generalisations about 'men' and 'women', emphasising polar differences, and universalising the experience of being a man or a woman, restricts individual and human possibilities. As a dominant paradigm in science too, sexual dimorphism may over-determine 'objective' research.[20] Reflecting similar movements in other areas of feminist theory, some scientists are trying to move away from the simple male/female duality towards a model that emphasises differences within a sex too. Studies are now examining sexual diversity within a species, even within a group, and inconsistent behaviour in an animal individual. But there is uncertainty among some feminist scientists about whether to go on emphasising the continuities between animals and humans, and male and female, or whether to stress the discontinuities and differences between animals and humans to keep up the assault on biological essentialism. If they continue with the former, it becomes crucial to challenge generalisations about animal behaviour, and to focus research much more on specifics. Choosing the latter course, arguing for human difference, means joining battle against the mobilised power of sociobiology, the new orthodoxy of popular science.

Sociobiology
The 'structural-functionalist' model of behaviour current during the greater part of this century argues that animal behaviour patterns

(including human ones) can be explained in terms of adaptive responses 'functioning' to serve individual and group needs. Sociobiology evolved from this model in the mid-1970s, realigning this explanation within biology – 'According to the sociobiologists, behaviours always evolve to maximise the reproductive fitness of individuals.'[21] Its emergence is seen by Sperling as an attempt to counter the rise of feminism, as its reductivism, determinism and biological purism run contrary to the politics of women's liberation, and seek to discredit it scientifically. Its tendency to 'inflate certain characteristics common to both humans and animals while underplaying or erasing the vast distinctions between them . . . [and its] disavowal of the uniqueness of humanity' renders this 'determination of society and culture through the genes' unacceptable to many scientists.[22]

However, not all feminist researchers have rejected sociobiology; some have used it to argue for a more pro-active model of female sexual behaviour. Sarah B. Hrdy and her fellow researchers, for example, have described patterns of exemplary non-sexist behaviour among some animals, and perceive 'female mate choice and female elicitation of male support and protection in rearing young as integral to the competitive strategies of females *vis-à-vis* other females'.[23] Attempts by feminists to redress the male bias of sociobiology, however, have not received wide academic support. It provides useful scientific buttressing for patriarchy. Indeed, an attraction, and a problem, of sociobiology is that it can be manipulated to support quite dubious social theories, and it is vulnerable to appropriation in easy equations and reductive formulas, which – passed off as science – is exactly the kind of material that suits entertainment television rather too well.

Popular biologism has its dangers. For example, the tenet that penetrative sex is an overwhelming, uncontrollable genetically programmed urge in the animal world can too easily be recruited to 'justify' aggressive sexual behaviour in the human male. And by concentrating so much on the reproductive imperative, sociobiology also normalises heterosexual sex, and renders homosexuality 'unnatural' (and bigotry therefore rational). Because of the way sociobiology is used, and the orientation of its most powerful publicists, it may be hard for lay people to muster counterarguments on its own terms. Shirley Strum's work, for instance, investigates other animal drives for pleasure and security, which could be used to argue strongly for the value and naturalness of same-sex relationships. It also exposes how marginal penetrative sex is in the fuller picture of animals' activities.[24]

Politics and storytelling

Sociobiology is presented on television as the obvious, unchallengable explanation for human behaviour. Alex Rowe, in an article advertising *The Trials of Life*, remarks:

> Humans made it, a human presents it, and a whole lot of humans will watch it – yet nowhere are humans mentioned. But by adding a touch of anthropomorphism to the narration and the titling . . . it [is] obvious that it is about us too. Sociobiology, *The Trials of Life* is saying (without saying anything about it), is simply one branch of ethology.[25]

The fact that sociobiology has its detractors is never signalled, here or in the programmes. David Attenborough's espousal of it inevitably gives it credibility with the public. But its politics are very important. With its discourse of inheritance, blood lineage, the family (using terms like monogamy and polygamy), territory, competition, and male dominance, it finds capitalist social structures and ruling-class concerns to be 'natural' in the animal world.

Sometimes patriarchy betrays its vulnerable points, such as in the closing words of *The Tale of the Pregnant Male*, a programme about seahorses, the only species in the world where the male gets pregnant:

> Seahorse fathers show that it's possible to be both a macho male and a caring parent, though why they in particular have such a tough time remains a bit of a mystery. On the other hand they are probably the only fathers in the world who can be really certain, one hundred percent, of the paternity of all their offspring.

Sexual politics can be seen to underlie this script (fittingly narrated by Attenborough); similarly, politics can be said to underlie academic scientific theories and methods too. Donna Haraway, rather than characterising the history of scientific development as 'progress', sees it as a sequence of 'contesting stories', myths that support particular political positions in relation to sex, race, class, and so on. She sees science as evolving 'through complex historically specific storytelling practices',[26] and sees the role of feminist interpreters of science as central in the current stage of the contest.

The challenge is how to mount the contest in the popular idiom, for the debate is still confined to the academic world. There is no doubt that the kind of topics feminist ethology is addressing could provide television wildlife programmes, even in their conventional form, with compelling material, such as the behaviour and role of infertile or post-reproductive females, sex as a pleasurable activity not necessarily dominated by the need to reproduce, or whether females ever express a preference for the less bullish males.[27] The continued resistance to gyno-focused stories has to be seen as political, contributing (perhaps unconsciously, though this is increasingly hard to argue) to the uneven balance of power in society. The politics is concealed behind the safety curtain of a classic genre, reliably uncontroversial, apolitical, whose established style demonstrates no difficulty in mediating between scientific and everyday discourse.

Perspective 3: media studies

Television natural history texts cannot be analysed simply as texts of science. The programmes are conceived and the scripts written with a different set of conventions and a different audience in mind from that of scientific research papers. They need to be seen as television texts too. There are a number of fronts in media studies on which feminist interrogation of television can and does take place. Three of the most fruitful in this context are the study of television audiences, their composition and the different relationships they have with a programme; the issues of representation and form, and the visual and narrative conventions employed by television in general (and television genres specifically); and the production aspect, the division of work and power in the industry itself.

Audience research

Current audience research is focusing on how different groups use and respond to different kinds of programme. Since the early 1980s the ethnographic study of television viewing has gained ground, noting not only the different positions in respect of perceived 'messages' that groups can adopt – making (in David Morley's terms) dominant, oppositional or negotiated readings, and subtle modulations of these within texts[28] – but also noting the uses to which television, and genres within it, are put by certain groups.[29] One audience group that has elicited particular attention is the family, since it is in the family context that a great proportion of television is viewed.[30] Just watching television together, these studies show, is for many families a high point, if not the climax, of family interaction, an opportunity for raising and discussing personal issues vicariously, and seeking and giving opinions.

Parents, and particularly fathers, still have the most control over programme choice.[31] Wildlife programmes are almost always transmitted in the slot scheduled as family viewing time, in the two or three hours before the 9pm watershed. Although they are not normally perceived, in critical or domestic circles, as gendered television (unlike soap operas and sport), a recent survey has found that men, far more than women, claim to have a particular affinity with them, rating them (collectively) second only to the national news as the programmes they prefer to watch. The women's top-ten chart does not feature them at all.[32]

There are a number of ways of looking at this 'emotional commitment' among men. The 'masculinity' of the conventional form and address adopted by the genre, as analysed earlier, may contribute to this sense of affiliation; so may other things, such as the photographic and technical virtuosity, the heavy emphasis on 'facts', and the use of quasi-technical terms (like thorax, marsupial or oestrus) which in context are self-explanatory but which serve to bridge the space between everyday discourse and the more male world of scientific discourse. Adults, and not only men, may like to feel they are educating themselves, and to feel that their children are benefitting from the same experience; but wildlife films also provide a link with a discourse familiar from childhood – they are, at base, stories about animals in a tell-and-show format, the words matched with illustrations.

In the context of both education and family viewing, one thing wildlife programmes provide, indirectly, is an opportunity for discussing sexual matters – the so-called 'facts' of life. For some children this is as close as they get to human sex-talk with their parents (some don't even get this far). Using the (animal) examples on the screen allows allusions to be made without getting personally involved. This mirrors the kind of communication Dorothy Hobson found among women at work, that is, 'the use of events within [television] fiction to explore experiences which were perhaps too personal or painful to talk about'.[33]

If wildlife programmes do have this educational function, families, and women and girls in particular, could surely be better served by a more gynocentric focus. There is still widespread ignorance, secrecy and embarrassment within families surrounding human female biology.[34] Indeed the whole natural history genre could be cast in a different educational mould and explore other topics – physiology, medical conditions, hormone activity, fertility, aging, and so on. But there is no 'demand' for this.

Representation: conventions and codes
Turning now from the viewing experience to the screen itself, to the strategies and devices by which the content takes form, it is useful to employ semiotics, which has been influential in literary as well as film and media studies. This focuses on the constructed nature of audio-visual texts and how meanings are made from them. Programme-makers always

claim their artistic choices and operations are made largely unconsciously – they just know what works, and they have rules and conventions to stick to – but the demystification of those processes is important in order to make the conventions, and the unconscious, visible, and to loosen the grip of the ideologies that are naturalised through them. The semiotic approach makes it possible to see how ideological connotations may be encoded in the images and language (and other technical practices) of a text, by showing that each element of an image or utterance could be different, and command a different connotative field.

Where gender issues are concerned, this is highly significant, since there is a tendency for television discourse – like the discourse of biological science – to be thought of as natural. In *The Tale of the Pregnant Male*, there are some interesting sequences which include a woman scientist, Amanda Vincent, who is end-credited as the film's scientific adviser but introduced only as studying the 'bizarre breeding behaviour' of seahorses. She is the first seen in a laboratory among tanks of seahorses (signifying 'scientist'), but the narration humorously describes her as a 'midwife' in a 'maternity ward'. In itself this is not particularly significant, but, taken with other aspects of the film, it can be seen as part of a systematic (even if unconscious) de-professionalisation of her role. Though she is (briefly, twice) granted the privilege of direct address, her quiet, North American delivery is sandwiched between blocks of Attenborough's voice talking authoritatively about her work and her findings. She is referred to throughout as Amanda ('Amanda's real interest is in their courtship and mating . . . Amanda has discovered that courtship takes time'); and the camerawork codes her very much as 'attractive young female', drawing on the conventions of western film aesthetics – lingering shots on her face, close-up of her dark eyes 'observing', low lighting that eliminates harsh shadows – making her the object of the viewer's gaze.

A feature of wildlife programmes that encourages passive acceptance of the text as neutral and transparent is their use of techniques associated with the realist mode, the conventional mode for fiction films. There might be an argument for developing a more Brechtian aesthetic for natural history programmes, to draw attention to the naturalising (reactionary) effects of realism. While the production team and its technology (cameras, lights, microphones, cables and suchlike) are kept out of view, one can almost forget the human work and creativity involved in the production process – and one certainly cannot see how scarce women are in the production teams.

The industry

Equal opportunities is becoming a serious issue in the television industry. Increasingly, attention is being drawn to the large discrepancy in the numbers of men and women employed in almost every sphere of television production – three to one in broadcasting overall – a discrepancy which is widening as management policies reduce the number of permanent posts in favour of temporary or contract work.[35] Natural history programmes are a particularly male bastion, as the credits at the end of the films will confirm. The nature of the work, particularly filming in exotic locations, can be exciting and adventurous, but the shoots may be endlessly protracted – not particularly suitable work for anyone with unsupported domestic responsibilities. Rather than modifying the working conditions to enable those with normal family demands to contribute, the demands of the job as it is presently organised determine who can be included in the projects.[36]

A new wildlife sub-genre is emerging that reflects this sense of exclusivity and specialism. How-they-shot-it programmes celebrate the film crew itself, showing their dedication, their daring and their mastery over prestigious high-tech equipment. They are often depicted as working for long periods in dangerous conditions, and enduring considerable discomfort, far from home – emulating in their way the heroes of other wildlife narratives. Recent developments in photographic and video technology, and the technicians' enthusiasm for showing them off, may indeed be determining one of the routes along which the genre is now developing, as the positive response to a series like *Supersense* (which tried to represent animals' sensory perceptions visually – and had its own spin-off *The Making of Supersense*) is read as a 'demand' for more. It may indeed be virtually impossible to break the patriarchal grip of this 'quality' genre without the macho work ethos being challenged from inside the industry.

The structures of the television industry, and particularly the wildlife film units, evince and reinforce the same patriarchal models and attitudes as the 'science' it purports to convey 'objectively'. In science as in other academic disciplines, an increase in the number of women has enabled a body of feminist work to start developing. Now a significant change is needed in the proportion of women holding positions of authority in the television industry – not just more individuals trained in the traditional masculine ways of thinking and operating, but enough women for an alternative critical culture to be taken seriously, and structural changes implemented. Then a reconceptualisation of natural history programmes might be effected in ways that could better serve the female viewing public.

Notes

1. Carl Gardner and Robert Young, 'Science on TV: a critique' in Tony Bennett *et al.* (eds), *Popular Television and Film*, London, British Film Institute (1981) pp. 171–93, p. 171.

2. See, for example, Gardner and Young, op. cit.; Neil Ryder *Science, Television and the Adolescent*, London, Independent Broadcasting Authority (1982); Roger Silverstone, 'Narrative strategies in television science', *Media, Culture and Society*, VI, 1984, pp. 377–410, also *Framing Science: The Making of a BBC Documentary*, London, British Film Institute (1985), and 'The agonistic narratives of television science' in J. Corner (ed.), *Documentary and the Mass Media*, London, Edward Arnold (1986) pp. 81–106; and Andrew Hart *et al.*, *Making The Real World*, Cambridge, Cambridge University Press (1988).

3. The previous year's programme on Severn Wildfowl, the BBC's first wildlife outside broadcast, was probably less influential in launching the genre than Walt Disney's imaginative film, *The Living Desert*, which was also released in 1953.

4. Roger Silverstone draws attention to the way science documentaries rely on narrative (mythic) forms to frame the more literal (mimetic) representations and arguments of science. He suggests that 'In the persistence of mythic forms, television adopts, but adapts, forms of traditional storytelling which link its products directly . . . with man's archetypal capacity for telling stories.' ('Narrative strategies in television science', op. cit. p. 388.)

5. See, for instance, Dick Leith and George Myerson, *The Power of Address: Explorations in Rhetoric*, London, Routledge (1989).

6. Ruth Bleier, *Science and Gender*, London, Pergamon (1984) p. 192.

7. David Attenborough, *The Trials of Life*, London, Collins/BBC Books (1990) p. 300.

8. Emily Martin, 'The Egg and the Sperm', *Signs*, XVI, 1991, pp. 485–501, p. 490.

9. Female field researchers seem to be given different treatment. Film profiles of self-sacrificial woman ethologists, such as Diane Fossey and Jane Goodall, concentrate not on an object of quest or a discovery, but on their personal adaptation to life in the wild, and their relationships with the primates they observe (a reflection, no doubt, on the necessarily slow pace of their research). Their femaleness, to a great extent, is the topic of these films, which have more affinity perhaps to the Tarzan legend than the folk-tale.

10. In *Quest in the Flooded Forest* Friedman Koester's wife Heide, though end-credited with her husband as having done the filming, is only mentioned once in the hour-long narration – 'Friedman's wife Heide accompanied them on their first trip to Cuyabeno' – and only seen briefly, at a distance.

11. A rather more paradoxical version of this story is appearing more frequently with the burgeoning of the conservation industry. In this version, the disequilibrium is not a mystery but a (potential) tragedy of nature, often one that is man-made: impending extinction or habitat destruction. Conflicting interests are measured against each other. It combines a doomsday script with a conservation script, ultimately taking an optimistic culture-can-win tone – if 'we' can generate the political will, 'we' can forestall disaster. Here is the environmental paradox: Man is the danger – trust Us.

12. Luce Irigaray challenges the value placed on Aristotelian logic and rational exposition and calls for a switch to two-ness and multiplicity. In terms of television science this would surely include the recording of doubts, contradictory readings and subjective responses.

13. The emotional effect of factors like the pace of the verbal delivery and the length of pauses cannot adequately be dealt with here; nor can factors like music or editing or camerawork (for instance, distance from the subject); yet each of these has an important rhetorical function.

14. One of Attenborough's film sequences shows a female wading-bird, a lily-trotter, destroying the clutch of eggs which a male (whose mate has recently been killed) has been hatching. His commentary frames the sequence in a rational explanation, based on genetic programming:

> She starts to smash them and he is unable to prevent her. They were on the verge of hatching. Having destroyed his brood she now offers herself to him, and the bereaved male mates with the murderer of his chicks. (*Continuing the Line*)

It is hard not to feel disgust at the pictures of nearly full-term embryos being hurled around in a frenzy, and to feel sympathy for the apparently distraught male, but the last of these commentary sentences deviates from the merely descriptive, and carries (largely through the words 'bereaved', 'murderer' and 'chicks') an emotive, even judgemental, dimension. It would have been possible to script the sequence to acknowledge the disturbing and complex range of emotions stirred in some viewers. But the unity and linearity of the programme's argument takes priority.

15. Donna Haraway, 'Primatology is politics by other means' in Ruth Bleier (ed.), *Feminist Approaches to Science*, Oxford, Pergamon (1988) pp. 77–118, p. 82.

16. Ibid., p. 79.

17. Bleier (1984) op. cit., p. 194.

18. Lynda Birke, 'Science, feminism and animal natures II: feminist critiques and the place of animals in science', *Women's Studies International Forum*, XIV, 1991, pp. 451–458, p. 453.

19. Ibid., p. 457. Indeed, the way animals are used and disposed of by filmmakers in the service of competitive entertainment television should also come under ethical scrutiny. In *The Observer* (22 March 1990) Ceri Griffiths of the Welsh Hawking Centre, who orchestrates predatory sequences for the BBC's Natural History Unit, explains that 'it would be impossible to get some of the shots in the wild, I thought everybody knew they were rigged,' and repeats the claim that it is 'the public [who are] demanding closer shots and more dramatic action in wildlife programmes'. The public should perhaps be more concerned at the concealment of this manipulation carried out in its name in programmes which use every strategy of film realism (including arranging the killing of the very creatures they are purporting to celebrate) to present to their trusting viewers the illusion of animal subjects observed 'naturally'.

20. Susan Sperling writes: 'For over two decades, an obsession with gender-role dimorphism (sexually differing behaviors) as an adaptive mechanism has impeded our understanding of the origins and maintenance of such sexually distinct behaviors in primates – behaviors that, after all, vary greatly both within and across species.' (Sperling, 'Baboons with briefcases: feminism, functionalism, and sociobiology in the evolution of primate gender', *Signs*, XVII, 1991, pp. 1–27, p. 6.).

21. Ibid., p. 3.

22. Evelyn Reed, from whom these quotations are taken, was an early and outspoken critic of sociobiology. The quotations are from 'Sociobiology and pseudoscience' in Reed, *Sexism and Science*, New York, Pathfinder Press (1978) pp. 34–53, p. 34, and 'Primatology and prejudice', ibid., pp. 8–33, p. 21.

23. Sperling, op. cit. p. 18. Haraway too claims Hrdy has 'centred females in her accounts in ways that have destabilised generalisations about what sociobiology must say about female animals or human women' (Haraway, op. cit. p. 108.)

24. See, for example, 'Life with the pumphouse gang', *National Geographic*, May 1975, pp. 672–91.

25. 'All us animals' in the supplement to the BBC *Wildlife* magazine, VIII, Oct. 1990, pp. 9–11, p. 11.

26. Haraway, op. cit. p. 79.
27. Donna Haraway notes that the concerns of Meredith Small's (prohibitively expensive) book, *Female Primates: Studies by Women Primatologists* include 'postmenopausal animals, female adolescence, female sexual exuberance, feeding strategies, mating systems explained from the point of view of female biology as the independent variable, and much else'. (Haraway, op. cit., p. 102.)
28. David Morley *The 'Nationwide' Audience*, London, British Film Institute (1980).
29. See, for instance, Dorothy Hobson, 'Women audiences and the workplace', Mary Ellen Brown (ed.) *Television and Women's Culture*, London, Sage (1990) pp. 61–71.
30. See particularly David Morley, *Family Television: Cultural Power and Domestic Leisure*, London, Comedia (1986), and James Lull, *Inside Family Viewing*, London, Routledge (1990).
31. A man in one of the families in Morley's research says: 'We discuss what we all want to watch and the biggest wins. That's me. I'm the biggest.' Morley (1986), op. cit., p. 148.
32. Source: British Market Research Bureau/Target Group Index, 1991.
33. Hobson, op. cit., p. 65.
34. The barrage of complaints following recent television advertisements for sanitary pads is evidence of this. See Judy Sadgrove's article 'High and Dry', *The Guardian*, 17 March 1992, p. 37.
35. The most recent comprehensive figures for Britain show a depressingly familiar picture of the division of labour in the skilled and technical jobs and in the influential positions in production. While production assistants, administrators and make-up personnel are overwhelmingly female, women comprise only 3–4 per cent of camera and sound technicians in the BBC and 'a typical ITV [Independent Television] company' has none at all. The higher up the scale in management and production the lower the proportion of women, but even on the lowest scale there are likely to be two-and-a-half to three times as many men as women. (Source: Institute of Manpower Studies, London, 1989.)
36. In the week before *Trials of Life* was broadcast, BBC Radio 4's Woman's Hour interviewed three women wildlife filmmakers: one of these specialised in producing 'back-garden' programmes and another producer admitted that being married to her cameraman made it easier to work abroad.

Repositioning feminist subjects

9 A child of war

JEAN GRANT

I came to write this paper when I was the only artist in a workshop* considering themes of identity and notions of the disappeared with a small group of Art historians. I became increasingly frustrated. The issues seemed oversimplified. The agenda wasn't mine and socio-historical contexts basic to an understanding of my work were not mentioned. In that workshop this artist had disappeared behind the constructs. The following is an attempt to 'read' my text. Text for me is installations or audio-visual slide shows. Perversely 'reading' it deprives me of nearly all my sensory tools. I am left with black and white silent and flat apart from the turning of the page. Please be patient with the pages; sit close and quiet before you begin to unravel the reflections of realities beneath the surface and connect with the action underneath.

*Maud Sulter, Hysteria: a Symposium on Women's Art History considering themes of Modernity, Identity and Notions of the Disappeared, Tate Liverpool Sept. 1991.

I was born in July 1940, 2 months after my father and his ship were blown up in Poole Harbour. No one seems to have any facts. He is a number on a War Memorial in Portsmouth.

I was brought up by a mother traumatised by the destruction of her husband. I was born to a mother who on waking from a birth during which she nearly lost her own life picked me up to cuddle me put her finger in my hand and discovered my hands were deformed.

I went to a charity boarding school for children whose fathers had been killed in the war. I was not considered suitable material for 'O' level art. Drawing kippers, fire buckets and mops bored me silly! . . .. I felt very alone, unable to identify with most of the girls and uninterested in the boys.

To me my life was normal I needed my own family to begin to learn of right and wrong and love and cuddles and all the snotty imperfection of family life.

To me the N. H. S. and the right to a free welfare state were my father's memorial 'what we fought for.' Beveridge's vision and Attlee and Churchill's promises that the war had made it impossible for things to ever be the same again are what I learnt constantly on the radio of my childhood.

I believe that most people at that time believed as I did, it was not a childish misunderstanding. The collective memory seems to have forgotten those promises, although many of us have thrived because of them. I because of my father could not forget.

Mrs Thatcher destroyed the memorial. I could not believe the Falklands was happening and the Gulf was even worse. Many of my images were dealing with bereavement. It became important to me that I try to recreate my father's last moments. What I have attempted to do has been ghastly and horrific, but brought me a feeling of comfort.

In the current politics I want to share my images.

Historically wars are always painted as glorious!

I find it impossible to believe that they were ever as portrayed.

The War Museum has a fascinating collection of paintings demonstrating this point. Many Artists are recording what they want to see, or the patron has instructed them to show.

More recently Artists painted from photographs in the safety of their studios. Richard Eurich is a typical example, he stated in his letter of application to become a war artist 'Now the epic subject I have been waiting for, the Dunkirk episode seems to me to demand the traditional sea painting of Van der Velde and Turner!'. . . . I know that is not how I feel. The artist who does more than record or do an exercise in their own style is very small.

Paul Nash is one of the few examples of an Artist dealing with emotion and fear. Julian Trevelyan also falls into this category. They are in a minority.

Sadly the Gulf Photographs on exhibition are similarly about style and portray a very sanitised event.

There is a collection of Women War Artists work, they also tend to have limitations.

Mary Kessel records what she sees in the City with great feeling and emotion but it is much as she did before and after the war and I wonder if her statements are more about society than the actuality of war.

Stella Schmolle is recording what she sees at a safe distance from the War zone. It may as well be a scout camp!

Dame Laura Knight entered the war campaign with gusto producing work for the war effort and our *splendid boys*.

Linda Kitson is the first woman to go to the front. She went to the Falklands and as a woman her work received a lot of publicity. She is reported as saying that she went in her professional role as a graphic artist and that the main difficulty she encountered was the cold.

I have always painted people. As a teenager it was ballet dancers enclosed in box like stage sets. Guildford Art School politicised me, gave me friends, male and female, I could identify with, and a sense of belonging.

Teaching and post graduate studies at the Slade isolated me again. I could not identify with Harold Cohen's abstractions, Coldstream's realist neurosis or Pop. My paintings of Greek myths became choruses of over life size, male, heads many of them screaming. My speciality as a lecturer was colour etching the relief seemed closer to reality.

I probably made the first photo gravure by a woman. Print unions were a closed shop in those days!

My first sea pictures are printed with relief so that as the viewer moves the sea swells up and down. The first blush was part of a goddess series with pigment running in the valleys of the relief.

I lectured at several art colleges, helped run a print workshop, sold work and gradually decided that all this was not for me.

In 'career terms' I had done surprisingly well. Women were unknown as lecturers in Fine Art departments in the early seventies.

My heads closed up, losing their features. I felt I would go mad if I continued. It seemed as if art was too dilettante and that it served no useful purpose for me or society, so as my images closed up I finished that phase of my life and married.

Over the next 20 years I had a family, worked in the peace movement and in the local community and enabled my children to learn at home. My life was very busy and exciting and apparently successful but I had bricked myself in.

During my marriage my only art work was potato cuts, family greetings cards, community newspapers, and assemblies on my bedroom window ledge. I felt that living was my creative statement. Ecrouid the monster took over.

About 5 years ago I started to draw quietly in bed sometimes on the backs of old envelopes, sometimes in tiny notebooks. It seemed very important that I did something small, humble and private, I did not want to make ART. I wrestled with gods, goddesses, serpents, female crucifixions and screaming heads, I just let them come and did not worry about style, image or saleability. They were mine and very precious to me. Over several years I took my ever increasing collection everywhere with me but showed it to people only once or twice.

I also bought an old kiln and started to hand build using my understanding of relief in a joyfully flexible way.

I found Marion Milner's books and felt a path I could identify with. She is a Jungian psychoanalyst. Her books explore her feelings about herself and her abilities.
'Foster the capacity to see for oneself rather than seeing only what one is told to see'.

Raynes Minns *Bombers and Mash* reinforced what I was remembering. She includes the following excerpt from *Living Together Again*, a War time publication to aid families deal with separation.

'To tell a child about a dead parent roughly or with uncontrolled emotion does real damage to the child's sensitive mind and feelings.

When the circumstances of life have been sordid or tragic it is better to leave out all detail and just quietly state the facts taking the child's attention forward to something new and interesting, such as "if daddy were here now he would have loved to see that new wireless set you have just made".'

Jean Dubuffet wrote: Art does not lie down on the bed that is made for it. It runs away as soon as one says its name. It loves to be incognito its best moments are when it forgets what it is called. His collection *L'art Brut* is in Lausanne.

Monica Kinley has a wonderful collection of Outsider Art and I saw an exhibition of some of her collection at the Cornerhouse in Manchester. I knew I was an outsider creating work from a deep need within, not part of a movement.

As a young woman I think my unconscious knew what I had to do, but in a typically female way I undervalued what it was. Jo Spence *Putting Myself in the Picture* p. 86, is discussing the same thing, the horror of war for a child, and the lack of acknowledgement to that child of what is happening. It is a horror that our society does not acknowledge, and yet our children not only have parents who may be damaged by the 1940 war but grandparents who were similarly damaged by the 1914/18 war.

Maybe through struggling to portray and understand my own feelings through my own work I have produced something closer to the feelings and fears of those usually women and children left at home. Something which the media has generally failed to do in war situations. Possibly, the armed services, politicians and most artists do not want to or can't accept or understand this point of view.

I had to go away from art and 'ferment' in order to find out that which it was worthwhile to communicate. Opting out in this fashion is not a hierarchical option, even in art circles, if you want a successful competitive career.

I did quite a lot of work relating to my father before the Dunkirk anniversary but the Gulf really set me off. It is a dreadful process to go through and yet wherever there is war innocent children without number have this sort of trauma to bear. The attempts to put Humpty Dumpty together again despite the mess the king's horses made. I felt it had to be seen. I am exhibiting now as often as I can and women come and thank me because it is the first time they have recognised their feelings about war being portrayed. Women whose husbands had been in the Gulf have said that although they had a lot of support whilst their husbands were away, they could identify with my screaming heads and recognise their feelings in a way the media did not. This recognition is very rich and important to me.

At the time it seemed it was my father I was putting together but now I think the process is about me I could not feel whole until I had completed it.

My father is mincemeat at the bottom of the sea. If a man is blown up it is even less organised than mincemeat.
Full fathom five thy father lies. Of his bones are coral made. Those are pearls that were his eyes. Nothing of him that doth not change into something rich and strange.
1940 must have been a good year for the fish

The death of Nelson. A national event even depicted as an epic scene at Madame Taussaud's waxworks. I seem to be talking about contrasts, contradictions and searching for resolution

When your father is blown up in the ocean he becomes disseminated. A swim is the best way to give him a hug.

My father is buried at sea with a bell for me to ring him. 'I will make a labyrinth to the bottom of the ocean, will I meet him or me? It must be my father for I am Safe on the shore. My father is mincemeat and the sun shines black. How can I talk to mincemeat. Do I have to give it a name?

Is it only I that can be angry? No the sea is angry. The sea takes him away on a raft.'

BE STRONG AND CRY

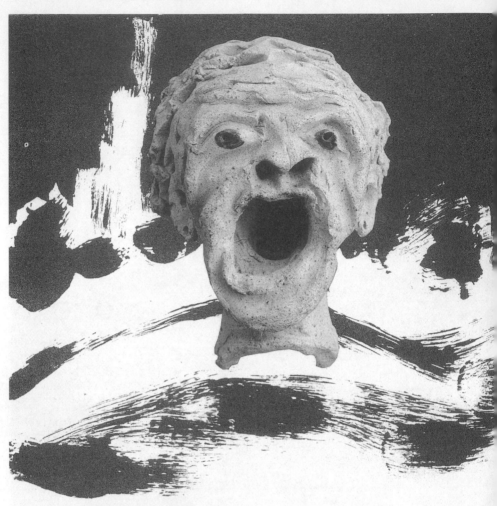

sea nymphs hourly ring his knell

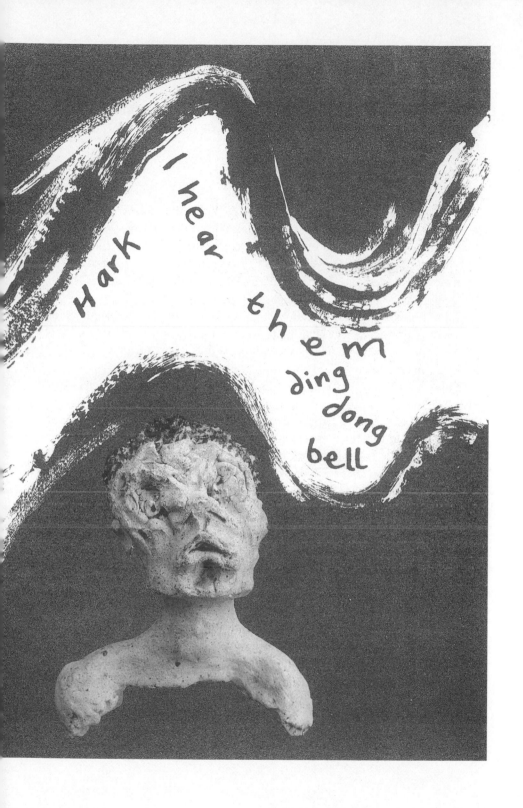

10 'I' the reader: text, context and the balance of power

LYNNE PEARCE

This essay takes the form of an autobiographical account of my own history as a 'gendered reader' and the sexual/textual politics involved in each of my many readerly incarnations or 'positionings'. My methodology here is to utilize the perspectives of critical hindsight to reveal how each new self-positioning arose in reaction to the inadequacies of the former, but was then itself abandoned as a new set of textual and political pressures closed in. The visual metaphor that springs to mind is of someone trying to cross a river by leaping from slippery stone to slippery stone; of being propelled precariously onwards, only to find each new footing no more secure than the last.

This recognition – that the rocks on which we stand as readers are ever-liable to be swept away from under us – also accounts for the ironic cast of my retrospective. It seems to me that this picaresque journey of ideological and ethical scrapes, of (inter)textual twists and turns, is not one that *could* be told 'straight'; that it is predicated upon the (postmodernist) recognition that none of us will ever make it to the (politically) safe ground on the other side of the river! Prompted into a consideration of 'irony as methodological strategy' by the editors of this volume, however, I have concluded that it was more especially the means by which I was able to *mediate* between my own experience and that of other (women) readers; irony enabled me to objectify and hence *specify* my experiences in a manner to which my readers will, I hope, relate.

To reflect upon the constraints, conditions and expectations imposed upon each and every one of us when we undertake to read a text as a woman, as a feminist, is, in itself, a profoundly political act and – however much we are forced to laugh at our efforts to protect our ethical integrity – it is, in my opinion, a useful form of intellectual narcissism. The particular focus of my self-scrutiny here – the relative power of *text* and *context* in the production of textual meaning – derives directly from the methodological issues raised by my book on Pre-Raphaelite art and literature, *Woman/Image/Text*, and also from my involvement with Sara Mills's edited collection of essays *Gendering the Reader*.[1] However, as the following narrative will attest, there have been many embarrassments and misadventures *en route* to these more mature reflections.

In the beginning which, in my case, lasted until at least half-way through my first degree, the thing that shall henceforth be known as 'the text' had one sure source of meaning, the author's, and one sure reader: me. As a student of literature, my role was to attempt to reach the author through his words (and, of course, I use the masculine pronoun advisedly); to reconstruct his meanings and intentions through a process of sensitive and polite probing.

The most curious thing I now remember about this time was my fondness for the pronoun 'we'. Despite the elitism of my 'sensitive' engagement with the text, I was always happy to share my responses with a group of anonymous but like-minded readers: as in the instance of my brave attempt to empathise with Stephen Daedalus in James Joyce's *Portrait of an Artist as a Young Man.* My senior school essays on *A Portrait* abound with sentences like: 'Chapter two is essentially a period of transition with regard to *our feelings* toward Stephen' and 'Unless the reader has himself reached the years of cynicism, bitterness is not an attractive quality (!)' Looking back over the essays, it is evident that I had to work extremely hard to empathise with Joyce's representative of male adolescence, but the 'anonymous' 'we' clearly gave me the means to grit my teeth and try. The fact that I was also sublimating my own gendered identity never occurred to me: English Literature as it was taught at school meant becoming a transvestite-reader on a permanent basis. No matter how complex the reader-positioning of the texts concerned, we were trained to respond as universalised male subjects.

It is also a significant comment on the limitations of English Literature as it was taught to me at university that my perception of the existence of a balance of power between author, text and reader only really became clear when I began my doctoral research. My Ph.D., on the nineteenth-century peasant poet, John Clare, was undertaken at Birmingham University, where the sudden blast of critical theory offered by the staff-postgraduate seminar (then led by David Lodge) turned me from a passive reader into a textual activist. It was the early 1980s: the time when the British academic system was desperately scrambling to catch up with Barthes, Derrida, Foucault, and, to my own particular peril, Mikhail Bakhtin. Suddenly the author was dead, the text 'untied', its meaning multiple, and the reader in a position of unprecedented power. With reckless confidence I set about releasing all the hidden voices from John Clare's now manifestly 'polyphonic' texts, employing deconstructive strategies to reveal their loss of faith in Romantic theories of language and the imagination.[2]

Powerful as I now was as a reader, however, I had yet to catch up with a sense of my gendered identity. Although I was teaching overtly feminist courses by this time, the material I was working with elsewhere failed to seem relevant to my work as a reader of John Clare. In terms of the text-reader equation, I can now explain this as the direct result of the 'false-consciousness' of my readerly supremacy. These were the years when I subscribed to the [Stanley] Fishian maxim that it is the method that the reader brings to bear upon the text that enables it to be heard and seen, which meant that I was entirely oblivious to the fact that the text might, in any way, be positioning *me*.[3] Hence I achieved the strange feat of talking extensively about the polyphonic and heteroglossic co-existence of different voices in Clare's poems, without considering the fact that they were all *male voices* which, although frequently addressed to a female subject *within the text*, nevertheless assumed a male reader. Because I thought it was I, the reader, who had made these voices audible by bringing my Bakhtinian theory to bear upon the text, both their gender and mine were irrelevant. It didn't bother me that these texts were excluding a female reader in terms of their positioning because I (as an existential female reader) had already bent them to my will. Looking back, this was the period of both my greatest power and my greatest blindness.

Thankfully the megalomania didn't last. At the same time that I, the postgraduate reader, was playing Faustus, another self was in the throes of a belated radical-feminism. A generation removed from the revolutionary events of the early 1970s, I am one of those who read Kate Millett and Germaine Greer alongside Catherine Belsey, Cora Kaplan, and Terry Eagleton: who caught up with the theory of first-wave feminism at the same time that its followers were charting its demise.[4] Looking back, I can see that what this produced was a peculiarly anarchic form of reader-schizophrenia. I, the reader, would read differently in different situations. Thus during the same period that I was completing my Bakhtinian liberation of Clare, I had also begun a fairly crude 'images of women' assault on Pre-Raphaelite painting. While one self was oblivious to the gendered positioning of a text because she thought herself free to do what she liked with it, another was steaming through the exhibition rooms of the Tate Gallery furious at the blatant exclusiveness of these male-authored icons. In one context I felt so powerful; in the other, so powerless.

My earliest work with the Pre-Raphaelites, then, which centred on a number of adult education courses I taught on Victorian Art and

Fig. 10.1 *Beata Beatrix* Dante Gabriel Rossetti
The Tate Gallery, London

Literature, was very much an attempt to expose and vilify the 'negative representation' of women in such texts. It is interesting to reflect how unproblematically 'the author' crept back into the equation at this point: 'John Clare' might have been consigned to permanent quotation marks, but the most reprehensible authorial intentions were ascribed to Dante Gabriel Rossetti. I, the reader, meanwhile assumed the role of heckler, instigating groups of cultured, middle-class female adult education students to mock and despise the texts that they were only permitted to view from the margins. It was a readerly scenario exemplified by Lucy Snowe's visit to the art gallery in Charlotte Brontë's *Villette*: the Pre-Raphaelite images of women, like Lucy Snowe's *Cleopatra*, were rejected on the grounds that they had been wrought for the salacious pleasure of a male audience.[5] My most memorable reader's statement from this period was a reference to the Pre-Raphaelite Brotherhood's 'penchant for sick and dying women'. See, for instance, Rossetti, *Beata Beatrix* (Fig. 10.1). Satire, I confess, had become a rather enjoyable reading strategy, and as it spread its seeds amongst my students, inculcated in us a sense of dissident group-power.

With the trashing and ridiculing of sexist and/or misogynist texts having noticeably declined in recent years, I am sometimes overwhelmed with nostalgia for the pleasure of such ribald malice. In an academic context it has disappeared, of course, because we are no longer so sure about who or what to ridicule: discourses, not authors, are now responsible for the anti-feminist world in which we live, and patriarchy is no longer the monolithic white-elephant we can blame for all our ills. For today's feminist reader everything, everywhere, is almost oppressively subtle, complex, and contradictory. Things (regrettably?) have gone beyond a joke.

As it happens, the book that finally came out of my work on the Pre-Raphaelites, *Woman/Image/Text*, is not entirely without jokes or the occasional flippant aside. However, any feminist aspiring to scholarly credibility in the late-1980s could not afford to be too cavalier. I, the reader, finally got round to putting pen to paper just as the paranoia over 'essentialist-thinking' really began to set in: the term 'woman' had by now become an epistemological minefield and, as all certainty over gendered identity fell apart, so, too, did the anxieties around reading increase. If it was no longer tenable to represent women as a group, where did that leave the woman reader, or, indeed, the feminist reader? Could there be any such thing as a reading position that was gendered, simplistically, male or female? How could a text direct itself to a male or female audience when those terms, in themselves, are inclusive of so many differences and contradictions as to render them meaningless?

The grim burden of these questions caused me, like many of my contemporaries, to abandon satire and polemic and to develop a new style of writing predicated upon the caveat. It is a style characterised by long and agonized sentences, sub-clauses, parentheses and footnotes. Theses, now, proceed with infinite caution: one step forward is followed by two steps back. Entire books are likely to end with a sentence which puts into question all that has gone before. We, as a community of feminist readers and critics, have found ourselves with a cleft stick which requires us to advance new theories (which are always demanding of *some kind* of generalisation), at the same time as recognising that the thing we are theorising – in my case, 'gendered reading' – is impossible to generalise about. The skill that we all most aspire to is therefore circumspection: how to succeed in getting through a book or article without tripping oneself up: a second's lapse of concentration and the essentialist assumption will be out, and you, the guilty party, will be shot down.[6]

In many ways *Woman/Image/Text* may therefore be seen as the moment when I, the reader, lost my nerve. Its readings of eight poem-painting combinations are a strange mixture of textual dexterity (reflecting the confidence I had gained through my post-structuralist training), methodological angst of the kind I've just described, and, most importantly, an increasing uneasiness about whether my readerly practices could be ethically and politically justified. I shall explain.

Alongside the growing demand for ever-greater critical complexity, 1980s feminist theory also required 'a positive approach' to textual analysis. Here, I have memories of publishers asking for a more 'up-beat' ending to books or chapters of books. Practising feminist criticism might be getting increasingly hard, but it must still be seen to be fun. Through the work of post-structuralist critics in literary and cultural studies, the fashion had been set for making the most recalcitrant of texts complex, exciting, and, of course, politically redeemable. Terry Eagleton's attempt to read Richardson's *Clarissa* 'on behalf of feminism' is a classic case in point, while in Kate Belsey's hands the manifest misogyny of Milton's *Paradise Lost* is blasted away to reveal exquisite points of doubt and contradition.[7]

Thus by the time I actually came to write *Woman/Image/Text* (summer 1989), I was obliged to put aside the feelings of gendered exclusion that many of the texts inspired and set about seeing how they could be positively reread. The question I posed myself, and which for a long time functioned as the working title for my introduction, was 'what can the twentieth-century feminist reader/viewer do with nineteenth-century male-produced images of women?'. Drawing upon the full range of 'deconstructive' reading strategies by then available to the feminist reader (for example, post-Althusserian Marxism, discourse theory, and recent work on spectatorship and pleasure in film and media studies) I found ways of undermining the dominant ideologies of the texts concerned and of inserting myself, the feminist reader, in their 'gaps and silences'.[8] By this means, a radical collusion could be wrought between myself and the women represented in the texts. Beata Beatrix might be dying (or, as Rossetti put it, 'rapt visibly towards heaven'), but her ghostliness and two-dimensionality are, in the last analysis, part of the discourse of masculine fear and impotence. The erotic threat presented by women in Pre-Raphaelite painting is circumscribed only by a formal and symbolic denial of their existential reality. Beatrice, as I suggest in my chapter, exults in her own ghostliness; smiles in our direction.[9]

Yet even as I used my post-structuralist reader-power to prise apart these texts and reappropriate them, I began to have grave doubts about the ethics and politics of doing so. To redeem the images concerned meant, more often than not, to read them out of context: to extract the text from the circumstances of its historical production and consumption. On the one hand this was reader-power being put to the most subversive of feminist uses, but on the other, it completely ignored the dominant reading position offered by the text itself.

Although *Woman/Image/Text* brought this dilemma to consciousness and made it part of its central thesis, the whole book was predicated upon the assumption that as long as we, as readers, are aware of what we are doing, such breaking of the rules is acceptable. In retrospect, I am less sure. When I come back to the paintings again now it is my sense of gendered exclusion which prevails. That I can, and indeed, have, read them against the grain of their historical production does not alter the fact that they have a *preferred reader* who is not me. The text I pretended was mine was all the time in dialogue with someone else.

The consequence of this loss of confidence in my readerly power was to turn away from male-authored texts altogether; and whenever I get lost in the sophistications of whether there is such a thing as 'women's writing', I hold on to this 'readerly response' as evidence that there must be. Indeed, as I thought more about the force of my own reaction I concluded that here, if anywhere, must be the definition of what we mean by women's writing: not writing by women, or about women, but, more especially, writing *for* them. However complex the categories 'male' and 'female' have become, texts *do* gender their readers, either explicitly or implicitly. While there will, of course, be some texts that are less specific in their address than others, at the two extremes there are many texts produced fairly exclusively for men or for women. Thus having spent so long attempting to redeem the former, I turned with joy and relief into the pages of the latter.

My attempts to formulate a theory for the specificity of address in contemporary women's fiction took me back, once again, to the work of Mikhail Bakthin. In an essay entitled 'Dialogic Theory and Women's Writing' I have argued that recent work on Bakhtin's theories of dialogic activity can be used to support the notion of a gendered exclusivity within certain female-authored texts.[10] Through linguistic strategies of direct and indirect address, through intonation and extra-literary context, it is evident that several women writers have successfully defined their audience as both female *and* feminist. Thus, once again, albeit for a short time, everything seemed very simple. There may be millions of texts from which, as a woman reader, I am excluded, but with an ever-increasing library of contemporary feminist writing, it became obvious where my energies should be directed. I resolved only to trouble myself with texts which spoke to me as a woman and as a feminist.

Unfortunately this second wave of readerly euphoria lasted little longer than the first. The texts I thought to be addressed especially to me turned out not to be so. What I had experienced as an intimate relationship between the chosen text and myself turned out to be but one of many. I soon saw that I could only ever occupy but *one* of the multiple positionings denoted by the category 'woman reader'. The text I had thought of as 'mine' was talking to others as easily as it talked to me. All the time I was reading, I kept overhearing scraps of conversation between the text and readers differently situated from myself. I became jealous and suspicious. I wanted to know what the text was saying to *them*: to the black women, the heterosexual women, the working-class women; to the women who were ten years older, or ten years younger, than myself. Once again I, the reader, felt excluded and unwanted. With so many *different* readers jostling for the position of preferred reader, I found it difficult to accept my own insignificance. De-essentializing the category 'woman' (as I knew I must) had de-essentialized me.

I have since discovered a number of texts which have helped explain the nature of this 'reader-jealousy' to me, as well as suggesting a possible way forward. One of these is Martin Montgomery's 'D-J Talk' (first published in *Media, Culture and Society* in 1986).[11] Part of Montgomery's analysis is concerned with the way in which the radio D-J's monologue is continually addressing different segments of the audience through 'identifiers' which include or exclude particular groups. For example, horoscope features identify and privilege the different star-signs in turn. The effect of this, as Montgomery explains, is that any individual listener will be positioned differently at different times and that: 'It is quite common for an audience to be in a position of overhearing recipient of a discourse that is being directly addressed to someone else' (p. 428).

While Montgomery welcomed this constant re-alignment of address as evidence that no discourse 'speaks from a single authoritative position' (p. 438), I, the erstwhile privileged reader, received the evidence with gloom. It was clearly true that none of my favoured feminist texts could exist in an exclusive relationship with any one reader-positioning, and my status as addressee was as tenuous as it had always been.

Since this 'second splitting' of the reader's ego I have, however, come to realise that my jealousy was somewhat misplaced. While it may be true that my favoured feminist texts have more readers than I originally thought, this does not irredeemably alter my special relationship to them. Indeed, after reflecting some more on Montgomery's model of shifting address, I realised that mutability does not necessarily equal promiscuity. 'Polyphony' which, in the Bakhtinian sense, demands that a text be comprised of a 'plurality of consciousnesses with equal rights', is not my *reader's* experience of contemporary feminist writing any more than it is my experience of the male literary canon.[12] The text may be comprised of many voices; it may effect multiple text-reader positionings, but this does not mean that it does so without preference or discrimination. As Stuart Hall observed in his work on encoding and decoding in television discourse as long ago as 1973, 'polysemy must not, however, be confused with pluralism'.[13]

Therefore, even as I showed in my work on John Clare that the voices *within* the polyphonic text can be hierachised according to the balance of power between speaker and addressee within the text, so, too, do I now propose a (mutable) hierarchy of reader-positionings.[14] Viewed in this way, a text like Alice Walker's *The Color Purple* becomes the site of a struggle for reader-privilege. Readers of different classes, races, and sexual orientations may turn hungrily from page to page for a sign of their own preferment. Sometimes their desire will be appeased; sometimes it will be disappointed. But either way, by the time they finish reading, a judgement will have been cast and they will know their place in the schema of the text's reader-positionings.

While, on the one hand, the existence of such textual preferment helps to explain why reading books, watching films, or looking at paintings continues to be such an exciting but nerve-racking occupation, it also offered me, the jealous reader, perverse consolation. Realising that one text might privilege me, even if another did not, confirmed that the dialogue between text and reader was, after all, a 'real' relationship; that it was subject to the same laws of selection, rejection and reciprocity as our interpersonal relations. If I, as a reader, have to learn to live with the continual possibility of rejection, then I may also enjoy the possibility of preferment. Acknowledging that the relationship between text and reader is inscribed by a volatile power dynamic in this way, permits desire even as it engenders fear. We may look forward to opening a new book, even as we are apprehensive of it. Moreover, by recognising this emotional dimension within the reading process we may come to a new understanding of its politics.

At the time of writing, this is where my story ends, though I don't pretend to have reached a rock any less slippery than those I have perched on before. In terms of the thesis I have been pursuing – the question of whether, in the production of textual meaning, it is text or reader who holds the balance of power – it is clear that I have now conceded renewed authority to the text. While I, the reader, exist in dialogic relationship with the text (any text), I am nevertheless *positioned by it*, and the challenge and excitement of the reading process depends upon my not knowing, in advance, if it will embrace me or reject me: position me as an ally or as an antagonist.[15] Yet to acknowledge that all texts operate codes of address in this way, that they make selections among their readership in terms of age, race, gender, class, education, is not to say that the reader is entirely disempowered. While hers may be a *reactive* position (it is the text which initiates the relationship), she has a degree of choice in how she may respond to her positioning, and this is where the *politics* of reading may ultimately be located. The feminist reader like myself, for example, must consider whether or not to pick up the gauntlet a male-oriented text throws at me; must decide whether or not to engage in a struggle for its 'meaning', either 'with' or 'against the grain'. Similarly, I must decide how to conduct my relationship with texts which position me as their 'ally': do I accept their intimacy at face value, or do I take the risk of probing deeper and establishing a more complex, more uncomfortable dialogue? For while I would now acknowledge that it is the text that initiates the relationship, I also believe that it is I, the reader, who must take responsibility for negotiating the terms upon which we are to proceed. Even as the text positions me, so may I (re)position my relationship to it.

Notes

1. See Lynne Pearce, *Woman/Image/Text: Readings in Pre-Raphaelite Art and Literature*, Hemel Hempstead, Harvester-Wheatsheaf (1991), and Sara Mills (ed.), *Gendering the Reader*, Hemel Hempstead, Harvester Wheatsheaf (1994).
2. See Lynne Pearce, 'John Clare and Mikhail Bakhtin: The Dialogic Principle', unpublished Ph.D. thesis, University of Birmingham, 1987. Part of my thesis focused on the polyphonic nature of Clare's asylum poem 'Child Harold' (written as a continuation of Byron's poem of the same name). In the Bakhtinian vocabulary, 'polyphony' means simply 'many voices' and my reading of this text analysed the many different personae adopted by the narrator and his fluctuating power *vis-à-vis* his 'addressees' within the text. A shortened version of this analysis was published as an article entitled 'John Clare's "Child Harold": A Polyphonic Reading', *Criticism*, XXXI, 2, 1989, pp. 139–57.

   Dialogic theory, as it has been developed by literary and other critics following in Bakhtin's footsteps, is predicated upon the general principle that no utterance (either written or spoken) is made in isolation, but is always dependent upon the anticipated response of an (actual or implicit) *addressee*. The reciprocal nature of this relationship is summed up in the following sentence from V. N. Voloshinov's *Marxism and the*

Philosophy of Language, Seminar Press, New York (1973): 'A word is a bridge thrown between myself and another. If one end of the bridge belongs to me, then the other depends on my addressee. A word is a territory shared by both addresser and addressee, by the speaker and his interlocutor' (p. 86). This principle of reciprocity is implicit in the work of all Bakhtinians whether they are dealing with 'the utterance' as a small, linguistic unit (the individual sword or sentence) or in terms of larger discourses.

   For further information about the work of Mikhail Bakhtin and dialogic theory see Katerina Clark and Michael Holquist's *Mikhail Bakhtin*, Cambridge, Mass. Harvard University Press (1984), or my own *Reading Dialogics*, London, Edward Arnold (1994).

3. Stanley Fish is America's most celebrated reader-response critic. See in particular *Is There a Text In This Class and Other Essays*, Cambridge, Mass. Harvard University Press (1980). See also the Introduction to Mills 1994 op. cit. for discussion of Fish's critical influence.

4. Kate Millett's *Sexual Politics*, London, Virago, 1977 (originally published in the United States in 1969) and Germaine Greer's *The Female Eunuch*, London, Paladin, 1971, were two of the key texts which launched the modern Women's Liberation Movement. Catherine Belsey's influential *Critical Practice*, London, Methuen, appeared in 1980, and Cora Kaplan wrote an important critical response to Millett's *Sexual Politics* which is reproduced in her collection of essays, *Sea Changes: Culture and Feminism*, London, Verso (1986). Terry Eagleton's work, from the 1970s onwards, has provided a model for much Marxist and feminist criticism: see in particular his *Literary Theory*, Oxford, Basil Blackwell (1983).

5. See Charlotte Brontë, *Villette*, Oxford, Clarendon Press (1984), pp. 278–93.

6. For an account of how anxious feminists have become about committing the 'sin' of essentialism see the 'round table discussion' between Marianne Hirsch, Jane Gallop and Nancy K. Miller ('Criticizing feminist criticism') in *Conflicts in Feminism*, eds. Marianne Hirsch and Evelyn Fox Keller, London, Routledge (1990).

7. See Terry Eagleton, *The Rape of Clarissa: Writing, Sexuality and Class Struggle in Samuel Richardson*, Oxford, Basil Blackwell (1986) and Catherine Belsey, *John Milton: Language, Gender, Power*, Oxford, Basil Blackwell (1986).

8. The reference to 'gaps' and 'silences' here is an allusion to Pierre Macherey's model of 'symptomatic reading' as outlined in his *Theory of Literary Production*, trans. Geoffrey Wall, Routledge, London (1978). For a brief account of what this type of reading practice involves see my *Woman/Image/Text*, pp. 5–15.

9. See *Woman/Image/Text*, pp. 46–58.

10. See Hilary Hinds, Ann Phoenix, Jackie Stacey (eds), *Working Out: New Directions for Women's Studies*, Brighton, Falmer Press (1992), pp. 184–93.

11. See Martin Montgomery, 'D-J talk', *Media, Culture and Society*, vol. VIII, no. 4, 1986, pp. 421–40.

12. 'A plurality of independent and unmerged voices and consciousnesses': see Mikhail Bakhtin, *Problems of Dostoevsky's Poetics*, (ed. and trans. Caryl Emerson) Manchester, Manchester University Press (1984).

13. See Stuart Hall, 'Encoding/decoding', *Culture, Media, Language*, London, Hutchinson (1980), pp. 128–38.

14. For my discussion of the power-relationship existing between speaker and addressee in John Clare's 'Child Harold' see the article in *Criticism* op. cit.

15. See Anne Herrmann, *The Dialogic and Difference: 'An/Other Woman' in Virginia Woolf and Christa Wolf*, New York, Columbia University Press, (1989). In this fascinating application of Bakhtin's dialogic theory, Herrmann compares the way in which Wolf's texts position their reader as a female 'ally', and Woolf's as a male 'antagonist'.

11 Remembering ourselves: memory, writing and the female self

SUSANNAH RADSTONE

Feminisms' quests for ways to live – or imagine life – beyond known, patri-archal bounds seek inspiration, enablement or solace in historical or mythical heroines. Feminist autobiography, too, often returns to the past – to childhood – in search of possible alternative futures. These various enterprises all apparently share a desire to 'remember' lost or hidden aspects of the past *for* feminism. A desire to return to, or recapture what has been lost arguably binds together a wide variety of feminist autobio-graphical, historical and even spiritual projects. This essay focuses, in the main, on a selection of feminist autobiographical works. It argues that though nostalgic desire drives each of the texts' excavations of memory, a clear distinction can be made between two types of nostalgic text. In what follows, I will be distinguishing between texts which 'repeat' and texts which 'work through' nostalgia.[1]

Carol Ann Duffy's poem 'In Your Mind' begins with a question: 'The other country, is it anticipated or half-remembered?'[2] Duffy's collection takes its title – *The Other Country* – from this first line. In this collection, as well as in her earlier work, this 'other country', figured alternately as place, as childhood, or as absent lover, glimmers in its hallucinatory pres-ence. The other country remains both tantalizingly close as well as uncompromisingly elsewhere. In 'Originally', the opening poem, both childhood and homeland are evoked in their absent presence:

> My brothers cried, one of them bawling *Home*,
> *Home*, as the miles rushed back to the city,
> the street, the house, the vacant rooms
> where we didn't live any more. (p. 7)

Here, it seems, the 'other country' is not anticipated, but half-remem-bered. Again, in 'Survivor', the 'other country', the past, haunts, and this time *diminishes* the present:

For some time now, at the curve of my mind,
I have longed to embrace my brother, my sister, myself,
when we were seven years old. It is making me ill . . .
. . . Why has this happened? I mime

the gone years where I lived. I want them back.
My lover rises and plunges above me, not knowing
I have hidden myself in my heart where I rock and
    weep for what has been stolen, lost. Please.
It is like an earthquake and no one to tell. (p. 33)

In their inscriptions of yearning, these poems, these bittersweet medita-
tions on memory evoke, more than anything, an overwhelming sense of
nostalgia. Nostalgia – once a medical term associated with the trials of
Swiss mercenaries forced to leave their native lands[3] – and then referring more generally to homesickness and now to yearnings for the past.
The Other Country seems to propose that its subject matter – hallucinatory, desired – belongs to the past: or does it? Perhaps not. The question
'The other country, is it anticipated or half-remembered?' comes at the
end of the collection, thereby prompting a rereading of all that has gone
before.

It would seem that feminisms' 'other countries' are best conceived of as
both half-remembered *and* anticipated. By 'other countries', I mean feminisms' utopias, or hopes for alternative ways of life. But what I mean by
remembrance needs further elaboration. Like the poem 'In Your Mind',
my aim here is to raise questions about the relationship between
memory's substance and the past – questions which raise further questions concerning our attempts to write, think and experience ourselves in
the present and for the future.

I am proposing that Duffy's work interrogates, rather than celebrates
nostalgia. For though many of the poems evoke sensations of nostalgic
desire with startling clarity, the work simultaneously acknowledges that
it is present circumstances which lend a particular glow, or nostalgia, to
phantasms of the past:

> Those unstrung beads of oil
> seem precious now, *now*
> *that the light has changed.*
> ('M-M-Memory', p. 36, emphasis mine).

But what drew me to Duffy's work first, and what I found irresistable and
compelling in it was its very nostalgia – its evocation of the hyper-reality
of lost homeland, lost childhood and lost love. In what follows, I will
attempt to interrogate and evaluate the lure of nostalgia.

Driving between my home – London – and my place of work – 160
miles away – I tuned to a radio review discussing Mira Nair's latest film,
Mississippi Masala, (United States, 1991) which concerns itself with
migrancy, displacement, loss of home; themes which recur in recent

descriptions of the postmodern condition.[4] But isn't it the case that recent women's autobiographical writing has evinced a *particular* concern with migrancy, emigration, loss of home? The radio programme's preview of the following week's agenda interrupted my musings on women and nostalgia with the following question: 'Why are we now more interested in Medea than in Oedipus?' In myth, the enchantress Medea's powers weakened in her husband's land, until his faithlessness prompted an anger which rekindled power: she murdered their children and burnt down the marital home. Medea deploys her restored powers to wreak a terrible revenge – a revenge that is also self-destructive since she loses her own children. The radio magazine's suggestion that Medea is currently upstaging Oedipus was prompted by Monstrous Regiment's recent production of Euripedes' *Medea*.[5] Monstrous Regiment (a feminist theatre company) lit upon Medea, no doubt, as a mythical heroine ripe for revival. And Medea was, after all, *some* woman: torn from her native land, exiled once, then exiled again, she remembered how to fight back. As victim and vanquisher of nostalgia Medea arguably offers herself up as a powerful figure around whom to weave a 'new' feminist mythology. My argument will position Monstrous Regiment's revival of Medea within this wider feminist context.

It would seem to be the case that Medea figures, in some guise or other, in many examples of recent feminist autobiographical or 'memory-work'.[6] Such recent work can best be understood, perhaps, as an attempt to re-inscribe knowingly – and in so doing to transcend – our historical inscription as 'woman'. But the question posed by all such work concerns the possibilities for inscribing a 'beyond' that arguably exceeds, but can only be attained in and through, history. One recurrent and familiar response to this problem involves the *remembering* of that which has been hidden in, or forgotten by history. Within the field of feminist psychoanalytic theory, this has led, for instance, to a particular focus on pre-Oedipal, rather than Oedipal stages of infantile development.[7] But if the call to 'remember' rings through the halls of feminist academia, several competing understandings of this project can be discerned. So my aim here is to evaluate and contrast (albeit crudely)[8] various 'theories and methods' of remembering and also to point out the different roles Medea – or at least a Medea-like figure – plays in each of them.

The first theory of remembering I shall discuss emerges in the work of Jane Flax, who in her article 'Remembering the selves: Is the repressed gendered?',[9] and in her book *Thinking Fragments: Psychoanalysis, Feminism, and Postmodernism in the Contemporary West*,[10] insists that 'remembering' must be seen as a primary task of empowerment for feminism, for 'without remembered selves', she asks, 'how can we act?'.[11] But how does Flax understand remembrance here, and what are the methodological consequences of her construal of the term? Though Flax's work seems often to oscillate between Enlightenment and postmodern understandings of the nature of knowledge,[12] where psychoanalytic theory is concerned, she comes down firmly on the side of object-relations theory – especially Winnicott, and against Lacanian theory.[13] According to object-relations theorists, the infant may project its destructive or aggressive impulses against an object (the mother) or a part-object (the breast), onto those objects or part-objects. For Flax, then, the 'remembered self' is a self which acknowledges its split-off objects and part-objects as part of itself. In this process of 'remembrance' a *core self* is formed, without which, argues Flax, we lose the possibility of creative or imaginative work in Winnicott's (postmodern as she sees it) transitional space.[14] In other words, without a core self – a remembered self – we cannot re-imagine ourselves *for* the future. In 'Re-membering the selves', Flax argues that under patriarchy, the woman's social self hides repressed autonomous and sexual selves. Remembrance, then, must bring to consciousness our autonomous will to mastery, our aggression and our sexuality. In Flaxian remembering, method is clearly rooted in object-relations therapy (Flax is a psychotherapist as well as an academic) and involves encountering, working through, and acknowledging as one's own, overwhelming feelings of destructiveness and aggression (self and other oriented), and fear of one's own and one's fantasised mother's rage. Perhaps *this* remembering, then, might be likened to an encounter with Medea – Medea as both split-off parts of the self and as fantasised pre-Oedipal mother.

Several pieces of feminist memory-work that make use of photography or video share certain theoretical underpinnings and methodological practices with this 'Flaxian' remembering.[15] Valerie Walkerdine has published two essays of memory-work, using as her raw material early photographs of herself from the family album. The first essay, published in Liz Heron's collection *Truth, Dare or Promise: Girls Growing Up In The Fifties*[16] took off from an image of Walkerdine as 'the bluebell fairy', or 'tinkerbell', to re-member her inscription within patriarchal discourses of proper working-class femininity. In her second piece, 'Behind the painted smile',[17] Walkerdine confesses that though she had originally included a second photographic illustration for that earlier essay, she had, in the end, forbidden its publication, since she found *this* image – the image of herself as fat child – unbearable, embarrassing and not admissible within the public arena. In the second, courageous, essay, Walkerdine sets out to do memory-work on this and other similar 'forbidden' photographs – to re-member herself through these inadmissable representations. Working with 'the bluebell fairy' image was all too easy, argues Walkerdine, since it allowed her to acknowledge her inscription within patriarchal dis-courses of feminine passivity, beauty and fragility while sustaining a sense of herself *as* properly feminine and beautiful.[18] The innovative method of memory-work Walkerdine deploys in her second, more recent essay, is clearly informed by a feminist reading of object-relations theory. By pro-jecting these images onto a wall and by etching and shading-in onto tracing paper the half-visible shadows under eyes and hidden expressions of anger and depression, Walkerdine remembers parts of a forgotten childhood self. What emerges in these revised images is the underside of 'the bluebell fairy': a depressed, demanding and angry child who, argues Walkerdine, reveals the repressed possibility of an actively sexual woman, a strong and powerful woman.

The hermeneutic governing Walkerdine's 'memory-work' is clearly shaped by that of psychoanalytic interpretation. But psychoanalysis' founding narratives are those of myth – and just as psychoanalysis claimed to discern the universal truths hidden in myths, might we not reread psychoanalytic textual analyses for the hidden myths that they screen? In Walkerdine's 'Beyond the painted smile', as well as in Flax's work, what we find is the myth of an archaic, powerful mother, re-mem-bered both as 'other' and as 'self'.

Like Medea, Sethe, the mother character in Toni Morrison's *Beloved*, commits infanticide: she murders her daughter, Beloved, to save her from a life of exile in slavery. But driven by her desire for fusion with her mother, Beloved returns from the dead, whereupon their identities merge: 'You are my face; I am you. Why did you leave me who am you?' asks Beloved.[19] Linda Anderson concludes her essay 'The re-imagining of history in contemporary women's fiction' with a reading of *Beloved*. For Anderson, this fusion between past and present, between subject and object, between mother and the child she murdered, negotiates what has seemed an impasse between feminism's twin desires to inscribe the female subject in, through and for history while gesturing towards her location in an unrepresentable region outside the socio-economic contract: 'Morrison reveals a complicated overlapping and enmeshing of meanings: she moves between history and its determinations to a subjectivity which lies beyond it in an imaginative realm which has yet to find a place.'[20] Following Kristeva,[21] Anderson aligns this unrepresentable region with 'the maternal'. But does this fusion between Sethe and Beloved enact such a negotiation? Or does it *re*-present Medea – subject and object of nostalgic desire? If this is the case, if this remembering, too, can be read as repetition, the retelling of the myth of an archaic pre-Oedipal mother, giver and taker of life, then can remembering ever do more than this, can representation avoid repetition?

Mary Jacobus opens her essay on feminist nostalgia by offering an alternative reading of the 'feminist attempt to recover memory (specifically, memory of the mother) beneath the myth – the contemporary feminist excavation of . . . [the] pre-Oedipal phase screened by the . . . Oedipal.'[22] Jacobus suggests that these remembrances might better be understood as acts of feminist nostalgia. Jacobus comes to her understanding of nostalgia as having a special bearing upon femininity through Jane Gallop's[23] reading of Lacan's re-writing of the Freudian castration complex. Gallop's reading points out that in Lacan, the boy's castration complex joins desire to threat, whereas for the girl, desire is joined to nostalgia: 'The boy's fear of losing what he has as the mother lost hers is matched by the female's regret for what she does not have (any longer)'.[24] 'The boy's fear is matched by feminine nostalgia', summarises Jacobus.[25] For Jacobus, feminine desire as nostalgia is produced at a moment of *Nachträglichkeit*: a remembering of the pre-Oedipal from the side of the Oedipal. From *this* side, the mythical object of nostalgic desire emerges, and emerges as phallic. According to Jacobus, then, it seems that nostalgic desire, feminine and feminist 'risks re-inscribing the fiction of the uncastrated woman who defends against castration anxiety, but does so at the price of denying sexual difference.'[26]

Remembering possesses two antonyms: forgetting and *dismembering*. If feminine remembering arguably defends against castration anxiety – a fantasy of dismemberment – can *feminist* remembrance remember what this nostalgia forgets? Can *feminist* remembrance *work through* (in the Freudian sense of stopping repeating)[27] the Medea-like creature of *Nachträglichkeit* to a beyond that might be our futures? In what remains of this essay, I will offer a reading of some texts which may be read as 'working through' feminine nostalgia, thereby anticipating the 'other country'.

The conclusion to Jacobus's essay on feminist nostalgia presents a reading of Rich's poem 'Transcendental Etude'[28] which points towards a revised theory *and method* of feminist remembering. *This* future-oriented remembering, argues Jacobus, both works through and is sustained by nostalgia. In turning over the *objets trouvés* in which a woman 'finds herself where she is not . . . the bits of yarn, calico, and velvet scraps' (Rich, 'Transcendental Etude'),[29] *this* remembering works through nostalgia's fantasies of plenitude (remembrance as defence against *dismemberment*) but is sustained by nostalgia's desire that things might be different.

Two texts which work through nostalgia, by turning over the *objets trouvés* (the objects both lost and found) of memory are Drusilla Modjeska's *Poppy*[30] and Eva Hoffman's *Lost In Translation: A Life in a New Language.*[31] The cover illustrations of both these loosely autobiographical texts include photographs from family albums. *Lost In Translation*'s cover displays a sepia photo of two young girls – sisters, with the older sister's arm around the smaller girl – mounted on an album page – an image which evokes nostalgic desire, and provokes readerly desire *for* nostalgia. The photograph on *Poppy*'s cover is again of two sisters, here an older girl holding a baby up to the mirror. And though this photo is not mounted on an album page, the rough texture of such pages is evoked by the cover design itself. But though both covers evoke and provoke nostalgia, neither text delivers it, since both interrogate rather than repeat nostalgia.

In Drusilla Modjeska's *Poppy*, a fictional daughter, Lalage, sets out in search of her lost (recently deceased) mother. Lalage's method is one of juxtaposing evidence. Fuelled by desire to know the mother she never knew, Lalage collects her evidence: 'The books Poppy read, the diaries she kept and the letters that were in her attic . . . An atlas, books on the history of Britain and maps that were detailed enough to show . . . the village where we lived when we were a family . . .'.[32] She interviews old family friends, and sifts through evidence, only to conclude that the mother she is seeking is not there: 'it doesn't tell me who she was.'[33]. She dwells on the opacity of old photos, which tell, not the story of her mother, but the story of bourgeois representations of the family, and she listens to oral histories which 'forget' her mother's nervous breakdown. These stories tell not the story Lalage desires – the story of Poppy, but the story of Poppy's inscription in history. Thus, when the evidence begins to coalesce – apparently promising plenitude, the fulfilment of nostalgic desire – Lalage turns away. But when she tries to look 'elsewhere' she produces a metaphor of mother as void: as a small child, she reports, she looked deep into her mother's belly button, but 'I couldn't make anything out,' she remembers, 'it was dark in there.'[34] So far, then, Lalage's quest produces Poppy's inscription as 'mother' or, beyond that, repeats the inscription of mother as terrifying darkness – a fantasy of the maternal which subtends her idealisation under patriarchy. But amongst the *objets trouvés* with which Lalage returns from the motherland to her home in the new world

(Australia), are the balls of twine that Poppy made, plaited from scraps of wool, cotton, thin strips of material, hair ribbon and crepe paper. Lalage explains that Poppy 'used the thread to tie papers, letters and old school reports into manageable bundles, or to wrap presents, or to hook a door-knob to a peg in the wall to stop it banging in the wind.'[35] For Poppy's daughters, explains Lalage, this thread was a bit of a joke: 'a metaphor Poppy made for her own life: Ariadne's thread'.[36] In *Poppy*, the juxtapos-ing of contradictory memories, histories and written evidence defeat nos-talgia's desire for an impossible return to plenitude. In place of fusion with an archaic, mythical mother, the text profers this thread, woven from the *objets trouvés* of a woman's life: metaphorical representation of a life that is at once fragmentary, elusive *and* coherent – a life sustained, according to Jacobus's reading of Rich's poem, not by 'the will to mastery . . . but by the will to change.'[37]

Like *Poppy*, which concerns itself both with the lost mother and the lost motherland, Eva Hoffman's *Lost In Translation* might be described as doubly nostalgic. As a young teenager, the narrator and her family were forced to leave their native land, Poland, and to take up residence in Canada. *Lost In Translation* tells the story, then, of how E-W-A Hoffman becomes E-V-A Hoffman. In the 'new world', experience – life without history – is schizophrenic. But like *Poppy*, *Lost In Translation* works through, rather than repeats nostalgia. The book's three sections are sub-titled 'Paradise', 'Exile' and 'The New World'. It is the relation between these three phases that the book sets out to 'remember'. By the end of *Lost In Translation*, 'exile becomes threshold, rather than bar, to a new *experi-ence* of the world – an experience suffused not by nostalgia for a mythical past, but by hope for an achievable future In the third section of *Lost In Translation* – in 'the new world' – the narrator remembers that her mem-ories of Poland and Polishness have been formed retrospectively, in the new language, in the new country. From this vantage point, the text's positioning of homeland, of motherland, as paradise, emerges as ironic. Eva explains that in the new country, 'I have only a memory of fullness to anguish me with the knowledge that in this dark and empty state, I don't really exist.'[38] But attempts to act out, rather than work through nostal-gia, refuse to deliver the longed-for plenitude: when she goes back to Poland, she feels as alienated there as in Canada, and reunion with a child-hood sweetheart only underlines the irretrievability of nostalgia's mythi-cal past. What *Lost In Translation*'s working through of nostalgia achieves is the acknowledgement of its homeland, motherland as *Nachträglichkeit*. What comes into focus more clearly, then, are the fragments of life in the present, from which Eva begins to envision her future: 'The sense of the future returns like a benediction, to balance the earlier annunciation of loss. It returns in the simplest of ways: in an image of a crooked Paris street, where I'll go on my vacation, or in a peaceful picture of myself, at my desk, writing. Quiet, modest images light up the forward trajectory, and these flickers that suppose a pleasureable extension in time feel very much like hope.'[39]

I'll end, then, with the question of methodology. *Poppy* straddles autobiography, biography, and family history as a daughter, Lalage, seeks her mother – 'remembers' her mother – via a range of methods: oral history, deconstructive textual analysis, and so on. *Lost In Translation*, though categorised as autobiography, seeks to 'remember' life in the 'motherland'. Like *Poppy*, then, *Lost In Translation*'s project bleeds over from autobiography to biography and family history. Towards the end of her essay on feminist nostalgia Mary Jacobus asks: 'Is there, then, no way for feminists to answer Woolf's call to "think back through our mothers" without mimicking the fetishist's refusal of sexual difference?'[40] This essay is about seeing a ghost – the ghostly figure of Medea rising up in feminist theory and memory-work. Following Jacobus, I have argued that Medea signifies the sheer difficulty of representing the mother in anything but male terms, as phallic or castrated – the sheer difficulty, then of writing ourselves, remembering ourselves, outside such terms. Jacobus felt that she could only begin to answer Woolf's call in *other* terms by performing what she herself acknowledges as a 'misreading'[41] of Rich's poem – a reading that sets aside Rich's unproblematised privileging of female experience and female particularity. *Poppy* and *Lost In Translation* both move beyond an initial encounter with Medea. In *Poppy*, Lalage confronts her longing for the mythical, powerful and mysterious mother. The book's project becomes, then, that of analysing the *myth* of Poppy. In *Lost In Translation*, Eva confronts her longing for the motherland – the land that granted Medea her powers. Here, the project is to analyse the *myth* of that motherland. In *Poppy* and *Lost In Translation*, Medea becomes then, not an answer to an impossible quest for origins, but the occasion for a new set of questions. What these quests deliver, finally, is a working through of nostalgia. Freed from nostalgia's repetitions, these texts anticipate the 'other country'.

Notes

1. Here I refer to Sigmund Freud's essay 'Remembering, repeating and working through' in *The Standard Edition of the Complete Psychological Works of Sigmund Freud* James Strachey (ed.), London, Hogarth Press (1953–74), pp. 147–56. (1914). In this essay, Freud distinguishes between acts which *repeat* unconscious resistance and acts of remembrance through which psychoanalysis bypasses resistance to make the unconscious conscious. I am suggesting, then, that feminist nostalgia might be regarded as a form of resistance against an acknowledgement of our historical condition. This aspect of my argument is indebted to Mary Jacobus' essay 'Freud's mnemonic: women, screen memories and feminist nostalgia', *Michigan Quarterly Review* 1987, pp. 117–39.

2. Duffy, Carol-Ann, *The Other Country*, London, Anvil Press (1990), p.55.

3. Starobinski, Jean, 'The Idea of Nostalgia', *Diogenes*, 54, 1966, pp. 81–103.

4. For a useful introductory discussion of the postmodern condition see David Harvey's *The Condition of Postmodernity*, Oxford, Blackwell (1989). For recent cultural analyses of contemporary experiences of exiledom, migrancy and loss of home, see *The Question of 'Home': New Formations*, 17, summer 1992.

5. Several productions of *Medea* were staged in London in 1992. The Almeida Theatre mounted their own production of the play, and Monstrous Regiment's production played at the Lilian Bayliss Theatre, Sadler's Wells.

6. Frigga Haug's *Female Sexualization*, London, Verso (1987) coins the term 'memory-work' to describe this book's collective autobiographical project. In this work, the focus falls on a collective remembering of the female subject's inscription within practices and discourses concerning the female body and female sexuality.

7. For a succinct summary of the issues at stake for feminism in the foregrounding of the pre-Oedipal see Margaret Whitford's entry, 'the pre-oedipal' in Elizabeth Wright's *Feminism and Psychoanalysis: A Critical Dictionary*, Oxford, Blackwell (1992). This entry provides an introduction to the most significant theorists in this field, who include Nancy Chodorow (especially *The Reproduction of Mothering*, Berkeley, University of California Press, 1978), Melanie Klein, and Julia Kristeva.

8. In this essay I am setting out to distinguish between two underlying tendencies within feminist 'memory-work'. In the first, nostalgia fuels a retrieval of what has been forgotten or lost by memory (see Flax, Haug and Walkerdine, for example). The underlying assumption here is that this retrieval will restore to us valuable missing aspects of, or understandings of, our social and personal experience. In the second (see Modjeska and Hoffman), it is this nostalgic quest itself which becomes the object of interrogation. My distinction is a crude one since I have not the space here to distinguish more rigorously between memory-work's inflection by different theories, such as those of sociology and psychoanalysis, or by different modes, such as those of poetry, autobiography, fiction and theory.

9. Flax, Jane, 'Re-membering the selves: is the repressed gendered?', *Michigan Quarterly Review*, 1987, pp. 92–110.

10. Flax, Jane, *Thinking Fragments: Psychoanalysis, Feminism and Postmodernism in the Contemporary West*, Berkeley, University of California Press (1990).

11. Flax, Jane, 1987, op. cit. pp. 106–7.

12. The Enlightenment theory of knowledge was grounded in concepts such as truth and justice, and in a belief that human beings were progressively gaining self-knowledge and greater capacities for self-rule through the exercise of reason. The contemporary legitimacy of the Enlightenment's grounding concepts and beliefs have been challenged by postmodern theorists such as Jean-Francois Lyotard. In *The Postmodern Condition: A Report on Knowledge*, Manchester, Manchester University Press (1984). Lyotard expresses the view that we are currently seeing the collapse of the legitimacy

of what he calls the 'grand narratives' of the west. Concepts such as those of 'universal truth' and 'justice', are understood by postmodern theorists, not as the grounds for an expansion of democracy and of universalist claims to human rights, but rather as forms of power, tied to particular regimes of knowledge. Though the distinction I draw in this essay between nostalgic texts and texts which interrogate nostalgia could be aligned with Enlightenment and postmodern theories of subjectivity, this would be to suggest too neat a fit between feminist issues and the postmodernism debates. There is a wide-ranging discussion concerning the relevance of and pertinence to feminism of the debate between postmodern and Enlightenment philosophies (for example, Linda Nicholson's *Feminism/Postmodernism*, London, Routledge, 1990), but to enter more fully into this question would be beyond the scope of this essay.

13. Though object-relations theory can be regarded as a revision rather than an overturning of Freudian psychoanalytic theory, these two tendencies within psychoanalysis are often characterised as offering competing understandings of the earliest years of infantile development. Unlike Freud and Lacan, for whom infantile development is understood to be driven by the *lack* of an object, object-relations theorists believe that from the earliest weeks, infantile development proceeds by means of relations formed with 'objects' which exist either in the external world or in the internal world of mental representations. The founder of object-relations theory was Melanie Klein, whose work gave rise to the school of British object-relations theory. D. W. Winnicott is one of the best-known of the British object-relations theorists. In his work, he stressed the ongoing significance for the infant's psychic well-being of its earliest experiences of the maternal environment. For further introductory material on Klein, Winnicott and object-relations theory see Elisabeth Wright's *Feminism and Psychoanalysis: A Critical Dictionary*, Oxford, Blackwell (1992), and Gregorio Kohon (ed.) *The British School of Psychoanalysis: The Independent Tradition*, London, Free Association Books (1987).

14. Flax 1990, op. cit. especially pp. 116–17. Flax draws here especially on D. W. Winnicott's *Playing and Reality*, London, Routledge (1989), (first published 1971: a book-length elaboration of his earlier 'Transitional objects and transitional phenomena' (1951), collected in D. W. Winnicott, *Collected Papers: Through Paediatrics to Psycho-Analysis*, London, Tavistock, (1958).) In this work, Winnicott focuses on the developmental stage at which the child's sense of boundaries between self and other are permeable and unfixed. He traces the child's creative use of 'transitional objects' in 'transitional space' to explore the foundations of culture and of art. For Flax, Winnicott's 'transitional space' and 'transitional objects' offer the beginnings of a model for a coherent feminist postmodern subject. Many advocates of postmodernism – feminists included – see a liberatory potential in postmodernism's fragmentation of the unified subject of Enlightenment philosophy. Flax stresses, rather, that work *in* postmodern or 'transitional space' *requires* a 'core self'.

15. See Annette Kuhn, pp. 58–72 in this volume.

16. Heron, Liz (ed.), *Truth, Dare or Promise: Girls Growing up in the Fifties*, London, Virago (1985).

17. In Spence, Jo and Holland, Pat (eds.), *Family Snaps: The Meanings of Domestic Photography*, London, Virago (1991).

18. Ibid. p. 36.

19. Morrison, Toni, *Beloved*, London, Chatto and Windus (1987), p. 216.

20. Anderson, Linda (ed.), *Plotting Change: Contemporary Woman's Fiction*, Sevenoaks, Edward Arnold (1990), p. 137.

21. Kristeva's writings on the 'speaking subject' stress that the acquisition of language and culture necessitates the repression of various preconditions *for* linguistic and

cultural competence, particularly the 'semiotic' and the maternal. The 'semiotic' refers to that register of signification which precedes linguistic order, culture and law. The 'semiotic' is linked to the infant's earliest impulses and drives and is linked to the 'maternal' space of undifferentiation. (Kristeva, Julia, *Desire in Language* (trans. S. Roudiez) Oxford, Blackwell, 1980.) It is in her essay 'Women's Time', (Moi, Toril (ed.), *The Kristeva Reader*, Oxford, Blackwell (1986)), that Kristeva most directly addresses the question of woman's place inside and outside history. Anderson acknowledges her indebtedness to this essay in the notes appended to her 'The Re-Imagining of History'. For a succinct introductory summary of Kristeva's thought, see Wright op. cit.

22. Jacobus, op. cit., p. 118.
23. Gallop, Jane, *Reading Lacan*, Ithaca, Cornell University Press (1985).
24. Ibid., pp. 145–6.
25. Jacobus, op. cit., p. 136. As I understand it, Jacobus cites Gallop in order to support a symptomatic reading of feminist nostalgia's imbrication with the patriarchal construction of femininity. Yet Jacobus seems also to suggest that feminist nostalgia registers a resistance to as well as an imbrication with patriarchal femininity. It is this agonistic view of nostalgia which informs the textual analyses with which I will conclude this essay.
26. Ibid., p. 133.
27. See note 1 above.
28. Rich, Adrienne, *The Dream of a Common Language: Poems 1974–77*, New York, Norton (1978).
29. Quoted in Jacobus, op. cit., p. 138.
30. Modjeska, Drusilla, *Poppy*, Ringwood, McPhee Gribble/Penguin (1990).
31. Hoffman, Eva, *Lost in Translation: A Life in a New Language*, New York, Penguin (1989).
32. Modjeska, op. cit., p. 11.
33. Ibid., p. 12
34. Ibid., p. 24.
35. Ibid., p. 15.
36. Ibid., pp. 15–16.
37. Jacobus, op. cit., p. 138.
38. Hoffman, op. cit., p. 108.
39. Ibid., p. 279.
40. Jacobus, op. cit., p. 135.
41. Ibid., p. 138.

12 Psychoanalysis and the imaginary body

ELIZABETH GROSZ

This chapter is part of a larger project on which I have worked for a number of years:[1] an attempt to rethink the terms in which subjectivity is usually understood in feminist theory. Subjectivity has tended to be conceptualised in terms that privilege and affirm the primacy of mind over body, a conceptual opposition that has characterised Western philosophy since its inception in ancient Greece. Even psychoanalytic theory has been generally understood, by feminists and others, as an account of the psychical production of masculine and feminine subjects, as if this can somehow occur or make any sense in isolation from the (cultural and social) specificities of sexed bodies. This chapter is an attempt to explain how psychoanalytic theory may be read as precisely an account of the psychosocial signification and lived reality of sexed bodies, rather than as an account of the genesis and functioning of the abstract processes of masculinity and femininity.

In focusing on, and giving primacy to, bodies in the constitution of subjectivity, I hope to be able to reclaim bodies from the status of pre-social, biologically fixed, inert, unchangeable given – the role they have been accorded by essentialist accounts of corporeality. In utilising psychoanalytic discourse rather than the more obvious discourses of science and biology, I hope to show that concepts like subjectivity and one's sexually differential value and status as masculine or feminine subjects not only rely on and retrace the contours of the sexually differentiated body, but moreover, are active ingredients in the constitution of bodies as social and cultural products. Where psychoanalytic theory requires an understanding of bodies as the grounds or raw material for the social production of subjects, in turn it also transforms the biological or natural status of the body, affirming it too as a fundamentally social product.

This chapter is an attempt to think subjectivity and especially the differences between the sexes, not in terms of the domination of the characteristics of mind, the mental sphere or the psyche, but in terms of bodies. My project is to think psychical depth or interiority in terms of the inscription and projection of corporeal surfaces. It is an attempt, as it were to turn bodies inside out and outside in. I want to experiment with the idea of circumventing or displacing the mind-body problem that has dominated western thought. I will explore the ways in which the psycho-analytic theory is able to problematise and provide other terms by which to understand the relations between the mind and the body, the inside and the outside, psychology and corporeality. Instead of relying on psychoanalytic accounts of the development of masculine and feminine character-istics, which most feminist theorists seem to focus on, I am here more interested in demonstrating how the ego, the very sense of self, is in itself linked to the subject's sexual and bodily specificity. This has clear impli-cations not only for those concerned with a feminist transformation of the power differential between the sexes, but also for those committed to anti-racist struggles: the form and specificity that is socially attributed to bodies mark the range and limitations of the subject's own self-under-standing and self-representations.

This understanding of subjectivity as a living-out of the specificities of the body, while only of indirect relevance to the visual and performing arts and media studies, and while not offering any specific feminist insights into the arts by way of policy or pragmatic projects, nonetheless threat-ens to reorient the terms in which the arts have been thus far understood. Supplanting the notion of the creative subject or the perceiving specta-tor/audience as beings who are primarily ideological and psychical agents with a notion of subjects as primarily corporeal beings, changes the ways in which the visual and performing arts have thus been produced and assessed. Traditional terms, of narrative content, of status as conventional or form-breaking, of depiction or characterisation of women and men as objects of representation, can be reassessed, and new modes of production and analysis, new modes of representation and new modes of corporeality can be explored. I am hopeful that this essay may at least begin to take up the challenge of engendering new intellectual models, new conceptual and representational practices that may more adequately be able to represent and produce subjects as sexually autonomous.

The ego as corporeal projection

Freud presents a startling account of the ego as a corporeal projection. This view confirms his claims in 'On Narcissism' (1914) that the subject only acquires a sense of unity and cohesion, that is, becomes an ego, over and above the disparate, heterogeneous sensations that comprise its expe-riences as a result of an intervention into nature. If the subject were merely a perceiving and experiencing being then there could be no way of unifying its experiences as the experiences of a single being, no way of asserting some kind of propriety over those experiences, no way of taking responsibility for them. The subject would simply be an aggregate of otherwise disconnected perceptual events, which give it no index of the existence of objects or the world. Before the advent of primary narcissism, the child is a (passive) conglomerate of fleeting experiences, at the mercy of organic and social excitations to which it may respond but over which it has no agency or control.

For Freud, the ego is what brings unity to the vast and overwhelming diversity of perceptions. It is a consequence of a perceptual surface: it is produced and grows only relative to this surface. Freud argues that the ego does not result from a preordained biological order, but is the result of a psychosocial intervention into the child's hitherto natural development:

> We are bound to suppose that a unity comparable to the ego has to be developed . . . there must be something added to auto-eroticism – a new psychical action – in order to bring about narcissism.[2]

This new action engenders primary narcissism (or what Lacan calls the mirror stage) at around six months of age. Narcissism, as Freud understands it, is a form of self-love, a mode of investing libido or sexual energy into one's own ego. Primary narcissism, that stage that engenders the existence of the ego, consists in a relative stabilization of the circulation of libido in the child's body, so that the division between subject and object (even the subject's capacity to take itself as an object) becomes possible for the first time. The ego is the result of a series of identificatory relations with the images of other subjects, particularly the mother or even its own image in the mirror. These identifications, which constitute what Lacan calls the imaginary,[3] are introjected or internalised, brought into the psychical sphere of influence of the ego in the form of the ego-ideal, the idealised model of itself to which the ego strives. At the same time, the ego is also a consequence of a blockage or rechannelling of libidinal impulses in the subject's own body in the form of a narcissistic attachment to a part or the whole of its body. In this sense, the ego is the meeting-point, the point of conjunction, between the body and the social. It is constituted from *internal* libidinal intensities and their relative stabilisation, and external identificatory inscriptions.

The subject cannot remain neutral or indifferent to its own body and body-parts. The body is libidinally invested. The human subject always maintains a relation of love (or hate) towards its own body because it must always maintain a certain level of psychical and libidinal investment, or more technically, cathexis. No person lives his or her own body merely as a functional instrument or a means to an end. Its value is never functional, for it has a (libidinal) value in itself. It is for this reason that 'Man' must be distinguished from animals. No animal kills itself in the presence of life-preserving conditions, no animal starves itself to death when food is readily available. The human subject is capable of suicide, of anorexia, because the body is *meaningful*, has significance, because it is in part constituted both for the subject and for others in terms of meanings and significances. The body can never be a mere object or instrument for consciousness, never a matter of indifference or insignificance.

Freud claims that the genesis of the ego is dependent on the construction of a psychical map of the body's libidinal intensities: the ego is not so much a self-contained entity or thing as a kind of bodily tracing, a cartography of the erotogenic intensity of the body, an internalised image of the degrees of the intensity of sensations in the child's body. He backs up his claims with reference to the 'cortical homunculus', a much-beloved idea circulating in neurological and medical circles in the nineteenth century:

> The ego is first and foremost a bodily ego: it is not merely a surface entity, but is itself the projection of a surface. If we wish to find an anatomical analogy for it we can best identify it with the 'cortical homunculus' of the anatomists, which stands on its head in the cortex, sticks up its heels, faces backwards and as we know, has its speech-area on the left hand side.[4]

The ego is a mapping, not of the real or anatomical body, but of the degree of libidinal cathexis or sexual energy the subject has invested in its own body:

> We can decide to regard erotogencity as a general characteristic of all organs and may then speak of an increase or decrease of it in a particular part of the body. For every such change in the erotogenicity of libidinal zones there might be a parallel change in the ego.[5]

The amount of libidinal intensity invested in the erotogenic zones – mouth, anus, genitals, eyes, including possibly even the entire surface of the skin – which Freud describes as 'erotogencity', the sites from which libido emanates, parallels changes that occur in the shape and form of the ego itself. If the ego is a libidinal reservoir, its 'shape' and contours vary both according to its libidinal investments in other objects, and according to the quantities of libidinal excitation that circulate in the subject's own body which are available for object-love through the sexual drives, which in their turn find their sources in the different erotogenic zones of the body.

The ego is ultimately derived from bodily sensations, chiefly from those springing from the surface of the body. It may thus be regarded as a mental projection of the surface of the body.[6]

Freud attributes a privileged role to the erotogenic zones, for it is clear that they play a disproportionately significant role in the formation of the sensori-motor homunculus, a mapping or registration of the passive (or sensory) and active (motor) interrelations between the subject's body and the world. The homunculus, the tiny 'manikin' registered in the brain, most notably in the cerebral cortex, is inverted like a mirror-image, but instead of being a point-for-point projection of the outside of the body, an accurate description of the body as it 'really' is, certain points of intensity are stressed above all others, leaving little or no room for the registration of other bodily zones. For example, the homunculus is usually regarded as highly overdeveloped in oral, manual and genital representations; It is particularly significant that there is no mention made in the relevant literature, of the female homunculus, and the ways in which it differs from the male.[3] Hysteria can, in a way, be seen as a response to this absence of representation, especially of autonomous representations of women.[4] In much of the relevant literature, the homunculus is *explicitly* described as male, and there is no mention of what this means for women.

Hysteria is a somatisation of psychical conflict, an acting out of resistance rather than its verbal articulation or conceptual representation. It is, according to Freud, a largely feminine neurosis. This may help explain how anorexia, a sub-branch of hysteria, is also an overwhelmingly feminine neurosis. It is a form of protest against and resistance to cultural investments defining what the 'proper' body is for women. (It is significant that there is no such 'proper' image for men. A wide variety of body-images remain perfectly tolerable.) The problem is not to provide women with *positive self-images*, but with *self-defined* images, whatever they might be – a much less patronising and more difficult project.

Although information can be provided by any of the sense organs, the surface of the body is in a particularly privileged position to receive information and excitations from both the interior and the exterior of the organism. This may help explain why the orifices are especially privileged in the establishment of erotogenic zones, and why the infant's psychosexual stages are part of the process of maturation which relies disproportionately on the cutaneous openings of the body's surface. However, in any case, the skin and the various sensations which are located at the surface of the body are the most primitive, essential and constitutive of all sources of sensory stimulation. The information provided by the surface of the skin is both internal and external, active and passive, receptive and expressive.[9]

The surface of the body, the skin, moreover, provides the ground for the articulation of orifices, erotogenic rims, cuts on the body's surface, loci of exchange between the inside and the outside, points of conversion of the outside into the body, and of the inside out of the body.

These are sites not only for the reception and transmission of information but also for bodily secretions, on-going processes of sensory stimulation which require some form of signification and sociocultural and psychical representation. These cuts on the body's surface create a kind of 'landscape' of that surface, providing it with 'regions', 'zones' capable of erotic significance; it serves as a kind of gridding for erotic investments in the body in uneven distributions.

The ego, then, is something like an internal screen onto which the illuminated and projected images of the body's outer surface are directed. It is the site for the gathering together and unification of otherwise disparate and scattered sensations provided by the various sense organs in all their different spaces and registers. It is also a registration or mapping of the body's inner surface, the surface of sensations, intensities and affect, the 'subjective experience' of bodily excitations and sensations.

The ego is not a map, photograph or a point for point projection of the body's surface, but an outline or representation of the degrees of erotogenicity of the bodily zones and organs. It is derived from two kinds of 'surface': on the one hand, the ego is on the 'inner' surface of the psychical agencies; on the other hand, it is a projection or representation of the body's 'outer' surface. In both cases, the surface is perceptual. Perception thus provides both the contents of the ego, and, to begin with, the earliest sexual 'objects' for the child. Moreover, in the establishment of the ego, perceptual processes are themselves sexualised, libidinally invested.

The ego is a representation of the varying intensities of libidinal-investment in the various bodily parts, and the body as a whole. Significantly, this notion of the body as a whole is dependent on the recognition of the totality and autonomy of the body of the other. The ego is thus *both* a map of the body's surface and a reflection of the image of the other's body. The other's body provides the frame for the representation of one's own. In this sense, the ego is an image of the body's significance or meaning for the subject and for the other. It is thus as much a function of fantasy and desire as it is of sensation and perception; it is a taking over of sensation and perception by a fantasmatic dimension. This significatory, cultural dimension implies that bodies, egos, subjectivities are not simply *reflections* of their cultural context and associated values, but are constituted as such by them, marking bodies in their very 'biological' configurations with sociosexual inscriptions.

It is significant that the two neuroses traversing the mind/body split, hysteria and hypochondria, in which there is a somatisation of psychical conflicts, are 'feminine' neuroses in which it is precisely the status of the female body that is causing psychical conflict. Anorexia is itself a kind of sexualisation (in a mode of renunciation) of the eating process, a displacement of genital sexuality. The body image becomes bloated, extended as the biological reality of the body becomes thinner and more frail.

Why is it that women are more likely to somatise their conflicts than men? Does this have anything to do with the female body-image? With the problematic rift of mind and body which women, even less than men, are able to live out and live with?

The ego is not simply bounded by the 'natural' body. The 'natural body', insofar as there is one, is continually augmented by the products of history and culture, which it readily incorporates into its own intimate space. In this, according to Freud, 'man' must be recognised as a 'prosthetic god', approaching the fantasy of omnipotence, or at least of a body well beyond its physical, geographical and temporal immediacy. If the ego is a mapping of the body, and if the body is able to incorporate a host of instrumental supplements, the ego (or at least its ideal) aspires to a megalomania worthy of gods:

> With every tool [man] is perfecting his own organs, whether motor or sensory, or is removing the limits to their functioning. Motor power places gigantic forces at his disposal, which, like his muscles, he can employ in any direction; thanks to ship and aircraft neither water nor air can hinder his movements . . . Man has, as it were, become a kind of prosthetic God. When he puts on all his auxiliary organs he is truly magnificent, but these organs have not grown onto him and they still give him much trouble at times.[10]

The once clear boundary between the mind and the body, nature and culture, becomes increasingly eroded. The very organ whose function it is to distinguish biological or id impulses from sociocultural pressures, the ego, is always already the intermingling of both insofar as it is the consequence of the cultural, that is, significatory effects of the body, the meaning and love of the body that is projected to produce the form of the ego.

Lacan and the imaginary anatomy

Like Freud, Lacan claims that the ego has no *a priori* status. It comes into being in the mirror stage, a phase in human development that occurs between about six and eighteenth months, in which the infant comes to recognise its own image in a mirror. The mirror stage provides the matrix or ground for the development of human subjectivity, the place and time from which the ego emerges. He seems to take Freud's comments about the ego being a bodily extension or projection very seriously. For Lacan, the ego is not an outline or projection of the real, anatomical and physiological body but is the body insofar as it is imagined and represented for the subject through the image of others (including its own reflection in a mirror). The mirror stage provides the child with an anticipatory image of his own body as a *Gestalt* or externalised and totalised image. The earliest recognition by the child of its bodily unity, that is, the recognition that its skin is the limit of its spatial location, is at the same time a misrecognition insofar as the image with which the child identifies belies the child's own sensory and motor incapacities. Lacan makes it clear that the mirror stage institutes 'an essential libidinal relationship with the body-image'.[11]

The imaginary anatomy is an internalised image or map of the meaning that the body has for the subject, for others in its social world, and for a culture as a whole. It is an individual and collective fantasy of the body's forms and modes of action. This, Lacan claims, helps to explain the peculiar, nonorganic connections formed in hysteria, including anorexia, and in such phenomena as the phantom limb. It also helps to explain why there are distinct waves of particular forms of hysteria, some even call them 'fashions', i.e. why hysterics commonly exhibited forms of breathing difficulty (e.g. fainting, *tussis nervosa*, breathlessness and so on) in the nineteenth century, which today have relatively disappeared and taking their place as the most 'popular' forms of hysteria today are eating disorders, anorexia nervosa and bulimia in particular.

Anorexia is arguably the most stark and striking sexualisation of biological instincts: the anorexic may risk her very life in the attainment of a body-image approximating her ideal. Neither a 'disorder' of the ego, nor as popular opinion has it, a 'dieting disease' gone out of control, anorexia can, like the phantom limb, be a kind of mourning for a pre-Oedipal (i.e. precastrated) body and a corporeal connection to the mother that women in patriarchy are required to abandon. Anorexia is a form of protest at or resistance of the social meaning of the female body. Rather than seeing it simply as an out-of-control compliance with the current patriarchal ideals of slenderness, it is precisely a renunciation of these 'ideals'.

Lacan argues that instead of observing and following the neurological connections in organic paralyses, hysterical paralyses reproduce various naive or everyday beliefs about the ways the body functions. In an hysterical paralysis, it is more likely that limbs which are immobilised are unable to move from a joint, whereas in organic paralyses, the immobilization extends further upward and encompasses many nerve and muscular connections not apparent to the lay observer. Hysterical paralyses, in other words, follow common sense views of the way the body works, especially those based on observation, visual appearance, rather than exhibiting any understanding of the body's underlying physiology.

In the phantom limb, the diseased limb has been surgically removed but continues to induce sensations of pain in the location that the limb used to occupy. In such cases, which occur with near universality in the surgical removal of mobile limbs, the absence of a limb is as psychically invested as its presence. The phantom can indeed be regarded as a kind of libidinal memorial to the lost limb, a nostalgic memory strongly cathected in an attempt to undermine the perceptual awareness of its absence. It does not completely undermine the experience of the absence of the limb, but results in the phantom feeling 'shell-like', 'empty', merely formal and abstract, different from the way other limbs feel to the subject. The subject's healthy limbs, for example, exert a certain weight or gravity which is absent when the limb is amputated. The phantom limb exhibits many curiosities and seems to follow 'laws' of its own very different from those regulating the rest of the body. It attests to the more or less tenacious cohesion of the imaginary anatomy or body schema.[12] Like hysteria, hypochondria and sexuality itself, the phantom limb testifies to the pliability and fluidity of what is usually considered the inert, fixed, passive biological body. The biological body, if it exists at all, exists for the subject only through the mediation of an image or series of (social/cultural) images, of the body and its capacity for movement and action. The phantom limb is a libidinally invested part of the body phantom, the image or *doppelganger* of the body the subject must develop if it is to be able to conceive of itself as an object and a body and if it is to take on voluntary action in conceiving of itself as subject.

This imaginary anatomy is at work not only in the everyday functioning of neurotic and perverse subjects where it functions most commonly at the level of the sexualization of parts or the whole of the body, and in the functioning of drives and their privileged objects, it is also crucial in explaining the symptomatology of psychosis. It is the precondition and raw material of a stable, that is, symbolic, identity which the child acquires as a result of the resolution of the Oedipus complex. Its reorganisation or decomposition witnesses psychotic breakdown.

The constitution of the subject's imaginary identity in the mirror phase establishes a provisional identity for the child, an identity which requires the stabilisation, ordering and placement of the subject in a sociosymbolic position where it can engage in symbolic and linguistic exchange with others. It also creates the conditions of possibility for the child's earliest and most primitive notions of milieu, context, environment or location.

Masculine and feminine

The question of biology and of the mind/body relation is raised once again, and in a most crucial and complex fashion, in Freud's account of the differences between the sexes. This is clearly the location of the most controversial and contested elements of his work. Yet even here, and in spite of Freud's clear biologism, there are also concepts and ideas which indicate a considerably more sophisticated understanding of sexual difference than many views commonly attributed to him. This is not to deny that there are still very major problems regarding his understanding of the differences between the sexes and particularly of female sexuality. Although this cannot be examined in detail, it is worthwhile indicating some of the major areas of feminist concern as well as those places in Freud's writing where, perhaps without his own knowledge or awareness, his position entails much that could be of value to feminist theory regarding the body and sexual difference.

Freud's account of the acquisition of masculine and feminine psychical positions can plausibly be interpreted as an account of the ways in which the male and female bodies are given meaning, and structured with reference to their relative social positions. Freud himself is not really concerned with the question of anatomy *per se*, seeking instead the psychical implications of anatomical differences. Nevertheless, he justifies his claims regarding the order of psychical events with recourse to a kind of confrontation the child has with (the meaning of) anatomy. His position can be best understood in terms of how meanings, values and desires construct male and female bodies (and particularly how their differences are represented). His postulation of the Oedipus complex and the castration threat can be read as an analysis and explanation of the social construction of women's bodies as a lack, and the correlative (and dependent) constitution of the male body as phallic.

The notions of phallic and castrated are not simply superimposed on pregiven bodies, an added attribute that could, in other cultural configurations, be removed to leave 'natural' sexual differences intact. Rather, the attribution of a phallic or a castrated status to sexually different bodies is an internal condition of the ways those bodies are lived and given meaning right from the very start (with or without the child's knowledge or compliance). There is no natural body to return to, no pure sexual difference one could gain access to if only the distortions and deformations of patriarchy could be removed or transformed. The phallus binarizes the differences between the sexes, dividing up a sexual-corporeal continuum into two mutually exclusive categories which in fact belie the multiplicity of bodies and body-types.

Although most psychoanalysts do not attribute sexual difference to the pre-Oedipal stages, and do not discuss the question of the sex of the body-image or the ways in which the body image does or does not include the sex of the body, it seems incontestable that the type of genitals (and later, secondary sexual characteristics) one has must play a major role in the type of body image one has, and the type of self-conception directly linked to the social meaning and value of the sexed body. Indeed, an argument could be made that the much beloved category of 'gender' so commonly used in feminist theory should be understood, not as the attribution of social and psychological categories to a biologically given sex, i.e. in terms of a mind/body split, but in terms that link gender much more closely to the specificities of sex. Gender is not an ideological superstructure added to a biological base; rather, gender is the inscription, and hence also the production, of the sexed body. Masculine or feminine gender cannot be neutrally attributed to bodies of either sex: the 'masculinity' of the male body cannot be the same as the 'masculinity' of the female body, because the kind of body inscribed makes a difference to the meanings and functioning of gender that emerges.[13]

Lacan says explicitly what is implied in Freud's understanding of sexual difference: while it makes perfect sense for the young boy, before he understands the anatomical differences between the sexes, to see others on a model derived from his own body morphology or representation, it makes no sense at all to claim that the girl too sees the whole world on a model derived from the *boy's* experience. Indeed it is the site of an amazing blindness on the part of these founding fathers of psychoanalytic feminism to claim that both the boy and the girl regard themselves, each other and the others in their world as phallic unless the phallus has an *a priori* privilege in the constitution of the body image. This is precisely Lacan's claim:

> All the phenomena we are discussing [that is, the various manifestations of the body image in psychical life] seem to exhibit the laws of *Gestalt*; the fact that the penis is dominant in the shaping of the body image is evidence of this. though this may shock the sworn champions of the autonomy of female sexuality, such dominance is a fact and one moreover which cannot be put down to cultural influences alone.[14]

Among Lacan's most deliberately provocative statements (in a body of work that abounds in provocation), it is unclear that the 'laws of *Gestalt*' entail the dominance of the penis in the body-image *unless* female sexuality is already, even in the pre-Oedipal stages when the body-image is being formed, construed as castrated. Now, in one sense this is true. If patriarchy requires that female sexual organs be regarded more as the absence or lack of male organs than in any autonomous terms, then, for the others in the child's social world, the child's female body is lacking. But for the child herself to understand her body as such requires her to accept castration long before the castration threat. What Lacan says is clear for the boy: insofar as the body image is a unified, externalised and totalising representation of the body, and insofar as the penis is 'part' of the male body, it clearly plays some role, even if not yet a dominant one in shaping the boy's body-image. But how it does so in the case of the girl is entirely obscure. When the penis takes on the function of the phallus which is only possible as a result of the Oedipal classification of female sexuality as castrated, as lacking the phallus, only then can it be said to be dominant in the shaping of the body-image for girls as well as boys. And even then, clearly the phallus does not have the same meaning for the girl as it does for the boy: at best, for the girl it represents a form of nostalgic fantasy for her pre-Oedipal and pre-castrated position, the position that I believe the anorexic tenaciously clings to, as the only period in which the female body is regarded as whole and intact; but for the boy it represents the social valorisation of the penis, an actual and not simply a fantasised part of the body.

If women do not lack in any ontological or biological sense (there is no lack in the real, as Lacan is fond of saying), men cannot be said to have. In this sense, patriarchy requires that female bodies and sexualities be socially produced a lack. This, in some social contexts is taken literally but also occurs at an imaginary and symbolic level, that is, at the level of the body's morphology and the body image. Psychoanalysis describes how this mutilated body image comes about, thus explaining the socially authorised social and sexual positions and behaviours appropriate to and expected from women; but it is unable to explain how this occurs (not only because it is unable to see that its analyses find their context in patriarchal culture and not just neutral 'civilization', but above all, because it is unable to see that its own pronouncements and position are masculine). On such a model, anorexia may be seen as a resistance to the castrated status accorded to women in our culture. It can be regarded as a mode of confirmation and acceptance of femininity only if the contradictory status of women and the female body in patriarchal cultures is ignored. It is a way of trying (often unsuccessfully) to negotiate a place in culture as a subject (and not just as a body).

What psychoanalytic theory makes clear is that the body is literally written on, inscribed by desire and signification, at the anatomical, physiological and neurological levels. The body is in no sense naturally or innately psychical, sexual or sexed. It is indeterminate and indeterminable outside its social constitution as a body of a particular type. This implies that the body which it presumes and helps to explain is an open-ended, pliable set of significations, capable of being rewritten, reconstituted in quite other terms than those which mark it, and consequently the forms of sexed identity and psychical subjectivity at work today. This project of rewriting the female body as a positivity rather than as a lack entails two related concerns: reorganisation and reframing the terms by which the body has been socially represented (a project in which many feminists are presently engaged in the variety of challenges feminism poses in literary, visual, and filmic representational systems); and challenging the discourses which claim to analyse and explain the body and subject scientifically – biology, psychology, sociology – to develop different perspectives that may be able to better represent women's interests.

Notes

1. The project has finally come to fruition in the form of a book, *Volatile Bodies. Towards a Corporeal Feminism*, forthcoming Bloomington, Indiana University Press; Sydney, Allen & Unwin. This chapter is a shortened and transformed version of the second chapter of the book.
2. Freud, Sigmund (1914) 'On Narcissism: An Introduction', in James Strachey (ed.) *The Standard Edition of the Complete Works of Sigmund Freud* vol. 14, London, Hogarth Press (1957–74).
3. For a more detailed explanation of Lacan's understanding of the imaginary, and the corresponding psychical orders of the symbolic and the real, see my reading of Lacan in *Jacques Lacan. A Feminist Introduction*, (1990), London, Routledge.
4. Freud, Sigmund (1922) 'The ego and the id' in Strachey op. cit. p. 26.
5. Freud (1914) op. cit. p. 84.
6. Freud (1923) op. cit. p. 26.
7. See for example, Cumming, W. J. K. (1988) 'The neurobiology of the body schema', *British Journal of Psychiatry*, 153 Supplement no. 2, 1988. Gorman, Warren, *Body Image and the Image of the Brain*. St Louis: Warren H. Green Inc (1969); and Reiser, Morton F. *Mind, Brain, Body. Towards a Convergence of Psychoanalysis and Neurobiology*. New York, Basic Books (1984).
8. I can recommend one paper in particular that not only articulates hysteria as a form of resistance, but focuses on anorexia as a mode of (unsuccessful) rebellion against the norms and imperatives of femininity that patriarchy imposes on women. See

Celermajer, Danielle, (1987), 'Submission and rebellion: Anorexia and a Feminism of the Body', *Australian Feminist Studies*, 5, pp. 57–70.

9.   In this context, the writings of Didier Anzieu are most instructive: he argues that the skin and tactility must be regarded as the primordial corporeal foundations for the operation of all the other senses, which can be understood as the incision of a cut or rim, the creation of an orifice on the body's surface. See in particular Anzieu, Didier, *The Skin Ego*. London, Karnac (1989); and *A Skin for Thought. Interviews with Gilbert Tarrab*. London, Karnac Books (1990).

10.   Freud, Sigmund (1929) 'Civilization and its discontents', in Strachey op. cit. pp. 90–2.

11.   Lacan, Jaques 'Some reflections on the ego', *International Journal of Psychoanalysis* 34, 1953.

12.   This notion is analysed in some detail in Schilder, Paul, *The Image and Appearance of the Human Body. Studies in the Constructive Energies of the Psyche.* New York, International Universities Press (1978).

13.   See in this context, the pioneer writings of Moira Gatens, (1990), 'A Critique of the Sex/Gender Distinction'. In Sneja Gunew (Ed.), *A Reader in Feminist Knowledge.* London and New York: Routledge. pp 139–60.

14.   Lacan (1953) op. cit.

Afterword

Feminist ideological perspectives are of fundamental importance in this book. So, too, is the desire to change normative codes not only at the level of theory, but in the very practice of our crafts as thinkers, writers and makers. These, indeed, are matters of principle: this is no abstracted idea we are talking about, this is our lives as women. How do we develop new, alternative modes of functioning within academe, within the arts and media, within society? One part of the answer has to be co-operative endeavour, and a related capacity to tolerate plurality of vision. This book stands as a marker to signal the feminist belief that matters of principle still count.

Among these matters of principle, two stand out. First is the project's bringing together of feminists of divergent experience and widely dissimilar public renown – from 'household names' to newcomers in publication – as part of a strategy aimed explicitly at questioning hierarchies of prestige and accepted notions of relative authorial credibility. These essays came out of the context of a conference – on Feminist Methodologies – organised by Penny Florence and Dee Reynolds at the Institute of Romance Studies, University of London, in January 1992. Like other feminist groupings, the Feminist Methodologies Conference deliberately sought to facilitate the networking of ideas between all women active in the field, regardless of affiliation or status, and hence to assert the right to speech. Every effort was made to seek out contributions from black women, and it is a reflection, perhaps, of their differing agendas as much as of their small number in academe so far that none was forthcoming. Awareness of whiteness, however, is an important strand within the collection.

Interdisciplinarity is the second principle. The wide range of research interests among feminists, as exemplified in this book, affirms the continuing need to scrutinise, to politicise, all corners of thought and practice; without this exposure, oppressive patterns of social formation will continue unabated, at best merely modified to accommodate changing circumstances. What the present volume demonstrates is the sheer variety of feminist work, yet at the same time the similarity of the preoccupations common among feminists from different disciplinary backgrounds. Perhaps even more crucially, this book reveals the extent to which forms of oppression themselves are similar – regardless of discipline.

Interdisciplinarity also plays a vital part within the work of most individual feminists. Belief in the value of working across discipline boundaries is not about trendy cross-referencing; it is about re-establishing links across false barriers in order to reweave the threads of knowledge and experience fragmented, finally, by the consolidation of the male professions in the nineteenth century. By asserting the value of shared interests, espousing a broadly common cause, feminists resist the containment imposed by the traditional academic 'field', while simultaneously exposing the fences for what they are: phantoms to keep us well-'disciplined'. Certain disciplines have lent themselves more immediately to interdisciplinary methods than others. Film and media studies, because more recently developed and, like cultural studies, more inherently populist and wide-ranging in their subject-matter than the older, more rigidly established disciplines, offer, indeed invite, cross-disciplinary investigation. Art History, despite the critical weight of modernist formalism and the vested interests of the art market, has, likewise, provided a locus for some of the most radical interdisciplinary interventions by feminists in recent years. Yet, discursively marginalised as women have been, their interests have been both on the edges and in the centre – whether confronting the canons of high culture or the male gurus of psychoanalysis, whether picking at the seams of popular science or examining personal and sociohistorical issues of childhood. But let us not underestimate ourselves: our attention to all such issues has transformed the ways they are perceived, has brought them into a new and uncompromising limelight. We have brought the margins to the centre and shown that, without edges, there can be no whole.

It is no coincidence that a central focus of concern in this book is the relationship between the verbal and the visual, word and image. The word, or language – that monolithic term used to distinguish the 'meaningful' among forms of human expression – has been accorded pride of place in western culture; it has been deemed all-powerful, the realm of the Symbolic, of patriarchal Law. Is this surprising? Is it not the inevitable product of a western patriarchal culture defending its own interests? Whether Freudian, or Lacanian, masculinist theorists have noticeably tightened their grip, rewritten their baseline, at key moments of women's struggle in the west for emancipation – for 'representation'. Theory, any theory, is both subjective and time-locked; as an active producer of cultural meaning, theory inflects the position of its theorist and is formed out of the needs of the theorist's own time. Feminists seek to uncover these underlying needs and to ask whom they serve, how and why; then to transform the differential bases thus inscribed by making theory anew, from women's own distinctive positions and subjectivities. In wishing to represent ourselves, accessing what has been relegated to the pre-verbal, and to the phase constituted as a world of boundless sensation – 'maternal chaos' – is vital. Included in this notion of maternal chaos are not only the mother and the infant – purportedly 'outside language' – but the visual sense, the realm of the image. In the search for ways to understand and describe the workings of the visual, feminists give new significance to that earliest of languages – the language of the image – and thus unsettle the omnipotence of the word.[1] Formed prior to verbal communication, the visual message retains elements which cannot be fixed or confined by the word – which is why visual images have an excess that resists reduction to logic, or to written language: immediacy, passion, terror, seduction – emotional excess which short-circuits reason to hit direct into the solar-plexus, or into the longing infant in us all.

One method characteristic of feminist intervention is that of breaking down the boundaries between theory and practice. Theory has traditionally been seen as a male sphere. Indeed, reason, logic, mental exercise have, in themselves, been gendered masculine – in contrast to practice, particularly visual arts practice which, through its physical materiality and sensuality, has commonly been gendered 'feminine'.[2] By giving new importance to and analysing the function of the actual material constituents in the formation of visual language – the language of mediums and making – we provide a fundamental means to decode that language, while simultaneously undermining the split between masculine and feminine. This approach has formed the basis of my own work as a feminist art historian, and is commonly found, too, in the theoretically inspired practice of much recent feminist art.[3] It is a method equally apparent in the comparable erosion taking place in feminist work between accepted literary and theoretical models of practice: autobiography (and hence the assertion of the feminist belief in the personal-as-political, and in the validity of individual witness) slides into history, into theory, into creative writing/making and back again. Safe, predictable boundaries of the 'subjective' and the 'objective' – of writer/text/reader, maker/object/looker

– are dissolved to challenge ideas of any eternal truth or fixed authority. Our brief, then, is ambitious. It includes not only representation as such, in all its senses, but representation as reception: investigation into how the 'audience' of the image/text is constructed – and can be deconstructed; into how we, as both consumers and producers, can dislodge those divisive paradigms which have reduced the personal and sensual richness of life to banal, monochrome abstractions.

Feminist history, and the insights it affords into the gendered premises of received history, is a vital component in feminist analysis. History helps us to call into question monolithic notions of masculinity and femininity, of class and race, by offering the detail of human social experience as material for complicating easy, universalising assumptions – a process which ensures that theory remains rooted in practice/experience, and does not become a free-floating abstraction. It assists us in refining and strengthening our theorisations by making it possible, for example, to locate changing notions of 'normality' at specific historical moments, and for specific ideological purposes, thereby identifying the normal as particular to a culture, rather than as a timeless phenomenon. Thus we are enabled to question western conceptions of the unitary self – a self which has excluded women – and to expose as ahistoric and erroneous those universals to which modern Eurocentric culture has traditionally been wedded. Engaging with the past not only enables feminists to write women's histories and to render visible women's experience; it is also the means to clarify the particular, changing forms and machinery of patriarchal power – and to recover the evidence of women's resistance to it. By locating 'binary divisions' within their specific socio-historical frameworks, and charting their transformations, we can expose this process of differentiation as an ideological mechanism for the suppression of dissenting voices, and as a guarantor of patriarchal supremacy. Feminist histories can demystify those powerful, formative beliefs which, like religion, philosophy, or psychoanalytic theory, have often served to police our thoughts through their hold on our emotions and unconscious. Equally, such dominant ideologies themselves (notably psychoanalytic theory) can be used as the means of their own undoing: in developing our own theorisations, feminists expose the supposedly oppositional 'self' and 'other' as but two sides of a single, psychic coin.

So we work to expose and subvert divisions between disciplines, between reason and emotion, and between theory and practice; to create spaces in which people can communicate without false boundaries. Feminism, in the 1990s, is a pluralistic enterprise in which widely differing approaches and methodologies, beliefs and concerns, mediums of expression can and must be encouraged, not simply to co-exist, but to combine forces. We are, I think, finally moving out of a phase in modern feminism which, because of the truly appalling discoveries we made about women's lives and experience, has tended to (re)produce a woman-as-victim syndrome. In thinking for ourselves, making for ourselves, and working together – as in the present book – we have the means to realise women's potential, our genuine stature and integrity, and to enjoy women's capacity to effect change in an unbalanced world.

Anthea Callen
University of Warwick
1994

Notes

1. K. Silverman, in *The Acoustic Mirror: The Female Voice in Psychoanalysis and Cinema*, Bloomington, Indiana University Press (1988), examines another formative pre-verbal experience, that of the maternal voice.
2. For further discussion, see A. Callen, 'Coloured views: gender and morality in Degas' *Bathers* pastels', in A. Benjamin, *The Body*, Special Edition of the *Journal of Philosophy and the Visual Arts*, London, September/October 1993, pp. 22–9.
3. See, for example, A. Callen, *The Spectacular Body: Science and Technique in the Work of Degas*, London and New Haven, Yale University Press (1994) and on recent feminist art, R. Parker and G. Pollock, *Framing Feminism: Art and the Women's Movement 1970–1985* London, Pandora (1987).

Select bibliography

Adler, K. and Garb, T. *Berthe Morisot* Oxford, Phaidon (1987)

Anderson, Linda (ed.) *Plotting Change: Contemporary Women's Fiction* Sevenoaks, Edward Arnold (1990)

Anzieu, Didier *The Skin Ego* London, Karnac (1989)

Anzieu, Didier *A Skin for Thought: Interviews with Gilbert Tarrab* London, Karnac (1990)

Arblaster, Anthony *Viva La Libertà: Politics in Opera* London, Verso (1992)

Attenborough, David *The Trials of Life* London, Collins/BBC Books (1990)

Baddeley, Oriana and Fraser, Valerie *Drawing the Line: Art and Cultural Identity in Contemporary Latin America* London, Verso (1989)

Bakhtin, Mikhail Mikhailovich *Rabelais and His World* Cambridge, Mass., MIT Press (1968)

Barker, Frances *et al.* (eds) *The Politics of Theory* Colchester, University of Essex (1983)

Barrett, Michèle (ed.) *Virginia Woolf, Women and Writing* London, The Women's Press (1979)

Barthes, Roland *Camera Lucida* London, Flamingo (1984)

Battersby, Christine *Gender and Genius: Towards a Feminist Aesthetics* London, The Women's Press (1989)

Beauroy, J. *et al.* (eds) *The Wolf and the Lamb: Popular Culture in France from the Old Regime to the Twentieth Century* Saratoga, Anma Libri (1977)

Belsey, Catherine *Critical Practice* London, Methuen (1980)

Belsey, Catherine *John Milton: Language, Gender, Power* Oxford, Blackwell (1986)

Benjamin, A. *The Body: Special Edition of the Journal of Philosophy and the Visual Arts* London, September/October 1993

Bennett, Tony *et al.* (eds) *Popular Television and Film* London, British Film Institute (1981)

Birke, Linda 'Science, feminism and animal natures II: feminist critiques and the place of animals in science', *Women's Studies International Forum 14*, 1991, pp. 451–458

Bleier, Ruth *Science and Gender* London, Pergamon (1984)

Bleier, Ruth *Feminist Approaches to Science* Oxford, Pergamon (1988)

Blind, M. (ed.) *The Diaries of Marie Bashkirtseff* London, Virago (1984)

Boffin, Tessa and Fraser, Jean *Stolen Glances* London, Pandora (1991)

Borsa, Joan 'Frida Kahlo: marginalization and the critical female subject', *Third Text 3*, 1990, pp. 21–40

Bowlby, Rachel *Just Looking* London, Methuen (1985)

Brown, Mary Ellen *Television and Women's Culture* London, Sage (1990)

Butler, Judith *Gender Trouble: Feminism and the Subversion of Identity* London, Routledge (1990)

Callen, Anthea *The Spectacular Body: Science and Technique in the Work of Degas* New Haven, Yale University Press (forthcoming 1995)

Carrier, David, 'Art history in the mirror stage: interpreting *Un Bar aux Folies Bergère*', *History and Theory* vol. 19, 1990, pp. 297–320

Carrington, Leonora *The Seventh Horse and Other Tales* London, Virago (1989)

Carter, Angela *Frida Kahlo* London, Redstone Press (1989)

Celermajer, Danielle 'Submission and rebellion: anorexia and a feminism of the body' *Australian Feminist Studies* 5, 1987, pp. 57–70

Chadwick, Whitney *Women Artists and the Surrealist Movement* London, Thames and Hudson (1985)

Chodorow, Nancy *The Reproduction of Mothering* Berkeley, University of California Press (1978)

Clark, Katarina and Holquist, Michael *Mikhail Bakhtin* Cambridge, Mass., Harvard University Press (1984)

Clark, T. J. *The Painting of Modern Life: Paris in the Art of Manet and his Followers* London, Thames and Hudson (1984)

Clément, Catherine *Opera or the Undoing of Women* London, Virago (1989)

Conrad, Peter *Romantic Opera and Literary Form* Berkeley, University of California Press (1977)

Conrad, Peter *A Song of Love and Death: The Meaning of Opera* London, Chatto and Windus (1987)

Corner, J. (ed.) *Documentary and the Mass Media* London, Edward Arnold (1986)

Dalotel, Alain *Paule Minck: Communarde et Féministe 1839–1901* Paris, Syros (1981)

Eagleton, Terry *Literary Theory* Oxford, Blackwell (1983)

Eagleton, Terry *The Rape of Clarissa: Writing, Sexuality and Class Struggle in Samuel Richardson* Oxford, Blackwell (1986)

Edelskin, T. (ed.) *Perspectives on Morisot* New York, Hudson Hills (1990)

Fish, Stanley *Is There a Text in this Class and Other Essays* Cambridge, Mass., Harvard University Press (1980)

Flax, Jane *Thinking Fragments: Psychoanalysis, Feminism and Postmodernism in the Contemporary West* Berkeley, University of California Press (1990)

Florence, P. *Mallarmé, Manet and Redon: Visual and Aural Signs and the Generation of Meaning* Cambridge, Cambridge University Press (1986)

Franco, Jean *Plotting Women: Gender and Representation in Mexico* London, Verso (1989)

Freud, Sigmund *The Standard Edition of the Complete Works* J. Strachey (ed.), London, Hogarth Press (1953–74)

Gallop, Jane *Reading Lacan* Ithaca, Cornell University Press (1985)

Garb, T. *Woman Impressionists* Oxford, Phaidon (1986)

le Garrec, Evelyne, *Séverine une Rebelle 1855–1929* Paris, Editions du Seuil (1982)

Gatens, Moira 'A Critique of the Sex/Gender Distinction' in Gunew, Sneja (ed.) *A Reader in Feminist Knowledge* London, Routledge (1990)

Gilbert-Rolfe, Jeremy 'Edouard Manet and the pleasure problematic' *Arts Magazine* vol. 62, no. 2, February 1988, pp. 40–4

Gorman, Warren *Body Image and the Image of the Brain* St Louis, Warren Green (1969)

Greer, Germaine *The Female Eunuch* London, Paladin (1971)

Grosz, Elizabeth *Jacques Lacan: A Feminist Introduction* London, Routledge (1990)

Grosz, Elizabeth *Volatile Bodies: Towards a Corporeal Feminism* Bloomington, Indiana University Press (1994)

Gunew, Sneja (ed.) *A Reader in Feminist Knowledge* London, Routledge (1990)

Hanson, A. C., *Manet and the Modern Tradition* New Haven, Yale University Press (1977)

Hart, Andrew *et al. Making the Real World* Cambridge, Cambridge University Press (1988)

Harvey, David *Consciousness and the Urban Experience: Studies in the History and Theory of Capitalist Urbanisation* Oxford, Blackwell (1985)

Harvey, David *The Condition of Postmodernity* Oxford, Blackwell (1989)

Haskell, Molly, *From Reverence to Rape: The Treatment of Women in the Movies* London, New English Library (1975)

Haug, Frigga *Female Sexualization* London, Verso (1987)

Herbert, Robert *Impressionism, Art, Leisure and Parisian Society* New Haven, Yale University Press (1984)

Heron, Liz (ed.) *Truth, Dare or Promise: Girls Growing up in the Fifties* London, Virago (1985)

Herrmann, Ann *The Dialogic and Difference: 'An/Other Woman' in Virginia Woolf and Christa Wolf* New York, Columbia University Press (1989)

Higgonet, A. *Berthe Morisot,* London, Collins (1990)

Higgonet, A. *Berthe Morisot's Images of Women* Cambridge, Mass., Yale University Press (1992)

Hinds, Hilary, Phoenix, Ann and Stacey, Jackie (eds) *Working Out: New Directions for Women's Studies* Brighton, Falmer (1992)

Hirsch, Marianne and Keller, Evelyn Fox *Conflicts in Feminism* London, Routledge (1990)

Hoffman, Eva *Lost in Translation: A Life in a New Language* New York, Penguin (1989)

Irigaray, Luce *Speculum of the Other Woman* Ithaca, Cornell University Press (1985)

Irigaray, Luce *This Sex which Is Not One* Ithaca, Cornell University Press (1985)

Irigaray, Luce 'The bodily encounter with the mother' and 'Women-mothers, the silent substratum of the social order' in Whitford, Margaret (ed.) *The Irigaray Reader* Oxford, Blackwell (1991)

Jacobus, Mary 'Freud's mnemonic: women, screen memories and feminist nostalgia', *Michigan Quarterly Review* 1987, pp. 117–39

Kaplan, Cora *Sea Changes: Culture and Feminism* London, Verso (1986)

Krakavitch, I. *Ce que veulent les femmes: Articles et Conférences de 1869–1894* Paris, Syros (1981)

Kristeva, Julia *Desire in Language* Oxford, Blackwell (1980)

Kristeva, Julia *Powers of Horror: An Essay on Abjection* New York, Columbia University Press (1982)

Kristeva, Julia *Revolution in Poetic Language* New York, Columbia University Press (1984)

Kuhn, Annette *Women's Pictures* London, Routledge (1982)

Lacan, Jacques *Le séminaire. Livre XX* Paris, Seuil (1975)

Lacan, Jacques *Ecrits: A Selection* London, Tavistock (1977)

Lacan, Jacques *The Four Fundamental Concepts of Psychoanalysis* London, Tavistock (1977)

Laplanche, Jean *Life and Death in Psychoanalysis* Baltimore, Johns Hopkins University Press (1976)

de Lauretis, Teresa *Technologies of Gender* London, MacMillan (1987)

de Lauretis, Teresa (ed.) *Feminist Studies/Critical Studies* London, MacMillan (1988)

Leith, Dick and Myerson, George *The Power of Address: Explorations in Rhetoric* London, Routledge (1989)

Lipton, Eunice 'Manet. A radicalized female imagery', *Art Forum* 13, November 1975, pp. 48–53

Lipton, Eunice *Alias Olympia,* London, Thames and Hudson (1993)

Lull, James *Inside Family Viewing* London, Routledge (1990)

Lyotard, Jean-Francois *The Postmodern Condition: A Report on Knowledge* Manchester, Manchester University Press (1984)

Macherey, Pierre, *Theory of Literary Production* London, Routledge (1978)

Martin, Emily 'The egg and the sperm' *Signs* 16, 1991, pp. 485–501

Matthews, Nancy Mowll *Cassatt and her Circle* New York, Abbeville Press (1984)

McClary, Susan *George Bizet: Carmen* Cambridge, Cambridge University Press (1992)

McGuigan, Jim *Cultural Populism* London, Routledge (1992)

Millett, Kate *Sexual Politics* London, Virago (1977)

Mills, Sara (ed.) *Gendering the Reader* Hemel Hempstead, Harvester-Wheatsheaf (1994)

Mitchell, Juliet and Rose, Jacqueline (eds) *Jacques Lacan and the Ecole Freudienne: Feminine Sexuality* London, Macmillan (1990)

206   Select bibliography

Modjeska, Drusilla *Poppy* Ringwood, McPhee Gribble/Penguin (1990)
Moi, Toril (ed.) *The Kristeva Reader* Oxford, Blackwell (1986)
Morley, David *Family Television: Cultural Power and Domestic Pleasure* London, Comedia (1986)
Morrison, Toni *Beloved* London, Chatto and Windus (1987)
Moses, Claire Goldberg *French Feminism in the Nineteenth Century* New York, SUNY Press (1984)
Mulvey, Laura *Visual and Other Pleasures* London, MacMillan (1990)
Nicholson, Linda *Feminism/Postmodernism* London, Routledge (1990)
Nochlin, Linda 'A thoroughly modern masked ball', *Art in America*, 71, November 1983, pp. 108–201
Parker, R. and Pollock, G. *Old Mistresses: Women, Art and Ideology* London, Pandora (1986)
Parker, R. and Pollock, G. *Framing Feminism: Art and the Women's Movement 1970–85*, London, Pandora (1987)
Pearce, Lynne *Woman/Image/Text: Readings in Pre-Raphaelite Art and Literature* Hemel Hempstead, Harvester-Wheatsheaf (1991)
Pearce, Lynne *Reading Dialogics* London, Edward Arnold (1994)
Peterson, Karen and Wilson, J. J. *Women Artists: Recognition and Reappraisal from the Early Middle Ages to the Twentieth Century* London, Women's Press (1978)
Pollock, Griselda *Vision and Difference: Femininity, Feminism and the Histories of Art* London, Routledge (1988)
Pollock, Griselda *Sexuality and Surveillance: Bourgeois Men and Working Women* London, Routledge (1992)
Pollock, Griselda and Kendall, Richard (eds) *Dealing with Degas: Representations of Women and the Politics of Vision* London, Pandora (1991)
Praz, Mario *The Romantic Agony* Oxford, Oxford University Press (1970)
Pribram, E. Deirdre *Female Spectators* Verso, London (1988)
Reed, Evelyn *Sexism and Science* New York, Pathfinder Press (1978)
Reiser, Morton F. *Mind Body Brain: Towards a Convergence of Psychoanalysis and Neurobiology* New York, Basic Books (1984)
Rose, Jacqueline *The Haunting of Sylvia Plath* London, Virago (1991)
Ross, Novelene *Manet's Bar at the Folies Bergère and the Myths of Popular Illustration* Ann Arbor, Michigan UMI Research Press (1982)
Rouart, D. *The Correspondence of Berthe Morisot* London, Lund Humphries (1957)
Ryder, Neil *Science, Television and the Adolescent* London, Independent Broadcasting Authority (1982)
Schilder, Paul *The Image and Appearance of the Human Body: Studies in the Constructive Energies of the Psyche* New York, International Universities Press (1978)
Showalter, Elaine *The Female Malady: Women, Madness and English Culture 1830–1980* London, Virago 1987
Silverman, Kaja *The Acoustic Mirror: The Female Voice in Psychoanalysis and Cinema* Bloomington, Indiana University Press (1988)
Silverstone, Roger *Framing Science: The Making of a BBC Documentary* London, British Film Institute (1985)
Spence, Jo *Putting Myself in the Picture* London, Camden Press (1986)
Spence, Jo and Holland, Patricia (eds) *Family Snaps: The Meanings of Domestic Photography* London, Virago (1991)
Sperling, Susan 'Baboons with briefcases: feminism, functionalism and sociobiology in the evolution of primate gender', *Signs 17*, 1991, pp. 1–27
Spivak, Gayatravi Chakravorty *In Other Worlds* London, Methuen (1987)
Stansell, Christine *City of Women* New York, Knopf (1986)
Steedman, Carolyn *Landscape for a Good Woman: A Story of Two Lives* London, Virago (1986)

Tambling, Jeremy *Opera, Ideology and Film* Manchester, Manchester University Press (1987)

Tickner, Lisa *The Spectacle of Women: Imagery of the Suffrage Campaign 1907–1914* London, Chatto and Windus (1987)

Tiemersma, Douwe *Body Schema and Body Image: An Interdisciplinary and Philosophical Study* Amsterdam, Swets and Zeitlinger (1989)

Voloshinov, N. V. *Marxism and the Philosophy of Language* New York, Seminar Press (1973)

Walker, Alice *In Search of our Mother's Gardens* London, The Women's Press (1984)

Walkerdine, Valerie 'Dreams from an ordinary childhood' in Heron, Liz (ed.) *Truth, Dare or Promise: Girls Growing up in the Fifties* London, Virago (1985)

Walkerdine, Valerie 'Behind the painted smile' in Spence, Jo and Holland, Pat *Family Snaps: The Meanings of Domestic Photography* London, Virago (1991)

Whitford, Margaret (ed.) *The Irigaray Reader* Oxford, Blackwell (1991)

Wilson, Elizabeth *Adorned in Dreams* London, Virago (1988)

Winnicott, D. W. *Collected Papers: Through Paediatrics to Psycho-Analysis* London, Tavistock (1958)

Witzling, Mara R. *Voicing our Visions: Writings by Women Artists* London, Women's Press (1992)

Wright, Elizabeth *Feminism and Psychoanalysis: A Critical Dictionary* Oxford, Blackwell (1992)

Index